BLOWING OUT THE DARKNESS

The Management of Emotional Life Issues, Especially Anger and Rage

Dr. David MacQuarrie, MD MA-ABS

Edited by Sarah M. Boyd. M.Litt.

authorHOUSE®

AuthorHouse™
1663 Liberty Drive, Suite 200
Bloomington, IN 47403
www.authorhouse.com
Phone: 1-800-839-8640

First published by AuthorHouse 1/28/2008

ISBN: 978-1-4343-4437-3 (e)
ISBN: 978-1-4343-4436-6 (sc)

Library of Congress Control Number: 2007907931

Printed in the United States of America
Bloomington, Indiana

This book is printed on acid-free paper.

Acknowledgements

Grateful acknowledgement is made to the following: to Warren Farrell for permission to quote from selections of his book *Women Can't Hear What Men Don't Say: Destroying Myths, Creating Love* (New York: Tarcher/Putnam, 1999); to W.W. Norton & Company for permission to use "The Belloc Ploy" from the book by Paul Watzlawick, John H. Weakland and Richard Fisch, *Change: Principles of Problem Formation and Problem Resolution* (New York: W. W. Norton & Company, 1974); and to Shambala Publications for permission to quote from the book by Ken Wilber, *A Brief History Of Everything* (Boston: Shambala, 1996).

Use of excerpts from the following publications are used on a free-trade basis after unsuccessful attempts were made to locate the author and/or publisher: Lori Gordon, *Passage To Intimacy: The PAIRS Program* (New York: Simon & Schuster, 1993); and Rupert Ross, *Dancing With A Ghost: Exploring Indian Reality* (Markham, Ontario: Reed Books, 1992).

I also thank Stephen Boyd for the front cover design and Karen Somers for the photo of the author.

Publication

The term **Blowing Out!** Is a registered trademark under the Canadian Intellectual Property Office.

Blowing Out The Darkness

--- The Management Of Emotional Life Issues,

Especially Anger and Rage ---

By Dave MacQuarrie, BSc MSc MD CRCPC MA-ABS

The idea of this book originated from the many workshops I have conducted on emotional issues. Personal experience and feedback from others have emphasized to me the profound need to challenge the dominant models of emotional management in our society. This book takes a new look at emotional issues with a process called Blowing Out!™

Although life's difficulties usually present themselves as individual struggles, I suggest that many of our emotional issues, especially those of anger and rage, are simply the tip of the iceberg of societal problems that we face. We need however to begin the work of healing at the individual level before we can resolve the systemic issues.

In part, this book offers practical tools for the management of emotional difficulties, especially those of anger and rage. It also suggests that most depression relates to how we abort our life energy, stuffing our emotions rather than exploring them effectively. Thus, depression is usually a "sociological disorder in a biochemical system" rather than a "biochemical disease." Additionally, the tools offered in this book can be expanded to any emotional issue with which people struggle and thus are applicable to any relationship or societal dilemma. Although I am most familiar with western society, I believe the ideas presented are applicable to any relationship and any society.

The Blowing Out! process explores the nature of conflict and suggests how to reach a place of willingness within oneself in order to cooperate with another person or persons and, thus, to achieve resolution. The willingness of the other person to cooperate then becomes the limitation. The book also provides an in-depth discussion of the skills one can use in conflict, especially when the other is non-cooperative. The identification and living of one's values are emphasized.

Concurrently, the book questions our society's long-term philosophic bases that underlie the problems of emotional issues. The Blowing Out! process provides means for the integration of emotion and cognition where one can think clearly at the emotional level --- the transrational level. This integration then leads to the ability to make and keep agreements with others, a skill that is sorely lacking in our global society.

Our society places great emphasis on objectivity and analysis in our approach to solving problems; and we have lost the ability to use the great skills that exist within the subjective. The major emphasis of this book is on relearning these skills that have been lost. The place of therapy is proposed as an investigation of the subjective --- an exploration of emotional depth as opposed to a "fixing" of a problem or an individual. The book suggests that the integration of the subjective and objective is essential for the survival of our species,

The final message of the book is the need to use anger wisely. Anger is both the most dangerous and most healing of emotions in our society. When clouded by issues of power, it fuels family violation as well as broader problems of systemic violation. Expressed cleanly, anger allows one to be honest, stating that this situation or event is one that is not acceptable.

It is my strong belief that we can live our lives differently. And in so doing, we can create a more effective society.

I have not created the Blowing Out! process in isolation. I have learned much from other therapists and from many clients. In this sense, I have had many mentors. For the most part throughout this book, I have attempted to provide appropriate references, but some sources have long been forgotten. I apologize for the occasional lack of reference and especially if I have misquoted anyone from the original source.

I have learned first-hand while writing this book of the need for authors to thank their family and friends --- the writing has had its daunting moments. For the many skills to which I have been exposed, I want to especially thank my wife Jan MacQuarrie, a trainer in Neuro-Linguistic Programming (NLP), and my friend Una Elliott who was Professor Emeritus of Education at the University of Toronto and a skilled practitioner of NLP. Because of the extensive editing provided by my daughter Sarah Boyd, I have invited her to be editor of this book.

Contents

Part C. The Philosophical

Part D. The Challenge

Appendices

SUBJECTIVE SKILLS EXPLORED IN THIS BOOK

DRAWINGS AND INSERTS IN THIS BOOK

PART A.
OPENING CONSIDERATIONS

CHAPTER ONE --- OPENING CONSIDERATIONS

Summary

This chapter introduces the basic purposes of this book. The primary purpose is to provide a means of thinking and acting within emotional issues such that we handle the difficult times of our lives safely and effectively. Only then are we available to cooperate with others to resolve the larger issues our society faces.

Throughout the book, anger and rage are used as the predominant metaphor to explore emotional difficulties. The skills, however, are equally applicable to all emotional issues.

It is intended that the book be both practical and philosophical. The practical component teaches the skills necessary to resolve even the most difficult of emotional issues. The book challenges the current models of emotional management by challenging the individual to find and live his or her authenticity as a human being. It is suggested that the route to this authenticity, and ultimately the route to societal change, lies in appreciating the importance of the subjective, especially the depth of possibility that exists within it. The book suggests that, as a culture, we have lost or forgotten many important subjective skills and that these skills can be regained.

Also developed in this chapter are preliminary concepts of life energy, emotion and the need for integration of the subjective and objective. Basic presuppositions are stated. The integration of emotionality and rationality (cognition) to achieve the transrational is emphasized as the route to maturation, both as an individual and as a society.

CHAPTER ONE --- OPENING CONSIDERATIONS

A science that does not incorporate spirituality is dehumanizing;
a spirituality that does not include science is delusional.

The above quotation is one I wrote myself (modified from a book I read years ago on chronic pain.) It is my truthfulness appearing as truth.

You, the reader, will interpret this quotation based on the connotations of the words, especially the words "science" and "spirituality." I cannot easily change the meanings given by you; I can be careful that I present clarity in my writings. I can also ask you to be careful of the assumptions that you bring to these words. My request to be careful of assumptions is one of the underpinnings of this book. Assumptions are a pervasive source of conflict.

We have many marvelous skills as human beings, especially the ability to have awareness and clarity. These words will become important as I proceed through the book's arguments. For now, let me define "awareness" as the "attention to one's spontaneously emerging perceptions," and "clarity" as the "ability to think at the emotional level." An additional marvelous skill that we have as human beings is our ability to put our experience into language. Language, awareness and clarity all dance with each other, mutually reinforcing each other. When used well, they strengthen one another; when used poorly, they limit one another.

To express our experiences in language allows us to share it with others. Yet, we can miscommunicate so easily. This tension will be explored as the book continues.

1.1. PURPOSES INTENDED BY THIS BOOK

A General Theory of Love[1] presents a comment from Blaise Pascal, a French mathematician who lived three hundred years ago: "The heart has its reasons whereof Reason knows nothing." The book then develops an integration between

---

1. T. Lewis, F. Amini and R Lannon. A General Theory of Love (Toronto: Random House, 2000) , p. 4.

neurophysiology and emotional experiences, especially those of love. In this book *Blowing Out The Darkness*, I attempt something similar: the integration of science and emotional experiences using anger as the predominant metaphor for exploration.

The mechanisms of anger and rage are easy emotions to grasp; they are also some of the most common emotions with which we currently struggle in our society. Although anger and rage will be the principal emotions described in this book, the concepts and skills are equally applicable to any emotional experience.

I am writing this book for a diverse audience. Some readers may want very practical tools for how to handle emotional difficulties, whereas others will want detailed explanations and justifications of the various concepts. I strongly believe that both of these needs require a paradigm shift in how we currently view and approach emotional issues and I suggest it is therefore necessary to write this book for multiple audiences. Bridging of the issues is essential. In so doing though, the development will require considerable detail. To simplify the process, I have therefore included short summaries of various sections throughout the book.

My overall purpose of the book is to present a variety of ideas and possibilities that allow you, the reader, an understanding of the mechanisms whereby we create our emotional lives. This understanding needs to be simple enough to be usable. It also needs to be accurate enough that the average person can bring corrective tools to his or her life, especially when this person is dissatisfied with the current state of what his or her life offers. Finally, I will relate this understanding to the fundamentals of who we are as conscious, self-reflective creatures.

I do not pretend here to present a rigorous scientific exposition with numerous footnotes and annotations. Rather, my intentions are four-fold. My first purpose is that the book will be practical --- almost like a cooking class that teaches skills rather than a cookbook that gives exact recipes. Human beings are not machines to which standardized procedures can easily be brought.

I will develop a methodology of anger management that I call Blowing Out!™ in contrast to the more common expressions of "blowing up" or "blowing down." This methodology appears highly successful, even in people who are initially reluctant. I once had a big, tough-looking guy as a client who was "mandated" by his wife to do something about his anger; he was told by her that the marriage was over if he did not. At the end of my weekend workshop on "Anger, Rage and Violation," he said to me: "Nobody gets into my head. You did." Subsequently, he and his wife voluntarily joined one of my ongoing therapy groups (see Appendix D for more details.)

My second purpose of the book is to challenge the dominant models of anger management. Under various guises, the therapy called Cognitive Behavioral Therapy (CBT) --- training the individual to out-think his or her emotional issues --- currently forms the major teachings of anger management. I suggest that this methodology is a good therapy in many cases; but it is not in keeping with our biologic design and represents an imposition on the emotional system, rather than an integration of the cognitive and emotional systems that would allow for optimal human function.

CBT tends to function from the perspective that if the client does things the "right" way, everything will be fine. The tendency to function from a deductive model is a weakness of any therapy and is principally limited by the maturity of the therapist using the tool. This tendency is, in many ways, a dominant characteristic of our society and, I believe, part of the problem rather than part of the solution.

While I believe CBT is an important and powerful therapy, it is most useful for those who are intellectually oriented and sincerely want to deal with their anger. It is generally not effective on those initially reluctant to change. These latter people have been described as "more hardened characters" or as "difficult to serve" clients. The model I am presenting has been very useful for these "more hardened characters," and as well provides a powerful model for those initially sincere in wanting to deal with their anger.

My third purpose of the book is to explore and challenge you, the reader, to find your authenticity as a human being, by which I mean the "the genuinely integrated complexity of being human." It is my belief that the Blowing Out! process is successful largely because it emphasizes and challenges the individual to be true to his or her self --- something for which (in my experience) all human beings strive. I further contend that a major loss of authenticity has occurred in our society because, as a society, we have lost any sense of ultimate purpose and relationship, a loss that is deeply embedded in our technological, post-modern world in which everything is relative.

The fourth purpose of this book is to explore the importance of the subjective. I define subjective as "that which arises from the internal processing of external and internal data by the mind." The mind is a feedback processor, responsive to the environment, such that multiple levels of response are possible for any given external stimulus. For example, in conversation with me, a male client tells me of being physically abused, how he had defended himself from the abuse and how subsequently he was charged as being abusive for what seems to have been an appropriate level of defense. I can be curious and angry and analytic, essentially all at the same time, when I consider how these difficulties of my client arose.

Even this example is too simplistic. It does not identify the complexity of responses that go on within me as my whole experience arises (the conversation with the client.) It ignores the multiple nuanced interactions between the subjective and objective that contribute to the creation of my whole experience, for example, my client's voice tone, my past experience with this same client and any other memories that influence my immediate experience. There is always this intimate, inseparable dance between the subjective and objective.

In this book, I will not resolve the complexity of that dance. Whole books have been written on the subject. What I want to do is illustrate features of the dance that I have uncovered. Underlying the four purposes of this book is the contention that THE major loss of our current civilization is the loss of exploration of the subjective, thereby devaluing the incredible skills that exist within a state of authenticity. I believe that the route out of this dilemma is for us to develop the skills of awareness and clarity. Awareness and clarity given expression through language allow us to recognize authenticity or its lack thereof.

In the chapters to follow, I will lay a foundation for what I hope is the true significance of emotional experience --- the richness it offers, how we trap ourselves and the ways we can escape these traps. This foundation is based on more than twenty years of exploration of emotional life issues, much of it at the personal level of myself or my clients. The foundation I develop will be consistent with many findings of modern neurobiology. I will develop my premises slowly, as I am stepping outside the cultural models in many ways. In so doing, I believe I am honoring our basic integrity as human beings. It does not mean that everyone will like what I have to say. For those who find my development too slow, I suggest first reading Chapter Three (Blowing Out!) for an overview of the practical, followed by Appendix D (Recidivism) to gauge the impact of what I am suggesting. Chapter Five (Individual Considerations: Therapy) further develops the book's emotional concepts. From there, you can choose to return to an earlier portion of the book to resume the development of its themes.

Throughout the book, I will refer to the words "mind," "body," "consciousness" and "other-than-conscious." I am not able to define these terms with accuracy --- whole books have been written on each one. Instead, I will assume you the reader to understand these words. At this point though, I will explain in more detail my use of the term "body-mind-heart-soul-spirit", written as all one word. By it, I mean the entirety of who we are as humans, regardless of particular belief systems. I suggest that the totality of who we are is awesome.

A key presupposition of the book is that experiential learning, learning that allows us to know who we are, is made powerful by an accompanying emotional shift that I call an "authentic feel-good" experience: we learn when we integrate emotionality with concept. To aid this idea, I have written the book in an oral style with many visual diagrams; and I often encourage you the reader to experiment with and feel out the ideas and tools that are being developed. I am attempting to simulate experiential learning, albeit inadequately. If I do not influence your emotional world with this book, you may at the very least gain many interesting ideas.

1.2. THE NATURE OF LIFE ENERGY

In the book, I will use repeatedly the concept of energy: life energy or life vitality. As reader, please pause at this moment and explore what is currently happening to you, mentally and inside your body. Perhaps you are excited and interested by the subject matter of the book, feeling light in the chest and kind of bouncy in your chair. Or maybe you are bored by it, making subtle motions of distrust with your facial muscles and are saying to yourself as you are about to put the book away: "Oh boy, what junk." Or maybe you are thirsty, feeling the beginning of dryness in your mouth; and you are about to get something to drink. All of these experiences are expressions of your current energy --- the vitality (or not) that you bring to your current experience of reading this book.

Although the term "energy" (more accurately, "life energy") is subject to much New Age interpretation, my intention when I use the word is to refer to our ability to perform work or initiate movement. This movement occurs both internally and externally as we process and respond to what is happening in our environment. The internal body experience, interpreted neurologically, is what I suggest is called "emotion." I will explain in more detail later in the book how energy and emotion are closely linked. For now, the best definition I have of "emotion" is a "biologically adaptive action tendency."[2] Emotion is a purposeful and useful beginning of action; everything you feel, think and do has purpose (often at the other-than-conscious level.) You do not have to like the experience or the emotion for it to be purposeful. Emotion may also be the end of action if you do not feel safe to continue the action into your current environment.

In describing energy and emotion, I will use the metaphor of fixing a car. If your car breaks down, you want to fix it so as to be able to accomplish your tasks

2. L. Greenberg and J. Safran. Emotion in Psychotherapy. American Psychologist, 44:1 (1989), 19-29 (p. 22)

more easily. If you know enough about cars and have the appropriate tools, you can move your car into your garage, take it apart, correct the defect, and put it back together. Off you go again. If you don't know enough about cars or don't have the appropriate tools, you will likely take your car to a mechanic who will disassemble it, correct the defect, and put it back together. Again, off you go. In either scenario there is a cost: time, energy/emotion, money or all three.

If we are to correct our emotional difficulties as individuals and as a society, there will also be a cost. One human being cannot change or fix another human being. Nor are we standardized such that our parts, especially our energy parts, are easily interchanged with each other. However, we can learn from each other, especially how our emotional systems work and what tools are useful for correcting the system, both our internal states and our external interactions.

1.2.1. HOW THE HUMAN EMOTIONAL SYSTEM WORKS

In this book, I am attempting to describe how the human emotional system works, essentially how we work as humans, so that the system can be brought back to healthy functioning. This is a book about tools that impact human lives in a positive manner, both in the short-term and the long-term. As such, it is meant to be a very practical book. My experience as a psychotherapist is that all of the tools presented can be both powerful and useful yet they may require you to stretch beyond your current "comfort zone" (or, more accurately, your current "familiar zone" --- we are creatures of habit.) In so doing, you may feel both excitement and discomfort.

Concurrently, I will present much theory. This information will hopefully allow you to understand and adapt the practical tools offered to your own needs, much as a chef who is knowledgeable of food chemistry can easily modify a recipe for a particular meal. The theoretical information is also intended to give you as the reader a perspective of individual problems within complex societal issues.

During my training workshops where I explore the tools of anger management, I always start by presenting the following as part of my visual slide presentation:

There are only two things I can tell others,

1) who they should be, or

2) who I am."

Then I add:

Both stances get me into trouble!"

What happens when one human being tells another human being who they should be? Generally the other person does not like it, especially if it persists. Eventually one person or both people get angry. This often results in the end of the discussion, generally with neither person learning very much. Alternatively, if I clearly tell someone who I am, including my stance as to what I believe life offers, they often want to tell me who I should be; again, there is the possibility of someone getting angry. None the less, I do strongly believe that, of the two alternatives, we as human beings can get our best possible outcomes if we each tell the other who we are and then negotiate the differences.

As such, the word "should" (and its many variations of "must," "have to," etc.) will not be used in this book --- I have no desire to tell others who they should be, only to tell them my truths of my years of exploring emotional issues, especially those of anger and rage. Within this precept, I will tell you my explorations of my own issues --- the place from where my truths originate. I will slightly modify the details to obscure the actual events. I have no interest in pointing fingers or blaming others, only to explore clarity of emotional experience. I will tell my own experiences because I have my own detailed and intimate knowledge of these experiences. No one else can know my truthfulness, nor can I truly know the experiences of my clients. Thus, I will often speak from a first-person point of view, principally using "we" to be inclusive. Sometimes I will address the reader as "you" to invite him or her to generalize my experiences. In both these ways of speaking, I am clear within myself that I am only telling you who I am, not who you should be.

1.3. WHO AM I?

So who am I? At the time of writing this book (with final editing in the summer of 2007) I am a sixty-four year old physician --- a specialist anesthetist --- with five university degrees in physics, biophysics, medicine, anesthesiology and psychological studies. I also have numerous diplomas in (and/or other exposures to) various therapies such as Gestalt Therapy and Neuro-Linguistic Programming. When I began my adult career, I intended to be a theoretical astrophysicist, someone who studies the development of the universe. Little did I dream that I would eventually study the inner universe rather than the outer one.

As far as I know, my family of origin was a well-educated family of the nineteen-forties. Many of my family members, both men and women, had university degrees, and some were highly respected in their chosen fields at the national or international level. The members of my family were, I believe, socially successful, but emotionally powerless; eighty percent were alcoholics by my definition (someone who uses alcohol to avoid life issues.) The story that I use to explain my family's emotional dynamics is that, as long as people kept their distance and interactions remained at a social and intellectual level, everything was fine. Social gatherings, however, were characterized by excessive drinking and loud, verbal arguments, often with physical fighting. Both my parents were alcoholics, and my father eventually committed suicide when I was eleven. Many other issues (including extensive teasing by other children and adults together with minor sexual abuse by a Scoutmaster) impacted my childhood, leaving me with a deep sense of isolation, shame and powerlessness.

The dynamics of my family that were especially impactful on me were the unspoken anger episodes that came out in subtle ways and the many double messages that I received, principally from my parents (implying "Do as I say, not as I do.") My way of surviving emotionally all this was to shut down my feelings and use my intellect to succeed. When I was fifty, my adult nephew told me a statement that aptly characterized my personality until I was in my early forties. As a child, he had been told: "Oh, yes, Uncle David, he's brilliant, but don't bother talking to him."

Parallel with my emotional pain was a profound sense of spirituality; somehow I knew that life had more to offer than was currently available to me but I just couldn't seem to access it. Starting at the age of eight, I had had a number of profound spontaneous mystical experiences culminating at age thirty-two in a sustained mystical experience called "Cosmic Consciousness" that lasted for three years.[3] However, at the times of my mystical experiences, I had no mentors to guide me in integrating these experiences into my daily life, and I experienced much despair in the struggle to do so as a result.

By the time I was forty, I was socially successful like the rest of my family. I was a skilled and respected professional anesthetist. At some deep level, however, I knew that I was likely to commit suicide, as did my father, if I did not do something differently with my life. I regularly went through what I called my "black cloud" experiences in which I felt deep despair and hopelessness, partly exaggerated by the fading of the peak states of peacefulness. If you had asked me then if I ever got angry, I would have said "Yes, every two or three years or so." I did not realize then that my "black cloud" experiences were actually my feelings of profound rage.

At that point, I was fortunate enough to become involved in adult growth experiences, initially Marriage Enrichment (a therapeutic movement of the

---

3. The name originates from the book Cosmic Consciousness wherein the author Richard Maurice Bucke researched spontaneous peak mystical states of consciousness prompted by his extended friendship with the American poet Walt Whitman. These particular states are characterized by profound peacefulness and joyousness. See Richard Maurice Bucke, Cosmic Consciousness: A Study in the Evolution of the Human Mind (New York: E.P. Dutton, 1969; Innes & Sons, 1901).

seventies and eighties.) From there I started going to experiential workshops run by excellent therapists, and my life changed, dramatically. For the first time ever, I recognized the possibility of shifting the pain of my life by my own choice. I didn't know then how much personal work it would take to do so but it was vastly superior to the choice of suicide. I also knew immediately that I myself wanted to be a therapist – it was the most creative endeavor I had ever encountered.

I have never liked the words "therapy" or "therapist." In this culture, such words have too many connotations, none of which are true for me, that the client is sick, helpless or needs to be told what to do. In my experience, therapy is the only field where I have found that the goal is growth as a human being. That the intention in relationship with others is to have "strength and power with" another human being rather than "power over" another human being. After a few years of taking workshops, I entered various programs to develop my skills of working with people in a therapeutic area. Since 1986, I have shifted my career to that of "therapist."

Early in my therapeutic journey, one of my mentors said to me that there were only two things I needed to learn: what I was feeling and what to do with what I was feeling. From him, I learned that I was feeling rage. At age forty, I did not know how limited my emotional world was, and I did not know how angry I was. At one point a few years into the process of my own growth, I described myself as the angriest person I knew. It would take a number of years of personal work to resolve this difficulty, especially since at the time there were relatively few resources available for changing emotional issues at an experiential level. From others (and from this first mentor), I learned what to do with what I was feeling. I have summed up my lessons in the words "emotional triangles" which I will discuss in greater depth beginning in Chapter Two (Section 2.3.2) of the book.

Although I write about my earlier years, all of it seems so remote now. Most of my emotional issues have been resolved and I give little thought to the pain I once experienced. I have a very successful marriage and three wonderful adult children by previous wives. There has been much pain for others and myself along the way and, although that saddens me on occasion, I didn't know any other options on how to resolve it. Frequently nowadays, I am profoundly grateful to be a tool for assisting others through their evolving pain of personal growth.

1.4. MAJOR DILEMMAS --- GROWTH AND WISDOM IN OUR SOCIETY

Much of this book arises from who I am. In order to present this information, I will make considerable use of metaphor and proverb. Metaphor and proverb offer the advantages of being simple enough to be understandable yet accurate enough to convey subtle and complex information. They get at both the conscious and other-than-conscious mind.

My experience as therapist for over twenty years is that five proverbs highlight the current major dilemmas of our society (see Figure 1.)

Figure 1: Some Proverbs As Used In This Book

- If you don't know where you are, you cannot get to where you say you want to be.

- If you always do what you've always done, you'll always get what you've always gotten.

- Life is not fair. It never was. Life is.
  - The best definition I have of life is "life is what happens when you are planning something else."

- The truth will set you free. But first it will make you miserable, and after, it can trap you in self-righteousness.

- The two most important things in life are reasons and results. And reasons don't count.

Two proverbs are especially important at this juncture in the book. The first one is: "If you don't know where you are, you cannot get to where you say you want to be." Imagine, for example, that you are in a big city such as Toronto in the province of Ontario, looking at a map of Ontario, wanting to drive to

Ottawa, almost five hundred kilometers away. The Ontario map offers you several different options as to how to get to your destination. You choose one, you get in your car and you drive to Ottawa. This will involve time and energy but will fundamentally be easy.

What would happen if you are actually deluding yourself (still thinking you are in Ontario) and are really in Vancouver, in the Province of British Columbia, several thousand kilometers away from Ottawa. The Ontario map tells you how to get to Ottawa from Toronto. If you get in your car and start driving, you will quickly find yourself lost and most likely blame the map as being inaccurate. The map is probably still a good map; it is not the difficulty. The map-reader does not have accurate information.

Everyone of us carries around a map inside our minds of how to interact with what life offers on our journeys. The map consists of our individual beliefs and values, our memories and expectations, of how we expect life to proceed. Our individual maps tell each of us how to respond to the events of the day: for examples, of how to interpret what our partners say, of how to behave with friends and colleagues, of how to think about life issues. We are generally not conscious of our maps until we encounter something that is difficult for us.

If our map does not contain relatively accurate information, we will easily get lost and be unable to get to where we say we want to be. From my perspective, as a species, we are frequently lost because we delude ourselves as to who and where we are in our life activities. We are reluctant to look at ourselves as being a major component of our maps.

The second proverb that I rely on heavily in this book is: "If you always do what you've always done, you'll always get what you've always gotten." Sometimes this proverb is considered negative. For example, in Alcoholics Anonymous, it is often used as "a definition of insanity," i.e. always doing what you've always done and expecting a different outcome. I suggest however that the proverb is not necessarily negative, for if you like what you are getting, keep doing what you are doing. It's obviously effective. But if you don't like what you are getting, you need to do something differently. And for that, you generally need a more complete or a different map.

This book will offer you skills on how to develop a more complete map of your own life's journey and of how to interact with the journeys of others. Some of the skills offered may be surprising to you. Please read the following paragraph quickly. Do not stop to analyze it.

****

Raednig Slikls

Aoccdrnig to a rscheearch at an Elingsh uinervtisy, it deons't mttaer in waht oredr the ltteers in a wrod are, the olny iprmoetnt tihng is taht the frist and lsat ltteers are at the rghit pclae. The rset can be a tatol mses and you can sitll raed it wouthit porbelm. Tihs is bcuseae we do not raed ervey lteter by it slef but the wrod as a wlohe.

****

For most people, the paragraph is amazingly easy to read, yet profoundly different from anything they were taught in school. The tools presented in this book may also ask you to step outside your customary views of how best to map your world; yet they can be amazingly effective in helping you to achieve the outcomes you want in your life.

1.4.1. THE NEED FOR INTEGRATION

As I will develop later in the book, especially in Chapter Six, I find it incredibly difficult to get adequate information in our society, especially what actually happens at the social level, with issues ranging from the environment to the psychopharmacology industry to the significance of spirituality. Numerous distortions exist, some of which are almost certainly deliberate (e.g. Watergate, Enron and psychopharmacological research.) In *A Brief History of Everything,*

Ken Wilber states the following: "ecologic wisdom does not consist in how to live in accord with nature; it consists in how to get subjects to agree on how to live in accord with nature[4]." Wilber discusses many stages of consciousness and describes in detail the need for integration, especially the integration of the subjective with the objective, what he calls the transrational. Wilber also notes that any attempt at a descriptive worldview is simply an attempt --- no description is absolutely accurate. All models of human experience are attempting to elucidate a consistent worldview of the same world, a worldview that is useful for human progress. He places great importance on what he calls the Pre/Trans Fallacy[5], wherein we confuse the display of irrational emotion with the emotionality of the transrational. Developing this latter skill of transrational emotion is what I refer to in this book as the skill of the subjective.

At our current societal level, we need skills for emotional management, skills that are effective both in the short term and in the long term. Only then can we learn to "agree on how to live in accord with nature." These skills must somehow bridge multiple facets of what we know to be human. They must include the physical, the biological, the emotional, the mental, the spiritual and all other components that serve to define us. They must include both subjective and objective.

1.5. SOME PRESUPPOSITIONS

If we are to find a way to live with compassion, humility and respect for all life, I suggest that as a species we first need to come to terms with the fact that we are short-term energy processors. This is both our richness and our tragedy as a species. Some of the presuppositions which underlie my thesis are listed below:

1. As a human being, I am a sensory-grounded short-term energy

---

4. Ken Wilber. A Brief History Of Everything (Boston: Shambala, 1996), p. 292.
5. http://www.pretrans.com/en/ptf.html

transformer. I take life energy from the environment, process it (neurologically and in other ways) at a sensory level into meaning (using my values, beliefs, memories and expectations) and then turn it back into life energy. Ideally, this will take the form of action in the environment, so that others can be energy transformers in interaction with me.

2. Everything I do (process, think, feel, act) is purposeful. (I am very well designed as an energy transformer.)

3. I am complex. Neurological processes compete within me for my internal energy. In *Plato's Republic*, Socrates speaks about the human mind as a ship in which the Sailors have mutinied and locked the Captain and Navigator in the cabin. Each Sailor then believes himself free to steer the ship as he pleases.[6] My mind has many competing facets.

4. I relate to other people in "emotional triangles," these being interactions between any two people and involving a third person or issue. These interactions allow the circulation of energy.

5. I am easily locked into my own self-righteousness. I highlight this aspect of human behavior with a Sufi story I modified long ago (source unknown.)

****

---

6. Lori Gordon, Passage To Intimacy: The PAIRS Program (New York: Simon & Schuster, 1993), p. 192.

Learning To Sail

On a certain island, the people longed to move to another land where they could have a healthier and a better life.

The problem was that that the practical arts of sailing had never been developed. Some people refused to consider alternatives to life on the island ("We made our bed; now we have to lie in it."), whereas others sought a solution to the problems locally without any thought of crossing the waters ("We just need to cooperate.")

From time to time, an islander would discover the art of sailing. Then, a student would come up to this person and start the following typical conversation.

"I want to sail to another land and have a better life."

"Great. For that to happen, you are going to have to learn to sail. Are you ready to learn?"

"Oh yes, yes, very much so, but I have to take my ton of cabbages with me."

"Cabbages? What cabbages?"

"Why, the food I will need on the other side, wherever it is."

"But what if there is already food on the other side?"

"I don't know that. I'm not sure there will be food and I have to bring my cabbages with me."

"But you won't be able to sail if you bring your cabbages with you — it's too much weight."

"Yuk. You call my cabbages weight; I call them my basic food."

"... you won't be able to sail."

"Hmmm. . . . I'm going to bring my cabbages to someone who understands my needs better!"

****

If you as reader struggle with long-term emotional pain as you read this book, think about what you carry with you and refuse to let go, that prevents you from exploring and learning the skills offered here. If you have been abusive or filled with rage much of your life or simply grieving a loss and want to stop these emotional processes, I invite you to reflect on what holds you back.

I do not suggest that this book offers a panacea or a solution to all of life's problems. I do believe that it offers a very powerful toolbox for resolving life's difficulties --- for learning how to sail. Throughout the book, I have made much use of summaries and personal commentary. I provide summaries (usually at the beginning of each chapter and in sections labeled "Some Implications Of ...") so as to maintain the bigger picture while developing the details. I also provide personal commentary (Author's Personal Commentary) as examples of how the processes have influenced my life. I tell of the impact of these processes on my own life because I am aware of the nuances, the subtleties; if I were to make up examples or tell of clients, the details would be more limited. In general, these summaries and personal commentaries have been written in a different font or style so that the reader may easily skip them if desired.

1.6. AN OUTLINE OF THIS BOOK

From the pre-suppositions and definitions I have outlined thus far, I will develop a model of energy and emotional management that I call "Blowing Out!" I call it Blowing Out! to distinguish it from the more common ways we tend to manage our difficulties, either blowing up (for example, exploding violently on others) or blowing down (for example, stone-walling.) Although I will address the issues of anger and rage most directly, I propose that the process of Blowing

Out! is applicable to any emotional experience and is a major, perhaps essential, route to the development of the transrational.

Moreover, I propose that the term "depression" as it is generally used, both in an everyday context and frequently in medical usage, is actually a sociological disease in a biochemical system, rather than a biochemical disease. I suggest that the skills of Blowing Out! are equally important to this pervasive societal dysfunction.

The remainder of the book will unfold its central argument in the following manner. Part B (The Practical) will develop the concepts and tools of the Blowing Out! process. In particular, Chapter Two will define the basic concepts that underlie the Blowing Out! process. While understanding these concepts is not necessary to use the Blowing Out! process, given that a dominant characteristic of our species is to seek meaning, the basic concepts support what the Blowing Out! process accomplishes, and consequently encourage the use of the tools.

Chapter Three will describe the Blowing Out! process in detail using, as illustration, the management of anger and rage. These emotional issues (as with all emotional issues) occur by taking data from the environment (the data in this case being called conflict), mixing it with internal experiences (values, beliefs, memories and expectations), creating meaning from the mixture, developing a plan of action from this meaning, starting to move into action (the beginning of action: emotion) and then continuing the action to completion so as to discharge the energy appropriately.

Unfortunately, we often stop ourselves from moving into action because we do not feel safe with our actions or the subsequent consequences of our actions. Commonly, underlying this stoppage is a feeling of powerlessness, often quite profound. Moreover, when we stop our actions, the energy accumulates and is available for later transactions. Potentially, as we stuff more and more energy over time, we become pressure cookers. We may experience panic attacks, violations of others (especially family members), depression and apathy, or all of these potential manifestations of being emotional pressure cookers. I name this stoppage as emotional "stuckness," the limitation of movement, physical and emotional, that results from the intention to avoid life's inherent pain.

Thus, emotional issues are made up of the following components: safety, energy, powerlessness and conflict. The Blowing Out! process consists of separating the components so as to manage their complexity in a safe and comprehensible manner. When we get stuck in our energy dynamics, it is possible, often essential, that we safely manage the short-term problem of our energy. Thereafter, we need to manage the long-term problems: why and how we feel powerless and the nature of the conflict.

Chapter Four will explore some essential skills that are necessary for the full utilization of the Blowing Out! process. The concepts of the previous chapters will be developed in this context to provide an effective toolbox in the management of anger and rage, tools that are appropriate to any emotional "stuckness."

Part C (The Philosophical) will expand on the ideas of Part B from a theoretical perspective. In particular, Chapter Five will explore issues pertinent to the individual, especially the nature of the therapeutic journey. The power of the subjective will be explored, and the tools of personal power will be developed.

Chapter Six will explore concerns at the societal level. As a culture, we use a variety of words for which there are no good definitions nor a good understanding of what is actually entailed in the use of each word. This chapter will suggest an appropriate understanding of words that in some fashion are significant to the emotional issues with which we struggle with as well as the traps we create about them: romance, spirituality, child discipline, and others.

Finally, Part D (The Challenge For The Reader) will explore the invitations of this book. Chapter Seven will summarize several processes I believe are necessary for our growth from the irrational to the transrational, both as individuals and as a culture. The final chapter, Chapter Eight, will briefly discuss what I call the world's best-kept secret.

The book closes with four appendices. Appendix A gives definitions of some of the words I use in this book. Although dictionaries are helpful, the subtle connotations and individual variations of some words are beyond the scope of a dictionary. Hence, Appendix A will develop the specific meanings I give the words I use in this book.

Appendix B lists some of the titles of books that I have found helpful in my own personal journey and in the writing of this book. Some of these books have been referenced in the main text; others are simply presented as information.

Appendix C lists short statements of what I call "?Truths?." These are statements I have collected over the years that are authentic for me. Some of my greatest periods of clarity have come from collecting and periodically reflecting on these statements --- they allow me to know my values and guide me in times of difficult decisions. For the sake of brevity and illustration, I have principally limited Appendix C to my truths about relationship.

Appendix D (Recidivism) is a brief compendium of statements by other people, all of whom have themselves attended the Blowing Out! weekend workshops, entitled "Anger, Rage and Violation." Several of these people (another therapist and a probation officer) frequently refer clients to me (both note the impact of the Blowing Out! process on their own clients who have attended the workshop.)

The various statements of Appendix D speak for themselves. A large number of people who come to my "Anger, Rage and Violation" weekend are there reluctantly. In the vast majority of cases, they leave with a profoundly different attitude. They often tell me that this is not the case with other programs they have attended. Although anecdotal, the feedback of others in Appendix D suggests the possibilities of how this type of work can be used to further the growth of all people, especially those who are most in need of hope for better lives.

I believe that the most important aspect of therapy is personal relationship. The therapist-client relationship is the vehicle of change; the exploration and risking of new behaviors by the client is the work of change. Is the effectiveness of my work as a therapist due to how I interact as an individual with my clients? Can the Blowing Out! process be adapted by others to get a similar outcome? Perhaps the answer to both questions is … "yes."

PART B. THE PRACTICAL

CHAPTER TWO --- BASIC CONCEPTS

Summary

This chapter discusses concepts that I believe to be basic to the understanding of emotional issues. The human brain is a series of filters designed to take information from the environment, process that information on the basis of past experience and future possibilities, and then formulate an appropriate response to execute action back into the environment. The major filters of the brain are: safety (survival), life energy (emotion: pain and pleasure) and awareness (which gives us the possibility of choice). The filters are accessed in the above order of importance, and precedence of which action to execute is given in this same order. Safety is paramount. Emotional energy is next. Choice follows. High levels of energy limit our awareness and thus limit our choices.

We are incredibly complex in how we function within these brain filters. Depending on what is happening, both within us and in our environments, our responses can be fairly stereotyped and rigid. This is especially so when our emotional energy is high. I use a metaphor called "Sailors On A Ship" to characterize this stereotypical feature of who we are. Often the Sailors are in mutiny; and a major need so as to function with awareness is to have an effective Captain on the ship.

Chapter Two next develops several metaphors of how our mind functions. These include the consideration of the mind as a pot of stew (the past) that is sitting on a stove being heated (the recent past) and stirred by a spoon (the current experience.) This pot is filled with energy. When empty, the mind is peaceful; when full, the mind is agitated. Actions (behaviors) empty the pot.

Major emotional difficulties occur when a pot is full, being heated, and we put a lid on it. In effect, we generate a pressure cooker and then manifest that pressure as panic attacks, family violations, depression and apathy. Another metaphor of the mind as a staircase offers suggestions about what behaviors may happen at various level of fullness of the pot. Recognizing the mind as a pot of energy means that it can be emptied.

A metaphor called "The Action Model" suggests that our emotional lives are governed by four major areas: relationship with others, our sense of our selves, the energy we bring to life (the pot) and the behaviors we bring to life (our actions.) When life is troubled, these same four areas become "Conflict" (relationship), "Powerlessness" (self), "A Full Pot" (life energy) and "Lack of Safety" (stopping our actions.)

We are not just individual energy processors; we live in interaction with others as social creatures. In so doing, we live within vast numbers of interconnected emotional triangles: interactions between any two people and involving a third person or life issue. Our interconnection with others is both our stability and a source of our emotional "stuckness." The ramifications of these interconnections are discussed in detail in Chapter Two, based on fundamentals of the laws of emotional triangles and laws of energy.

Understanding and effective management of these laws allow us to be successful in our relationships. But when the areas of Conflict, Powerlessness, A Full Pot and Lack of Safety are mashed together, we are likely overwhelmed and lost in a morass of emotional difficulty. We need to separate out the four components of our emotional lives so as to live effectively. Separating them out will form the underlying principle of the Blowing Out! process to be developed in Chapter Two.

The final metaphor of Chapter Two is called "The Pointing Finger" and highlights an individual's connection to his or her emotional triangles. He or she can point a finger at others (blame), can focus on the situation or can focus on him- or herself as the agent of change.

CHAPTER TWO --- BASIC CONCEPTS

This chapter will explore some basic concepts that form the underpinnings of the Blowing Out! process (see Figure 2.)

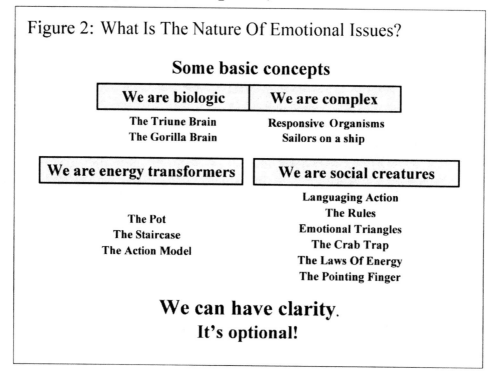

Figure 2: What Is The Nature Of Emotional Issues?

Some basic concepts

We are biologic	We are complex
The Triune Brain The Gorilla Brain	Responsive Organisms Sailors on a ship

We are energy transformers	We are social creatures
The Pot The Staircase The Action Model	Languaging Action The Rules Emotional Triangles The Crab Trap The Laws Of Energy The Pointing Finger

We can have clarity.
It's optional!

A fundamental assumption in this book is that we need an accurate map. A map is a collection of details about a particular subject that is accurate enough to be useful and simple enough to be effective. The map is not the territory; the map is simply a way of comprehending the territory so as to make travel easier. As human beings, we need an accurate mental map; we need concepts that are accurate enough to be useful and simple enough to be effective in our day-to-day lives. This mental map has to take into account our biological nature as well as our capability for clarity and depth of experience.

Some of the landmarks of this map are shown in Figure 2. I have divided the concepts into four areas. I would caution the reader again that the concepts simplify what actually happens. Hopefully, they provide a map that is accurate enough, one that contains the essential data but does not contain so much data that the user is overwhelmed. In addition, the concepts need to impact the other-than-conscious mind for them to be effective in learning. The bottom line is that we can have clarity. It's optional. It is not guaranteed.

2.1. WE ARE BIOLOGICAL --- THE BRAIN

Throughout much of the history of Western civilization, our basic biology as human beings has been ignored. Many religions have emphasized body as sinful and mind or spirit as the major aspect of life. We have split mind from body in our major philosophies. Yet not only are our bodies biological but so are our minds. Recognition of this fact of our basic biology is primary in coming to terms with our emotional issues.

I often tell my clients: "My body is my source of information." Indeed, all biological organisms are designed to receive information (sensation through sensory systems) and act on that information (action --- response through motor systems.) All information travels from our bodies to our minds. The purpose of the mind is to act as a delay loop between sensation and action. The system is well-designed --- not omnipotent, just well-designed. It is so well-designed that our bodies almost always knows our truths and what actions are appropriate, long before we am ready to acknowledge this information consciously.

Action clears out any clutter in the mind's delay loop that prevents new information and new possibilities from arriving. Action can be discharge specific to the accumulated clutter (this is what I need to do---so just do it!); or it can be non-specific discharge (exaggeration, role play, anger discharge in safety, etc.) My experience is that both options satisfy our biological system, provided that the action is developed to completion. In other words, if at first you don't succeed, do anything else that is different. Although I personally experience the impact of action in clearing the clutter most clearly in my work as a psychotherapist, my belief is that it is applicable to the entirety of our everyday lives.

2.1.1. THE TRIUNE BRAIN

It is essential to understand the development of the human brain in order to process emotional issues effectively. The model of "The Triune Brain"[1] provides a starting point in our understanding (see Figure 3.)

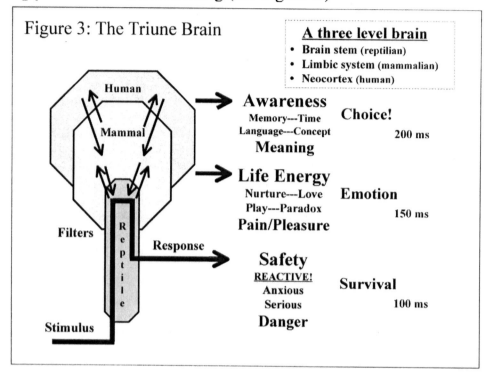

Figure 3: The Triune Brain

A three level brain
- **Brain stem (reptilian)**
- **Limbic system (mammalian)**
- **Neocortex (human)**

Awareness
Memory---Time
Language---Concept
Meaning
Choice!
200 ms

Life Energy
Nurture---Love
Play---Paradox
Pain/Pleasure
Emotion
150 ms

Safety
REACTIVE!
Anxious
Serious
Danger
Survival
100 ms

The Triune Brain model is an anthropological model of the human brain that outlines at least three different major evolutionary stages of brain development.

Our basic brains are similar to those of reptiles. The reptile characteristically appears very somber to the world, is primarily interested in survival and has rapid reactions when threatened.

On top of our reptilian brain, we have a mammalian brain (principally the limbic system). With the addition of mammalian structures, the human brain achieved the ability to respond emotionally --- to play and nurture, and to sustain our anger and "negative" emotions. Mammals play or nurture their offspring, whereas reptiles, for the most part, do not. As illustration, I invite you to step

---

1. Paul McLean. The Triune Brain In Evolution: Role in Paleocerebral Functions (New York: Plenum, 1990).

into and note the differences between any experiences you may have had playing with turtles or snakes versus playing with dogs or horses.

The third stage in our brain development is that of the human brain (the neocortex and especially the frontal lobes) which is the cognitive brain wherein we give meaning and significance to events in a much more complex way than all other known species. This ability has granted us much greater choice as to how we respond to our world, both immediately and over the long-term.

Information entering our brains follows a very particular order. The vast amount of information (about 99%) that you and I are taking in at this moment enters the reptilian brain first. Smell (the remaining 1%) enters the mammalian brain directly, whereas nothing enters the human brain straightaway. In other words, the information we take in is, for the most part, processed and responded to at sophisticated but evolutionarily primitive levels below consciousness. This characteristic may be called reflex or instinct but it essentially represents the filtering of the brain to reduce and simplify the volume of information that we consciously have to process.

2.1.1.1. THE NATURE OF FILTERS

I invite you, the reader, to pause for about ten seconds and look around your surroundings for objects that are colored "red." ….. Now look around for objects that are colored "blue." …..

While you were looking for objects colored "red," where were the objects colored "blue?" Likely, you did not see them because you were filtering for the color "red," discarding "blue" as insignificant for the moment. This exercise is what the brain does all the time --- it filters and initiates responses. The kind of filter and response depends on what level of the brain is doing the processing.

The reptilian brain filters for "safety." If information entering the brain is perceived and interpreted at the reptilian brain level as threatening, we go into survival mode --- so-called freeze, fight or flight mode. We then act from this mode, possibly in very destructive ways. The filtering and response by the reptilian brain occurs well before conscious interpretation. For simplicity's sake, I generally say it takes about 100 milliseconds (ms) for the reptilian brain to respond and about 200 ms for conscious awareness of that response. The actual times are probably double these figures. The important message is that, if operating from the reptilian brain, we act before we are consciously aware of what we are doing. If a behavioral response occurs before reaching the human brain, we often say to ourselves, "Now why did I do that? I didn't mean to do that!" Good excuse, but not accurate --- we were simply making choices from a brain level below consciousness.

As illustration, there have been several times in my workshops when members of the Armed Forces have asked me to not use a laser pointer during presentations. Although I never point the laser beam directly at the participants (hence there is no danger to their eyes), I have been told that the beam nonetheless reminds these Armed Forces members of conditions they have experienced on the battlefield, and is a major source of anxiety for them. In asking me not to use a laser pointer, these individuals are presumably filtering the environment from the perspective of safety, independent of the actual circumstances where the pointer is currently used, in the classroom, to highlight information on a display screen.

After the initial processing of the reptilian brain (with or without actual behavioral response), the information percolates up to the emotional brain and then eventually to the human brain. At the emotional brain level, information is filtered for "life energy." Is it painful or pleasurable? If painful, I will likely start to move away from the source of information; if pleasurable, I will move towards it. The mammalian brain introduced to our biology the ability to evaluate the environment in much more sophisticated ways than the reptile, including the ability to nurture and play. The ability to respond to complex energy such as "play-fighting" was also greatly enhanced. Witness from your own experiences how much more sophisticated a dog is as a pet versus interacting with a turtle as a pet.

--- Author's Personal Commentary ---

A personal description from my past may help. When I was a child, some of my family members were doctors and lawyer. They often talked about the extreme violence of local biker gangs. Since then, if I encounter someone dressed in black leathers, for example, in a mall where I am perfectly safe, I initially move away from that person. They could be the nicest individual but my Reptilian Brain filter says "Danger!"

In contrast, when I see a woman out of the corner of my eye whom I consider to be beautiful, I start to turn my head well before my conscious choice intervenes (this being a common male pattern.)

Eventually information from the emotional brain is passed to the human brain which has the fundamental filter of "awareness." The development of the human brain allowed for greater sophistication in human culture, making available the ability to comprehend time (in the form of past memories and future planning) and to use language (which allows for contact at a distance, especially conceptual contact.) These two abilities have given us the capability of making meaning of our environment and transmitting it from person to person through language.

Thus a person's behavior into the environment is dependent both on the data received as input from the environment and the filter brought to the data. Much of what we do in life is react to a situation, especially with our immediate response. We react from whichever filter is doing the interpreting rather than accurately and more fully assessing the data from all three brain levels before deciding on which action to take. Our immediate response and our long-term response may be at odds. For example, as discussed in Chapter One, getting people to agree on how to live in accord with nature" requires an integrated long-term response.

2.1.1.2. THE GORILLA BRAIN VERSUS THE HUMAN BRAIN

An additional feature of the human brain that is of major importance to our emotional health is our unique post-conception phase of brain development (see Figure 4.)

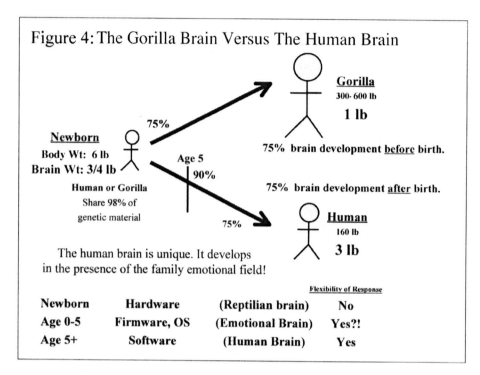

Figure 4: The Gorilla Brain Versus The Human Brain

The newborn human and the newborn gorilla have similar body weights and brain weights. Total body weight for each is about six pounds and the brain weight is about three-quarters of a pound[2]. Genetically, humans and gorillas have approximately ninety-eight percent of their respective DNA in common. However, a fully-grown adult gorilla typically weighs three hundred to six hundred pounds[3] with a brain weight of one pound[4]; that is, seventy-five percent of the gorilla's brain has developed before birth. An adult human being, on the other hand, typically weighs approximately one hundred fifty pounds with a brain weight of three pounds; that is, seventy-five percent of the human brain develops after birth, in the environment of the family, and exposed to the family emotional field.

---

2. http://faculty.washington.edu/chudler/facts.html
3. http://www.comozooconservatory.org/como_zoo/animals/gorillaB.shtml
4. http://faculty.washington.edu/chudler/facts.html

Part of our uniqueness as human beings is that our post-conception phase of brain development allows our brains to become much larger than the birth canal. But it also exposes us, and our brain development, to the intricacies of the family life into which we are born. The newborn is designed to copy the family's emotional field as his or her primary model of how to respond to the world. The newborn copies family dynamics (actions, emotions and behaviors), not rules of conduct or beliefs. Most of a human's brain growth is complete by age five. Yet, because the rules of conduct are often at odds with the actual behaviors of family members, this copying and coping is also a major source of pain and confusion for the growing child. Note the common family rule, "Do as I say, not as I do."

An analogy is useful here, between the human brain and a computer. The newborn human brain is like the hardware of a computer, limited in responses and waiting for the operating system and software. From the age of five onwards (the age at which we generally go to school and by which time our brains are relatively developed), we are adding software --- various programs on how to accomplish tasks such as reading and writing, mathematics, the study of history, etc. The intervening time from age zero to five represents the development of the operating system, the interface between the hardware and software, the inner and outer world.

On a computer, it is relatively difficult to change the hardware whereas, with only a little knowledge of computers, it is relatively easy to change the software. If you don't like the program, you can exit, erase the program and start up a new one.

The operating system is more tenuous. You don't get to just quit it because you don't like how the computer is operating. Yet if you know what you are doing, it is actually quite easy to change the operating system (it can be messy otherwise.) We often think that early childhood experience is irreversible; on the contrary, I believe that it is at least partially reversible with good care. A schoolteacher friend of mine once told me that "a child seems to recover *if* conditions which allow him or her to develop 'normally' are present between the ages of five & ten.[5]" As a therapist of twenty plus years, I frequently witness the ease with which all human beings can change if they have the right tools to influence their emotional lives. In my experience, the emotional brain is incredibly plastic under the right conditions; it is a place of profound awe for me.

2.1.1.3. SOME IMPLICATIONS OF THE TRIUNE BRAIN

a. Our brains are designed for survival, not community. As humans, we tend to place high value on community, on interacting socially based on rules of conduct. However I suggest that community only becomes accessible to brain functioning after our survival needs are met.

b. Our basic responses to life occur through the filters of our survival needs and our emotional energy, and not what we think "should" happen from our human, or cognitive, brains.

c. Our primary emotional experiences develop out of the emotional patterns of our families. These are deeply embedded in our emotional brains.

d. The rules of conduct that we live by are also learned in the family and are secondary influences embedded deep in our emotional brains. Often the rules are at odds with our emotional lives. The unhealthiness of our family rules is a primary limitation, potentially throughout our lives. For example, the rule that "children should be seen and not heard" was very suppressive of my childhood development and remained a major influence until only a few years ago.

e It is possible to change our emotional patterns, at least the secondary patterns. But they do not change easily by imposing new rules of conduct

---

5. Personal communication.

from the human brain above. Like a young child with a toy, they change when provided with options that are more interesting.

f. We are capable of compassion and clarity, of mature cognition, and can use our emotional energy effectively if we can integrate the components of the triune brain. In so doing, we can achieve a transrational state which includes safety, the appreciation of emotionality and the choice of which values are important to us in the present issues. This concept of integration will be important throughout the rest of the book and will be referred to as the integration of safety, energy and choice.

2.1.2. WE ARE COMPLEX

Our complexity as human beings is both our richness and our tragedy. If we can integrate all three levels of our being, our complexity can be awesome; if we are not integrated, then we can be dangerous. The following sections will discuss in greater detail various implications of our status as complex organisms.

2.1.2.1. WE ARE RESPONSIVE ORGANISMS

Modern neurophysiology has begun to unravel how the brain stores information for future use, especially memory and pattern (see Figure 5 on next page.)

A neural impulse (a stimulus) arrives at a simplified neural network (a collection of neurons that interact with each other.) In the newborn's immature brain, new information may stimulate neurons in a random fashion. As one neuron stimulates another, a pathway develops. Something within our neurophysiology allows this first pathway to retain its pattern of response such that the next stimulus of a similar nature will traverse the same pathway again. For lack of a better term and better information, I label this process of pattern development as

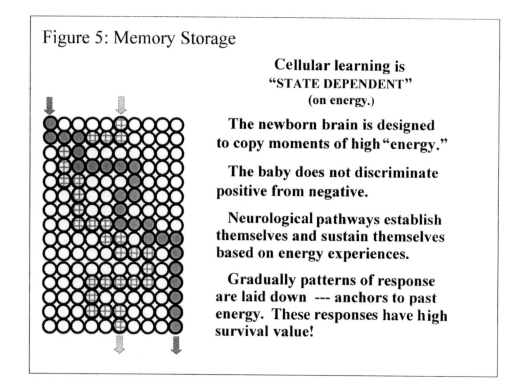

Figure 5: Memory Storage

Cellular learning is "STATE DEPENDENT" (on energy.)

The newborn brain is designed to copy moments of high "energy."

The baby does not discriminate positive from negative.

Neurological pathways establish themselves and sustain themselves based on energy experiences.

Gradually patterns of response are laid down --- anchors to past energy. These responses have high survival value!

"high energy-dependent.[6]" Different pathways will be developed (and different response patterns result) depending on the type of emotional field. The more emotionally stimulating an event is (painful or pleasurable), the more likely a neural pattern will be laid down for it to occur at a subsequent time. Different pathways will be developed (and different response patterns result) depending on the type of emotional field operating in the environment of the newborn (the family dynamics.)

Over time in the newborn's brain, a collection of high energy-dependent pathways will group together in common emotional themes to form "state-dependent" response systems. These are relatively self-sustaining, overall response systems in which individual responses are triggered by certain energetic (emotional) states associated with the common emotional theme. Consider, for instance, how the newborn interacts with the mother, both of whom are biologically designed to interact with each other. The mother feeds, cuddles and plays with the newborn, while the newborn learns how to respond to the

6. See Chapter Six on "Limbic Attractors" in T. Lewis, F. Amini and R. Lannon, A General Theory of Love (Toronto: Random House, 2000).

mother. When the newborn smiles, it gets a reward of excited response from the mother, thereby reinforcing that particular pathway in the newborn's brain. As the newborn grows into an infant, it learns a whole new repertoire of actions that get a response from mother, thus gaining rewards for these neural pathways in the infant's brain while other pathways, not rewarded, fade in intensity. I label this collection or set of pathways (in the infant's brain) as its "mummy" part. In other words, the infant's "mummy" part is a state-dependent response system within the infant whereby certain actions or characteristics are evoked only when the mother is around (see Figure 6.)

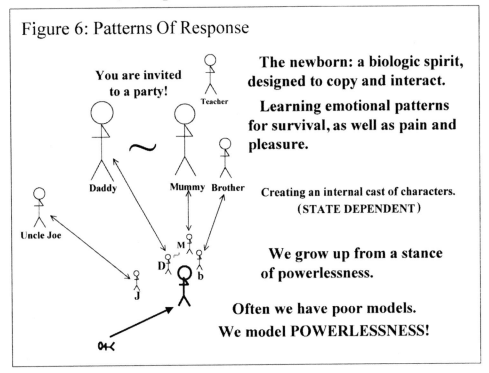

Figure 6: Patterns Of Response

You are invited to a party!

Teacher

Daddy   Mummy   Brother

Uncle Joe

The newborn: a biologic spirit, designed to copy and interact.

Learning emotional patterns for survival, as well as pain and pleasure.

Creating an internal cast of characters.
(STATE DEPENDENT)

We grow up from a stance of powerlessness.

Often we have poor models.
We model POWERLESSNESS!

At the same time as the infant is learning to interact with the mother, it is also interacting with the father. Because the father is a different person than the mother, a different repertoire of actions and behaviors from the infant will elicit a different set of responses in the father. So too then is the baby's "daddy" part different than its "mummy" part.

From time to time, the baby experiences the mother and father in conflict with each other. As the infant attempts to assimilate life's experiences into some coherent pattern, its "mummy " and "daddy" parts will also experience an internal conflict as a result. The overall health of the family, including its many intricacies in how it addresses conflict, will determine the health of the baby in significant ways. If the family dynamics are healthy, then the baby's "mummy" and "daddy" parts will likely be healthy. But if the family dynamics are unhealthy, then the baby's "mummy" and "daddy" parts will also be unhealthy. In other words, if our parents have only limited skills at managing emotional issues, and they themselves feel powerless to deal with life's many issues, we are designed from birth to model them in their powerlessness.

Take, for example, a family where the father feels constantly discouraged as a result of working two jobs and having to be up at five o'clock a.m. every single morning. Meanwhile, the mother is exhausted from looking after all six children at home. When the infant awakens at three in the morning, cold, wet and hungry, the mother and father are likely going to argue over who has to get up this time and look after the baby. This emotional energy will be copied into the baby's brain development and be identified as normal. Or say the mother and father are drug addicts who go at each other "tooth and nail;" this energy will also be incorporated into the baby's brain development as normal. Thus, the baby's "mummy" and "daddy" parts will develop patterns that are deemed normal but are in fact ineffective.

At this early phase of development, baby identifies the emotional energy of the family emotional field as "ideal" --- regardless of the adult perception of "positive" and "negative." This is the only experience the baby knows. Even if socially successful, the family may be emotionally immature, as in, for example, the many alcoholic or dysfunctional families who nonetheless achieve a high degree of social success. As the reader, how many really healthy families do you know?

Around two years of age, the infant becomes a toddler and begins to discriminate between positive and negative experiences and to recognize choice. The painful components of choice also become more prominent, in that the toddler is extremely limited in his or her power to exercise choice and influence others.

In order to cope with his or her growing awareness of powerlessness, the toddler develops "blinders" to the pain of it --- a distortion of experience. The toddler does so by copying and creatively responding to his or her family environment. He or she may choose unconsciously to become "the pretty ballerina" or "the straight-A student", "the hockey star" or "the street bully," whatever works to ensure his or her survival in the family and the rest of the world into which he or she has entered.

As the toddler grows into an older child, depending on the circumstances to which he or she is exposed, many other parts develop inside of him or her. For example, there may eventually develop a stubborn child (a child who wants his or her own way), a helpful child, an internal critic or many other characters, effectively creating an entire internal cast of characters. In this sense, the child learns to respond to different people and situations with a gradually expanding repertoire of responses --- all part of the process of becoming an emerging adult. Again, the overall response system is state-dependent in that it is relatively self-sustaining and is dependent on individual responses triggered by commonly-grouped energetic (emotional) themes.

Another important component of a child's sense of powerlessness, as my schoolteacher friend mentioned above has pointed out, is a "child's need to be recognized. Every child will find some way so that he or she can be recognized both by his [or her] peers and by the adults in his [or her] community. Where positive recognition is not received by the child (in the child's eyes), a pattern of 'negative,' often antisocial behaviors may develop, both with regard to the child's peers and the adults of the child's community. In my opinion, almost all the negative behavior found in children under the age of twelve is the result of attention-seeking where the positive attempts have not been recognized. The goal is recognition. There is almost no perceived difference in the child's mind whether this recognition is positive or negative. The child *will* receive attention from others.[7]"

_____
7. Personal communication.

2.1.2.2. Sailors On A Ship

If not managed by awareness and choice, we live these state-dependent response systems in an other-than-conscious fashion, subject to the whim of the environment and our own reactivity. The complexity of this state-dependent development is expressed in the following metaphor (see Figure 7.)

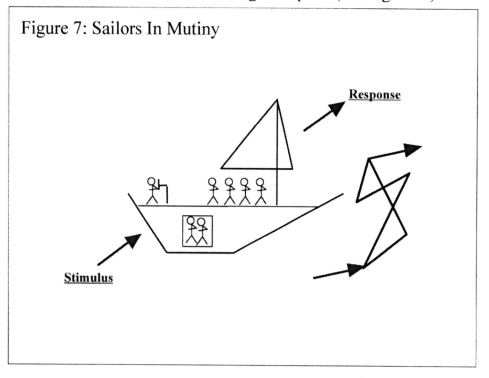

Figure 7: Sailors In Mutiny

Response

Stimulus

"The human mind is very much like a ship where the sailors have mutinied and have locked the captain and the navigator in the cabin. Each sailor believes himself free to steer the ship as he pleases. First one sailor and then another takes over the helm, while the ship travels on a random and erratic course ... these sailors cannot agree on a goal and, even if they could, they do not know how to navigate the ship to reach it.[8] ...."

--- Author's Personal Commentary ---

To illustrate the above metaphor, I often tell the story to my clients of

8. Lori Gordon, Passage To Intimacy: The PAIRS Program (New York: Simon & Schuster, 1993), p. 192.

my own experience with potato chips. Pretend it is Friday afternoon, the end of the week, before suppertime. I'm wandering around the kitchen, and I open a cupboard door. Before I am even conscious of what is in the cupboard, my Sailor #1 (the Potato Chip Kid) spots the large bag of potato chips and immediately reaches for it. Just before I touch the bag, my Sailor #2 (Critic Voice) pipes up, "You idiot, you know what you are going to do. Eat the whole bag!!" Then my Sailor #3 (Dr Dave) says, "No, no, no. We talked about this last week, and we recognized it is a problem. We decided to limit our intake to a small bowl of potato chip.)" The Potato Chip Kid says gleefully, "Yeah, potato chips!!" The Critic Voice now responds, "I don't trust you people." Dr Dave says, "No, we decided on our course of action and that is what we will do."

So, I go and get a small bowl and fill it with potato chips. I carefully close the bag for another time, and I go sit in the living room. Twenty minutes later, I suddenly realize I am sitting with an empty bag of potato chips on my lap. Reliably, by the time I eat the last three potato chips, I am saying to myself, "I don't even like potato chips this much. I feel awful."

The next day, Dr Dave plans another strategy, forgetting the sabotage and how it occurred.

The point of my story is that each Sailor carries state-dependent energies (values, beliefs, memories, expectations) that need coordination and integration. To continue with the metaphor of Sailors On A Ship, please see Figure 8 on the next page.

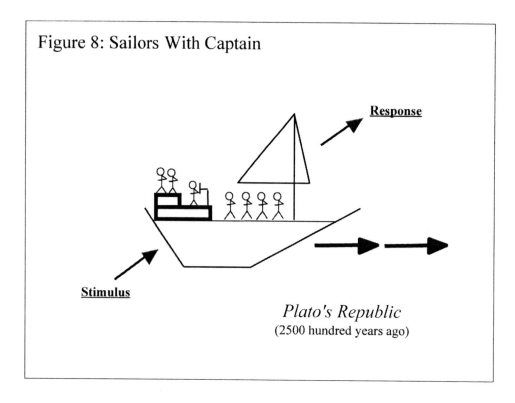

Figure 8: Sailors With Captain

Response

Stimulus

Plato's Republic
(2500 hundred years ago)

"The task of the individual is to quell this mutiny and release the captain and the navigator. Only then is he free to choose a goal and steer a direct course to reach it."

From *Plato's Republic*[9]

Twenty-five hundred years ago, even Plato recognized our complexity and tendency to have subpersonalities (also called parts, functional identities, or other names) and our ways of being in internal conflict with ourselves. Almost all of the clients I encounter can easily apply this metaphor to themselves as accurate of their internal states.

Our different parts likely arise in early childhood as we copy our parents and other significant persons in our lives in an attempt to assimilate the world around us. However, we do not know how to handle the complexity of our subpersonalities at this early age (if we ever do.) We do not know how to integrate them and we frequently experience our parents' confusion of struggling with their own Sailors, even as we grow into adults ourselves.

9. Lori Gordon, Passage To Intimacy: The PAIRS Program (New York: Simon & Schuster, 1993), p. 192

a. We are complex as human beings and generally poorly integrated. We have numerous internal conflicts as we encounter our own sailors in mutiny within ourselves.

b. At a simplistic level, our lack of integration is symptomatic at the level of meaning (alcoholics often talk about "analysis paralysis"), but it arises at the energetic (or emotional) level. It is possible that, if we change the emotional dynamics of our lives, we might also change our cognitive and conceptual understanding of our world.

2.1.2.3.1. Understanding Versus "Overstanding"

Our general lack of integration as a species is consistent with what I experience in a therapeutic context. Internal change does not often occur from the top level down (of the Triune Brain), the type of reasoning generally called "understanding" (see Figure 9.)

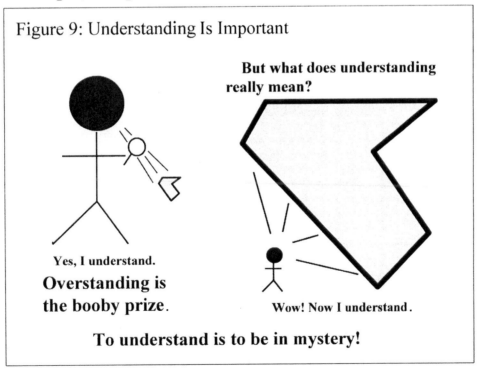

Figure 9: Understanding Is Important

But what does understanding really mean?

Yes, I understand.
Overstanding is the booby prize.

Wow! Now I understand.

To understand is to be in mystery!

A cartoon I draw for clients shows a stick figure standing with a magnifying glass examining an object. The stick figure is saying: "Yes, yes, I understand." A second frame shows the same object greatly magnified with the stick figure standing under it, exclaiming in awe: "Wow, I understand. What mystery. What profound mystery!" I consider this second frame to be true "understanding"; I call the first frame is "overstanding" and believe it is a predominant model of our current society.

2.2. WE ARE ENERGY TRANSFORMERS --- THE MIND

We are short-term sensory-grounded energy transformers. This premise is one of the primary presuppositions of this book and underlies every other concept and metaphor.

2.2.1. THE POT

The best metaphor that I know to describe how we are short-term sensory-grounded energy transformers is to visualize the human mind is a pot of stew (see Figure 10.)

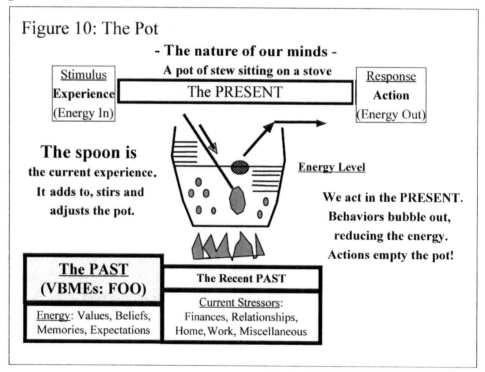

Figure 10: The Pot

Imagine a pot of stew with multiple ingredients, sitting on a stove being heated. The ingredients (such as potatoes, carrots, etc.) represent the energy associated with our values, beliefs, memories and expectations (VBMEs.) Most of these come from our distant past, usually childhood (all the things we learned consciously and unconsciously from our parents and significant others.) The heat represents the stresses of our recent past: finances, relationships, work and home situations as well as the many other miscellaneous events of the last few days. All of it --- the ingredients and the heat --- represents our past --- our distant past and recent past. As the pot is heated, the contents percolate and occasionally ingredients come to the surface. When they do, we become aware of them as our present experiences (in the form of thoughts and feelings.) If the ingredients come to the surface with enough energy, they pop out of the pot (as behaviors --- actions in the present.) For this to happen, we have made some kind of a decision, consciously or unconsciously. When the action pops out, the energy in the pot is diminished. Actions empty the energy of the pot.

The spoon is the present environment, the "here and now," and it adds to and stirs the pot. The spoon is composed of what is happening outside ourselves in our current environments and, more significantly, what is important to our VBMEs within our current environments. We are designed to filter out all that is unimportant to our VBMEs (recall the exercise above with the red filter), and we especially attend to our survival (reptilian brain) and what is painful or pleasurable to us (emotional brain.)

As the reader, please look around right now and notice what gets your attention. As you do so, also notice what other thoughts, feelings and sensations occur within you. Perhaps you notice a picture on the wall that triggers a long-forgotten memory. Perhaps you notice a coffee cup and your thirst comes to the foreground. Of all the possible things around you which you could have focused on, how did you choose those particular items to attend to? And how much emotional energy did you attach to your choice?

This process of attending to the environment is very fast, often as brief as 200 ms (less than a quarter of a second) from the start of the sensation to the beginning of your behaviors. The process can be slowed down with awareness and intention, which I will discuss at further length later in the book.

2.2.1.1. THE LID

Unfortunately, when we do not empty the pot, there are significant consequences, in both the short-term and the long-term (see Figure 11.)

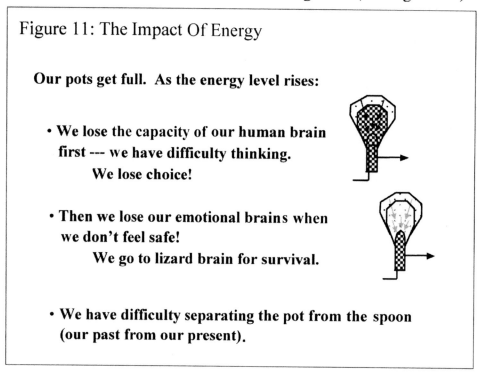

Figure 11: The Impact Of Energy

Our pots get full. As the energy level rises:

- **We lose the capacity of our human brain first --- we have difficulty thinking. We lose choice!**

- **Then we lose our emotional brains when we don't feel safe! We go to lizard brain for survival.**

- **We have difficulty separating the pot from the spoon (our past from our present).**

First, energy builds because experiences are not completed. As the pot gets filled by this energy, the intensity makes it difficult for relatively neutral data to get to the level of the human brain, not without first being contaminated by our preconceived VBMEs (values, beliefs, memories and expectations.) In effect, we do not think clearly. Perhaps we are hypervigilant or sleepy or find some other way of avoiding the intensity of our energy level. Second, as our energy further intensifies, as the pot gets even more full, our reptilian brain is engaged and we do not feel safe. As this accumulation of energy proceeds, we have difficulty distinguishing the spoon from the pot, our past VBMEs from what is actually happening in the present. This three-fold process of not thinking clearly, not feeling safe and not being able to distinguish past from present continues until we say to ourselves, or someone else says to us:

"Put a lid on it!"

When a full pot is sitting on a stove being heated, what happens when you put a lid on it? Although the lid may stop spills and prevent more ingredients from getting in, the pot fundamentally becomes a pressure cooker (see Figure 12.)

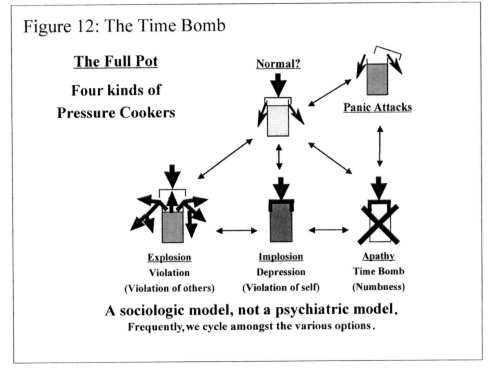

Figure 12: The Time Bomb

The Full Pot

Four kinds of Pressure Cookers

Normal?

Panic Attacks

Explosion
Violation
(Violation of others)

Implosion
Depression
(Violation of self)

Apathy
Time Bomb
(Numbness)

A sociologic model, not a psychiatric model.
Frequently, we cycle amongst the various options.

As biological creatures and pain avoiders, an additional feature of ourselves as pressure cookers is that we lose consciousness of the pressure. We accommodate to it --- it becomes "normal" and therefore persistent.

For simplicity sake, I recognize four types of pressure cookers. Generally we cycle amongst all four but we also each have our favorites.

a. Panic attacks --- the lid is loose and easily pops off. We feel anxious and agitated, wanting to run away and hide.

b. Family violations --- the pressure builds up and we explode, resulting in emotional and physical abuse.

c. Depression --- "de'pressure" rises and we implode. (I personally consider this to be the biggest factor in modern day depressive illness.)

d. Apathy --- "I don't get angry. I get even." In the worst-case scenario, someone takes a submachine gun and kills twenty people.

The above categorization is not a psychiatric model (which has to do with diseases of the mind); it is more of a sociologic model (which has to do with the organization of society.) For example, according to current psychiatric models, the dominant approach to depression is to consider and treat it as a "biochemical disease." While I recognize the possibility of intrinsic biochemical defects (and believe them to be important in some cases of depressive or manic-depressive illness, as well as other diseases), even here though, my experience is that many psychiatric diagnoses fit the patient to the label, a well intended approach but essentially stemming from our reluctance as a society to deal with human issues. Rather, I believe that the vast majority of depression in our society is "a sociologic disease (the way we live our lives) in a biochemical processor (our bodies and brains.)" Our brains respond biochemically to how we manage our energy choices in our behaviors and environments.

2.2.1.2. THE STAIRCASE

So how does the pressure cooker happen? Well, ... life happens!

I use the metaphor of a staircase to emphasize the gradual filling of the pot, as well as the gradations that can occur within the level of energy in the pot (see Figure 13.)

At the bottom of the staircase, the pot is relatively empty. At the top, it is full, perhaps with a lid on it.

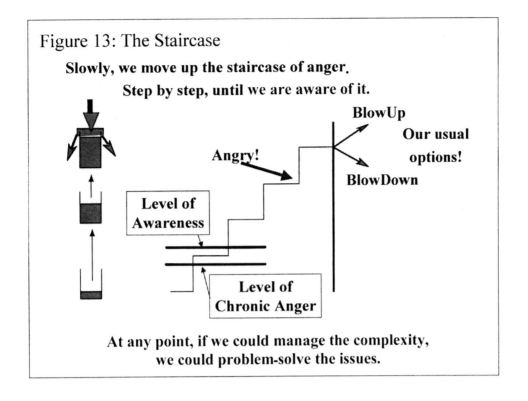

Figure 13: The Staircase

Slowly, we move up the staircase of anger,
Step by step, until we are aware of it.

BlowUp
Our usual
options!
Angry!
BlowDown

Level of
Awareness

Level of
Chronic Anger

At any point, if we could manage the complexity,
we could problem-solve the issues.

We are generally quite peaceful with an empty pot. But then something happens that is a trigger for our energy --- tied to our values, beliefs, memories and expectations (VBMEs.) Our pots get a little fuller and we become "frustrated, confused, whatever ..." but not yet clear as to what exactly is happening internally. The experience remains below our conscious awareness. The difficulty that triggered our energy continues and we note that we are becoming angry (or experiencing some other uncomfortable emotion, one that is not safe for us to feel.) Our pots are getting fuller. If we feel safe, likely we will do something to resolve the difficulty, some form of problem solving. Often, the difficulty is one that is recurrent and such that we have not been able to resolve in the past. We want to ignore the uncomfortable feeling so we push it down below consciousness, especially if it hooks some major issue of our childhoods (for example, the situation reminds us of an unresolved argument with a family member.) Our pot gets fuller, perhaps very full by this point. Sooner or later, we reach our limits. And we either explode (blow up) or stonewall (blow down), unable to internally process and unable to control the situation.

Unfortunately, the Staircase effect represents a trap (see Figure 14.)

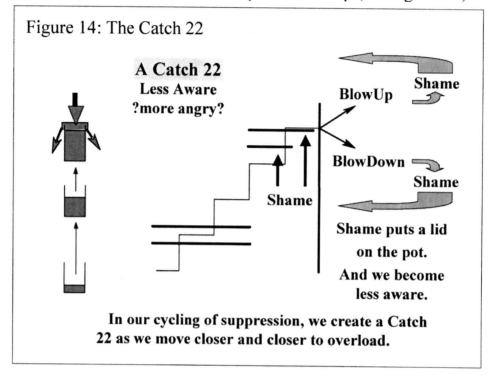

Figure 14: The Catch 22

A Catch 22
Less Aware
?more angry?

BlowUp

Shame

BlowDown

Shame

Shame

Shame puts a lid on the pot.
And we become less aware.

In our cycling of suppression, we create a Catch 22 as we move closer and closer to overload.

As we climb the staircase (and especially when we blow up or blow down), we recognize a problem; but usually it is one that we have had many times before and have not resolved. We feel our powerlessness and begin to criticize ourselves for not being "perfect" or see ourselves as victims being "abandoned" or do whatever is our favorite way of beating ourselves up emotionally. This is the process of shame or guilt. This process does not empty the pot nor does it take us off the staircase. Effectively, it puts a lid on the pot. We accommodate to the increasing pressure by getting used to it; gradually we go numb to the pressure. At this point, we are full pots, being heated on the stove, with lids on the pots. Or, putting it another way, we are sitting at the top of the staircase, waiting …

2.2.2. THE ACTION MODEL

Another way to think of the pot is as what I call the action model --- a stimulus-response process, or more accurately, a sensation-action process (see Figure 15.)

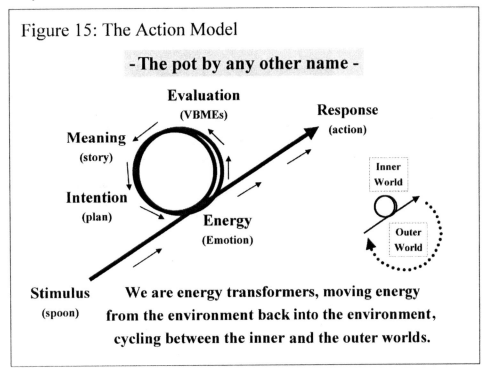

Figure 15: The Action Model

- The pot by any other name -

Evaluation (VBMEs)

Meaning (story)

Response (action)

Intention (plan)

Energy (Emotion)

Inner World

Outer World

Stimulus (spoon)

We are energy transformers, moving energy from the environment back into the environment, cycling between the inner and the outer worlds.

The model appears linear but is actually composed of two interlocking circles, one within the mind and one in the external world. Its linearity emphasizes that we are energy transformers, moving energy from the environment, back into the environment.

To illustrate the process of the action model, I will lay out the various steps involved. To start, some event happens. If it is significant, it reaches the level of interpretation, of which we may or may not be conscious. We apply interpretation by filtering it through our values, beliefs, memories and expectations (VBMEs) and creating meaning of the event. This meaning is actually a fiction, a story, since it is always contaminated (sometimes heavily) by our VBMEs. From this story, we develop a plan of action, an intention to act in relation to the meaning we have created. Our nervous system begins to shift; our muscles begin to tighten; our blood vessels and other neurological systems activate. We are in the beginning of action or "e-motion" (one meaning of the prefix "e" is "from.") This information of shifting muscle tension is then fed back to our nervous systems. We are feedback systems --- we need to be to learn from the environment. If we are attentive, we also give this new information a name: "feelings." Then we act. In so doing, we gather new information to further develop our stories. We also create meaning --- our story that we carry with us (and chew on if we are unable to act.) I will call this story, the story of our "Ghosts" and will develop the concept of Ghost in the next chapter. For example, we have a conversation with someone wherein we are frustrated but unable to do anything about it. Once that person has left, we then continue the conversation in our heads --- with the Ghost of that person. As the reader, I imagine you have done this process many times. If we do not move into action, the Ghost persists. To my knowledge, the only way to empty the pot is to move into action in some fashion. Even in the act of forgiveness, we struggle internally (with tense muscles) and then relax as we let go of our concerns.

2.2.3. SOME IMPLICATIONS OF BEING ENERGY TRANSFORMERS

Many of our struggles as human beings become clearer when we recognize ourselves as energy transformers. Consider the following:

a. The spoon can add to the pot and stir it up, perhaps whip it up. But if a spoon stirs the pot of stew and a carrot comes to the surface, do you say that the spoon caused the carrot to exist? You might say that the spoon has a role in bringing the carrot to the surface perhaps, but as for causing it to exist --- certainly not! Why then do we say that others or other circumstances cause our feelings? Why then do we blame others for our thoughts, feelings and behaviors?

b. We give our interpretations to the behavior of others (how they stir our pots) depending on our past experiences, often with the same people. Often, a current misunderstanding depends more on the past than the present, on how much is already in the pot.

c. We will trust others (as spoons in our pots) if we interpret their behaviors as being both well-intended and consistent with their words --- the stirring is dependable. The same could be said for our being trustworthy: what do we intend in our behaviors and how do we act from our intentions?

d. Actions empty the pot. A useful question to ask ourselves is: What do usually we do with our energy, especially when stressed? There are two circumstances under which people can generally feel peaceful temporarily. If you go to a gymnasium and work out vigorously for an hour, you are relaxed; nothing bothers you for a while. Alternatively, you find a friend who will authentically listen to you about what is happening in your life right now, without criticism or judgment, ... just really listening. You will come away peaceful.

Note that both of these are actions. In the first case, the muscular action is exercise. In the second, it is talking out our story. Energy is stored both in muscles and story. Actions empty the energy.

e. Much of our difficulty in life results from our inability to resolve our past issues and from carrying that pain (and lack of resolution) into the present. The question to ask here is: How do we resolve our past?

f. We do not easily resolve our past principally because we do not feel safe with our emotional energy --- we weren't safe as children, and we collapse into childlike subpersonalities when we are stressed (our emotional brains represented in one or more of the Sailors on the Ship.)

g. Nor does our society know how to handle "negative" emotions --- we are taught to "blow down" at least until we have an excuse to "blow up" (playing sports, getting drunk, road rage, etc.) Or until we really explode.

h. As energy transformers, we cycle between our inner and outer worlds. It keeps the energy moving.

i. The emotional brain is in some fashion timeless. Our Ghosts will persist and energize our actions, perhaps for years, until some resolution is reached.

j. When we are moving energy, we often do not stop to consider what energy is being moved. If another Sailor then comes to the helm, we may then identify what we just did or felt, and perhaps judge it as inappropriate (as compared to being effective for this particular sailor who has done the action.) This rapid shifting of Sailors is a major source of internal conflict.

2.3. WE ARE SOCIAL CREATURES --- HOW WE FUNCTION

Our families of origin are where our emotional brains develop and where we first learn how to interact with others. We learn the rules there. This is our past. Our present evolving families and work relationships are where we act out the rules.

How did all this rule-bound processing of information come about? In addition to our basic biology, the ability to language our experience is part of the rule development in that language allows us to name our internal experiences and to share them with others.

2.3.1. WE GROW UP IN FAMILIES --- THE LANGUAGE OF ACTIONS

Imagine I'm a two-year-old playing with toys (see Figure 16.)

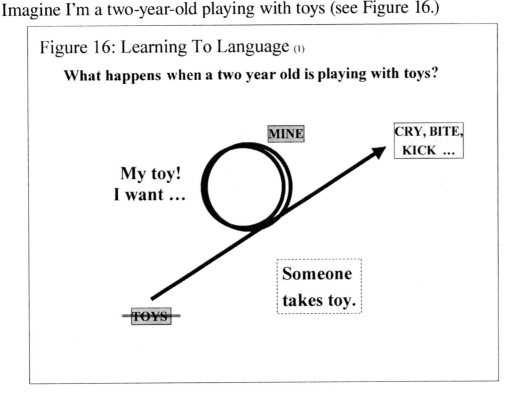

Figure 16: Learning To Language (1)

What happens when a two year old is playing with toys?

MINE

CRY, BITE, KICK ...

**My toy!
I want ...**

**Someone
takes toy.**

TOYS

Another child takes the toy. As a two-year-old, I have a value of "Mine!" by this age. The missing toy becomes "My Toy!" "And I want my toy back!" So I bite, kick, grab, scream --- whatever it takes to get my toy back. This is normal, healthy two-year-old behavior.

Then a parent comes along and tells me three new things, each of which is a new message which will have major implications for the next eighty years or so of my life (see Figure 17.)

Message Number One: "STOP!" This means I have to shut down my energy, because a big person, someone on whom I am absolutely dependent for survival,

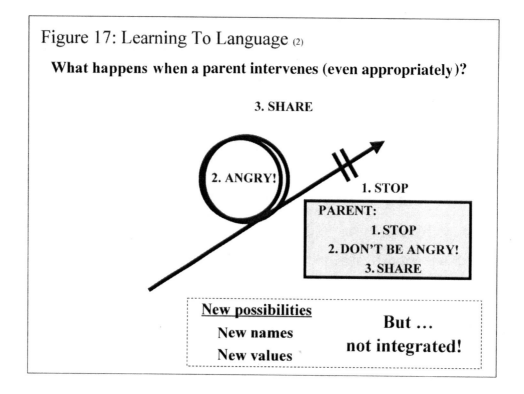

Figure 17: Learning To Language (2)

What happens when a parent intervenes (even appropriately)?

3. SHARE

2. ANGRY!

1. STOP

PARENT:
1. STOP
2. DON'T BE ANGRY!
3. SHARE

New possibilities

New names

New values

**But ...
not integrated!**

is upset. In other words, I am not safe; I am in danger; I will be abandoned. I may not have enough language yet to understand the words but I understand the energy or feelings.

Message Number Two: "DON'T BE ANGRY." As a two-year-old, I am actively engaged in the process of learning language. For the rest of my life this internal energy state, this beginning of action that I am currently experiencing, will be called "Angry." I may lose conscious awareness of the body feeling but my neurological systems will remember. Furthermore, I will learn several different kinds of anger, depending on the circumstances.

Message Number Three: "SHARE." Yet my parent may not show or tell me how (perhaps they will simply yell at me.) Even if they do demonstrate sharing, likely they demonstrate how to share peacefully. They are just giving me new words which do not really have an impact on me --- it is energy and actions that impact.

The next morning at breakfast, I see my parents exchanging newspapers and moving coffee cups back and forth between each other, smiling when they do so. I think: "This must be sharing --- I like it when mummy and daddy share." Some time later, I see my parents are in an argument, yelling at each other. I say to myself: "Oooh. Mummy and daddy are angry! ..... But wait a minute ..... mummy and daddy are angry..... They said 'Stop' --- they're not stopping. They said 'Don't Be Angry' --- they're being angry. They said 'Share' --- hmmph, I guess you share only when you are peaceful and you don't share when you're upset."

Under other circumstances and in similar fashion, I will learn to name "sad," "happy," "silly" and many other words that describe my internal experiences (learning at the same time that these words have subtle but important distinctions.) If one behavior does not get me my goal, I will use another to get what I want. I am goal-orientated; I want my parents to respond to me with positive energy. To do so, I will learn to misname my internal experiences. For example, speaking as the author again, I learned as a child that I would be teased if I was angry, and nurtured if I was sad. Which behavior do you think I displayed most? Sadness, of course, because it got me my goal of positive energy from my parents. In fact, I had so successfully transformed my anger into sadness that it was not until the age of forty-four that I realized that most of my adult sadness and despair was actually rage.

As a result of seeing significant others display the many subtle but important distinctions of emotional experience, most two-year-olds gradually absorb these many complexities, and learn to have internal conversations with themselves as well to have internal conflict with themselves (amongst the various Sailors). Rarely does the child integrate the complexity effectively, especially if the child's parents have not integrated the complexity themselves. Perhaps, as an adult, the two-year-old can integrate --- perhaps. Likely the child says something like: "I'm never going to be like my parents." Then at the age of forty or so, he or she realizes just how much he or she really is like them (or the exact opposite in reaction to them, but still living from a need to avoid pain.)

2.3.1.1. WHAT ARE THE RULES BEHIND OUR ACTIONS

In our attempt to survive our families (healthy or otherwise) and become adult individuals, we know that there are rules of behavior as to how to succeed. We know consciously some of the rules --- the societal rules of polite behavior called etiquette. We also know our family rules which are similar yet somehow more covert, and not quite matching to the societal rules. Even the societal rules are somewhat erratic. We sometimes meet people who are highly successful at the level of accomplishment and societal reputation, yet find out later that they are in fact closet alcoholics or philanderers, not people we want to model.

Occasionally we meet people who are incredibly healthy at the emotional level (although they may initially seem like quite ordinary people). We may wonder how they could be so lucky. But are they really lucky or are they skillful? What are the rules by which they have gotten to be so healthy?

As we wonder about them, we tend to compare our inside reactions with their outside behaviors, not seeing the internal complexity of the other, especially not their internal struggle to maintain their own rules. We focus outside them to discover what has contributed to their success rather than question what skills they use. It is necessary to focus outside to gather data but the data we need concerns the internal skills that they are using. Even more importantly, we need to translate these skills into actions of our own lives.

2.3.1.1.1. Guilt And Other Difficulties

The major rules are rules that allow us to avoid pain --- our primary biological predisposition. These rules allow us to interact with one another in a way that minimizes differences amongst ourselves (and hence minimizes overt conflict in our relationships.) We also want to avoid naming the significant differences since naming them might mean overt conflict also.

In particular, two rules tend to dominate us, rules we don't usually name, but that run us (see Figure 18.)

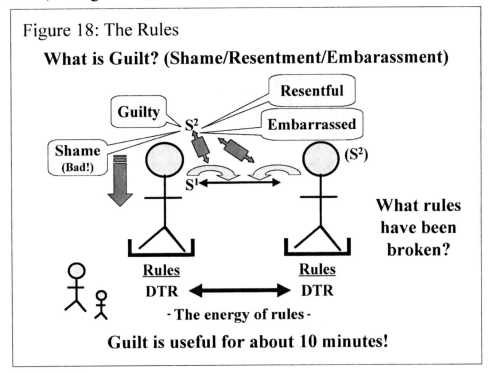

Figure 18: The Rules

What is Guilt? (Shame/Resentment/Embarassment)

What rules have been broken?

· The energy of rules ·

Guilt is useful for about 10 minutes!

It is important to name these rules if we are ever to change them. One of the most profound statements I know in this regard comes from the Scottish psychiatrist R. D. Laing: "Until you can see through the rules, you can only see through the rules.[10]"

The first unnamed rule is "Don't talk about the rules" (which I have shortened to DTR.) As children, when we questioned our parents or others as to what they were doing, we would often be teased or shamed for asking the questions. We learned that, "we don't hang out our dirty laundry in public in this family." Or we learned that there is a "dead elephant in the middle of the room and that everyone walks around it; people smell it, but they don't talk about it. Thus we learned it isn't safe to talk about the rules.

The second unnamed rule is "Everyone's rules are the same." Of course, we think they are; we grew up in the same family. And now as adults, we can't talk about the rules to clarify them and discover our differences; to do so, we would have to break Rule Number One. Although this first rule applied years ago when we were children, our emotional brains do not easily update to new realities, if indeed they are substantially different.

These two dominant rules create certain major dilemmas within individual people. The first dilemma is usually called "Guilt." Some part of me (Sailor #1) has a thought or chooses to act in a certain manner. This thought or action then gets evaluated by another part of me (Sailor #2) who decides that the initial thought or action breaks our internal rules. I then criticize myself (from Sailor #2) but I cannot name the internal conflict for that would mean talking about the rules (DTR) and bringing them to consciousness. This internal conflict is usually called "Guilt" because I feel I have done something wrong at a very significant level while not being exactly sure what it is that I have done.

The second dilemma is created when another person break my rules (which are my rules and not necessarily his or her rules.) My Sailor #1 and Sailor #2 are then in a bind --- the other has broken the rules and should know that he or she has broken the rules; rule number two says that our rules are supposed to be the same. But because we cannot talk about the rules, I will silently bear a grudge against the other; this internal conflict is called "Resentment."

The third dilemma, "Embarrassment," occurs when I break the rules and project that the other will criticize me (since our rules are supposed to be the same.) Again, I will internalize the conflict since to name the conflict would be to break the rules further. Finally, if I break the rules and I project that the other will think me wrong as a person, the fourth dilemma of "Shame" is created, which is a more significant emotional state than "Guilt" because it implies that I am intrinsically bad in breaking the rules.

On the one level, the rules of our society and families are crazy but they often run us nonetheless. The intention is to keep us safe and within our familiar environments. While these are not necessarily bad intentions, my stance is that these four emotional states are truly useful for about ten minutes only. For, in

---

10. I have been unable to track the specific source although I believe it to be: Ronald David Laing, Knots (London: Penguin, 1970).

about ten minutes, I can usually figure out the unnamed rules and make an appropriate, conscious decision on how to proceed. I will explain how to do this as the book unfolds.

2.3.1.2. SOME IMPLICATIONS OF GROWING UP IN FAMILIES

We get into many situations of internal conflict, especially between what we should do and we want to do. This occurs when we look at what others do (their outside behaviors) and compare ourselves --- our internal worlds with their external worlds --- and find they don't match. We think: "Everyone else seems to have it together. What's wrong with us?" And what is it that our parents really wanted us to stop when we were two years old? Our anger? Our desire for the toy? Most of the time it is that they simply didn't want us to create conflict, because they didn't like conflict.

What are we supposed to do with our energy? Especially if we are not safe to express it? Generally we have to shut it up inside ourselves. We think to ourselves, "That is what everyone else does." Alternatively I suggest in this book that the only way for the energy to be discharged is in action. A vitally important distinction of this book is the difference between anger-assertion, saying who we are and what we want, and anger-violation, treating another person as an object and taking what we want by force.

2.3.2. WE INTERACT --- WE LIVE IN EMOTIONAL TRIANGLES

Thus far, I have been discussing the biological and sociological dilemmas of being human as an individual and have not emphasized the dilemmas of being in relationship with others. Families are our earliest social groups. Then we move into larger groups where, theoretically, we are "grown up." Even if we have numerous ways to manage our life energy so that we am not stuck with our anxiety, or we have numerous ways of changing our past experiences so that we create new and more effective, more joyous, outcomes for ourselves, we still live in relationship with others. Many of these relationships are cooperative and pleasant, especially when we put effort into them.

Some are not. What do we do with our alcoholic friends or abrupt colleagues who are unwilling to cooperate with our needs? Or with friends or family members who say they will do something and then don't do it, even after several attempts to negotiate a resolution.

The concept of emotional triangles (see Figure 19) has been the most important and useful concept I have ever encountered in this regard, dramatically shifting how I work with people, both professionally and personally. Everything that occurs in our lives occurs within emotional triangles. Each triangle consists of ourselves, a second person and a third person or issue common to us both. Figuratively and literally, when we consider the number of people and issues in our lives, we exist in thousands of interlocking triangles.

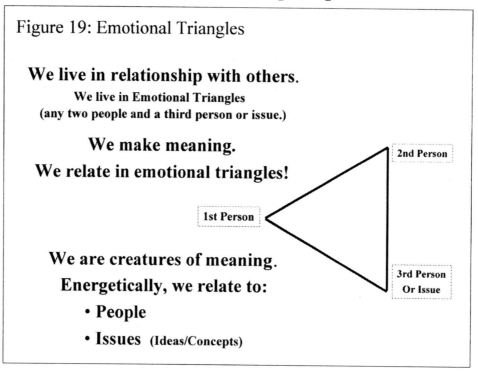

Figure 19: Emotional Triangles

We live in relationship with others.
We live in Emotional Triangles
(any two people and a third person or issue.)

We make meaning.
We relate in emotional triangles!

2nd Person

1st Person

3rd Person
Or Issue

We are creatures of meaning.
Energetically, we relate to:
- **People**
- **Issues** (Ideas/Concepts)

--- Author's Personal Commentary ---

As an example of how many emotional triangles I personally exist

within, consider my current marriage. I have three adult children while my wife has four adult children; including ourselves, that makes for nine people in total, or forty-nine emotional triangles (mathematically, the total number of participants, minus two, squared.) If each person has a life issue pertinent to them (nine people and nine issues), this would entail 144 triangles (the mathematics get complicated.) When you take into account the spouses and children of our adult children, and my clients and other people that I encounter regularly, you can see that the number 144 represents only a small portion of the many thousands of triangles that exist within my life. As the reader, how many people and issues are involved with in your life?

We form triangular emotional relationships in order to exchange energy. Emotional triangles take into account that, as humans, we relate to people and ideas. Additionally, our emotional triangles can be either external (with other people) or internal (with our other Sailors within.) In other words, we form triangles in many different ways, both with other people and with concepts --- triangles carry energy for us.

In any system, everything is related to everything else. When one person or issue changes, the dynamics of all relationships to which the person or issue is connected must change (in some way, small or large, thereby giving different attention to different things.) The impact on any one relationship may be minor or major but all of our relationships will change. Thus, because of the multitude of emotional relationships that impact us, any one relationship is always unstable, potentially shifting in response to changes in other relationships. Witness what happens when someone marries --- many family relationships change, not only the in-law relationships but also those within the nuclear family and existing friendships as a result of shifting family loyalties.

Despite the inherent instability of individual emotional triangles, the network of relationships will respond in such a manner as to keep the overall system fairly stable, shifting back and forth until a new equilibrium is reached. Two of my mentors (Jorge Rosner and Edwin Friedman) have indicated that, in their experience, the system requires approximately three months to re-establish equilibrium. The interlocking of emotional triangles thus allow us to move energy round in a fairly stable fashion. This interlocking is the nature of any system --- we call it stability or the familiar. It is also be a place of emotional "stuckness" or resistance to change.

2.3.2.1. THE LAWS OF EMOTIONAL TRIANGLES

There are three laws of relationship contained in the concept of emotional triangles (see Figure 20.)

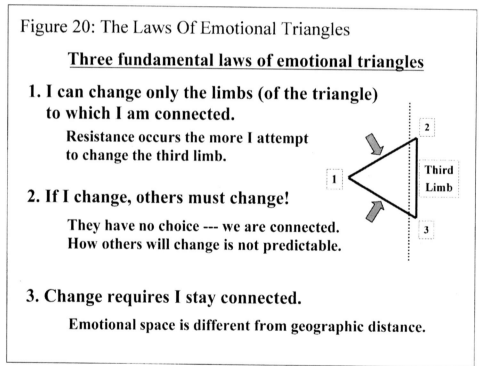

Figure 20: The Laws Of Emotional Triangles

Three fundamental laws of emotional triangles

1. I can change only the limbs (of the triangle) to which I am connected.

Resistance occurs the more I attempt to change the third limb.

2. If I change, others must change!

They have no choice --- we are connected.
How others will change is not predictable.

3. Change requires I stay connected.

Emotional space is different from geographic distance.

These laws are applicable to every triangle and to all triangles simultaneously.

1. Within any one triangle, we can change only the limbs to which we are

   directly connected. When we attempt to change the third limb, the limb to which we do not have direct connection, we can create an impact but the outcome is unpredictable. When we persist, the outcome becomes more predictable. We will create resistance to our efforts; we will create "STUCKNESS." As a result, we will pick up pain from the third limb.

One of the most dramatic examples of the first law of emotional triangles comes from William Shakespeare. He was no fool when he wrote *Romeo and Juliet*. The story likely survives because we know its emotional truth at the other-than-conscious level. In the play, the two families of the lovers wanted to keep Romeo and Juliet apart. Based on the first law of emotional triangles, it was absolutely predictable that Romeo and Juliet would come together in a manner that would cause pain for both families --- mutual suicide, in this case.

2. If we ourselves change, others must change; we are all connected. Change in one relationship will ultimately have an impact on all other relationships in our lives, perhaps a small impact, perhaps a massive one. But specifically how the relationships will change is unpredictable.

The more effective our change in impacting the system, the more resistance we may encounter. This is because others will have to change and they may not like it, even if the change is healthy. Consider what happens when someone stops smoking. For the first week, people congratulate the person heartily but generally by week two, the remarks are usually something like "You're so irritable these days! I liked you better when you were smoking." This kind of comment is the attempt to restore the system to its original state (even if the original state is not desired at the conscious level) and is a form of sabotage; sabotage is part and parcel of change. And the system will likely require about three months to re-stabilize at its new equilibrium. I often tell my clients that the work of change is thirty percent self and seventy percent responding to the sabotage of the system. The sabotage isn't necessarily consciously intended. It simply represents the resistance of others to change within their own systems.

3. Change requires that we stay connected. Emotional space is different from geographic distance. The essential skill is to stay connected with other people while remaining non-anxious at the same time. Usually, our anxiety is such that we want change to occur in the other person, which zaps us of our energy. Instead, we need to manage our own energy effectively, especially our anxiety.

Fundamentally we have three options in how to interact with other people in a healthy manner (see Figure 21.)

Before I discuss these three options, what do I mean by "a healthy manner?" A healthy exchange of energy defines an individual in relationship to another; it states "This is who I am; who are you?" My contention is that direct interaction between individuals will always be healthy in the long-term if the intention is growth of self and/or other. It is a stance of integrity; it will not necessarily be pleasant or fun. I further contend that any healthy exchange of energy will improve the over-all health of the emotional system even though the manner in which this will occur is not predictable.

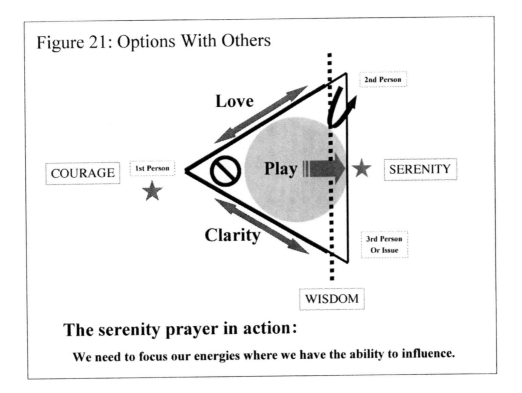

Figure 21: Options With Others

Love

2nd Person

COURAGE 1st Person Play SERENITY

Clarity

3rd Person
Or Issue

WISDOM

The serenity prayer in action:

We need to focus our energies where we have the ability to influence.

With the above understanding, I will now discuss the three options for interacting with another in a healthy manner:

a. We can put energy into improving the relationship between ourselves and the other. Anything we do in a manner that adds growth is likely to be effective, at the very least will promote the health of the system. I call this energy "Love" (of which forgiveness is a big component.) Moreover, if our intention is truly to reveal who we are without imposing on the other, even our anger-assertion can be a component of Love.

b. We can put the energy of "Clarity" (which I define as the ability to think at the emotional level) into the issue by developing our own perspective and our best guess as to the other's perspective. We can study what actually needs to happen with the issue-at-hand (given the needs of ourselves and others.) We can ask ourselves here "What is our own 'stuckness' that limits the resolution of the issue?"

c. While the above two options are usually effective in cooperative relationships, they are not necessarily so in uncooperative relationships. Here, we can manage our anxious energy through "Play" which is best accessed when we activate our human brains rather than our reptilian brains. The *Webster's New World Dictionary*[11] defines "play" as "an activity whose sole aim is diversion or amusement." In play, we utilize the unstable energy of the emotional triangle in a way that blocks the ability of ourselves and other people to get involved in any third limb of the triangle, by acting in a way that is unexpected to the situation but challenging in a non-threatening manner. Because play is unexpected, it disrupts our getting caught in our own anxious energy. It also disrupts our reactivity to another person's anxious energy --- we are able to respond in a way that challenges the other person to deal with his or her own energy. Play is the most difficult option to enact since we are so easily caught in our own anxiety about our own rules and about how others will perceive us. Yet it is a powerful process when utilized well. And we play best when our pots are empty.

In summary, emotional triangles give us all a practical way to live the Serenity Prayer.

---

11. Webster's New World Dictionary: College edition (Toronto: Nelson, Foster, Scott Ltd, 1959).

"God grant me the serenity to accept the things I cannot change;

The courage to change the things I can;

And the wisdom to know the difference.[12]"

I cannot change the third limb of my emotional triangles; I can interact with its elements only. I can change those limbs to which I connect directly, myself and my relationships with others. Furthermore, I can distinguish the different limbs from one another, myself and my relationships with people from the elements of the third limb.

2.3.2.2. THE CRAB TRAP

One of my mentors, Edwin Friedman, was deeply appreciative of fundamental biological principles as the underpinnings of growth. He frequently told the story of how to catch crabs in the North Atlantic Ocean.

First I need to explain how lobster traps work (see Figure 22 on next page.)

Like crabs, lobsters are crustaceans, bottom-dwelling ocean creatures. Generally, lobster traps are rectangular boxes with a rope and float attached. The inside of the trap consists of two chambers with one-way entrances. One chamber is open to the ocean; the second chamber only connects to the first. Bait is placed in the second chamber, and the trap is dropped overboard by the fisherman. Lobsters smell the bait and then search around for an entrance. They push through the opening into the first chamber and then drop down the few inches to the base of the trap. Eventually they enter the second chamber where the bait is located. Once they have eaten the bait and attempt to leave, they have great difficulty getting up to the opening that was so easy to enter from the opposite direction.

Twenty-four hours later, the fisherman comes back to the trap, brings it to the surface and opens it to remove the living lobster. Off they go to the market.

---

12. http://www.aahistory.com/prayer.html

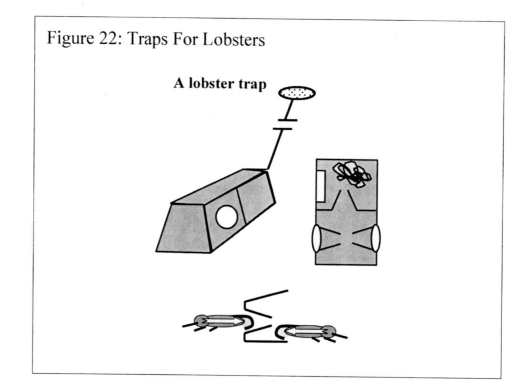

Figure 22: Traps For Lobsters

A lobster trap

Now for the crabs. There are some complex crab traps; for example, spring loaded, no exit when sprung. Besides being expensive, generally they do not last long in salt water.

In order the catch crabs, the simplest and most effective crab trap I've heard of is to take a large wooden box, say six feet by six feet by three feet, with an open-mesh chicken wire bottom. There is no top to this trap. Put some ropes on it and attach a float (see Figure 23.). Weigh the trap down with rocks (for weight), put lots of bait in it and push the trap over the side where crabs are likely to be. The box sinks to the ocean floor; the float marks where it is. It doesn't look like much of a trap, but come back in twenty-four hours and see how many crabs are caught.

Similar to lobsters, crabs smell the bait in the trap and climb the walls (three feet is an easy climb for crabs; not so for lobsters.) Soon there are twenty or so crabs in the box and the feast begins. When the bait is all gone, the crabs are now trapped. But if they climbed into the box, what stops them from climbing out?

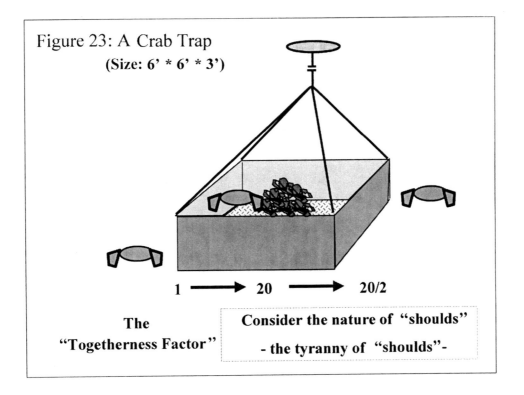

Figure 23: A Crab Trap
(Size: 6' * 6' * 3')

1 ──▶ 20 ──▶ 20/2

The
"Togetherness Factor"

Consider the nature of "shoulds"
- the tyranny of "shoulds"-

Their basic biology! Crabs are social animals; once they have formed a group, they have a strong biologic urge to remain as a group. If one of the crabs attempts to leave by climbing the walls of the inside of the box, the others will pull it back into the box. If another crab tries to leave the box, the others (including the first crab that attempted to leave) will pull it back into the box. If a third crab insists on attempting to leave, the others will kill it --- they will tear its claws off in their effort to keep it in the group rather than let it exit. Biologists call it the "Togetherness Factor." Twenty-four hours later, you come back and bring the trap to the surface. There are twenty crabs, perhaps two dead but eighteen still alive. Off you go to market.

Humans also have the basic biology of the "Togetherness Factor." We too are subject to the crab box; we have no choice in this. For we too are social creatures, and get anxious about the third limb of emotional triangles, the limb we are unable to control. Still we attempt to control it. We attempt to control the activities of others so as to sooth our own anxieties. Or, others want to control us so as to sooth their anxiety. Our crab trap is the word "should" and we will kill to defend it! You only have to witness the many wars of the past century to know how deeply we defend the word "should." It's not right or wrong; just our basic biology. The word "should" is our stability as a system and our sense of community, as well as the trap we set for ourselves in how we respond to individuals who want to be different and step outside the box. "Should" can be a dangerous word!

2.3.2.3. THE LAWS OF ENERGY

In addition to being social creatures, we are emotional creatures. It is another major component of our basic biology. Our laws, our philosophies and our literature discuss the bounties of communing with each other by treating each other with love and respect. Yet we often contravene this kind of positive energy. How do we do this and to what purpose? From my perspective, there appear to be three laws of energy that permeate our energy dynamics and account for many of our behaviors (see Figure 24.)

The first law of energy is that we all want positive energy. To my knowledge, without exception, every human being wants to be loved, acknowledged and accepted. It is a very high need for us as a species and one that permeates our philosophies, our spiritualities and our behaviors.

The second law of energy is that it is easier to get negative energy than positive energy. For example, to get negative energy from you, I simply have to insult you. Likely you will get angry and argue with me, especially if we have an ongoing relationship. To get you to respect me and honor me, however, is much harder work on my part, depending on what is in my pot and how I am currently being heated.

The third law of energy is that negative energy is much preferred to no energy --- to living in a vacuum. If we are short on energy (feeling lonely, bored, etc.), we will do almost anything to get attention. And which type of energy are we likely to go for? Negative energy, of course. It's much easier to get.

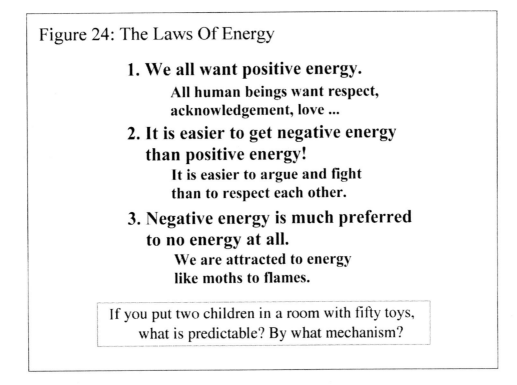

Figure 24: The Laws Of Energy

1. We all want positive energy.
 All human beings want respect,
 acknowledgement, love ...
**2. It is easier to get negative energy
 than positive energy!**
 It is easier to argue and fight
 than to respect each other.
**3. Negative energy is much preferred
 to no energy at all.**
 We are attracted to energy
 like moths to flames.

If you put two children in a room with fifty toys,
what is predictable? By what mechanism?

The three laws of energy sound simplistic yet they underlie much of what we do on a daily basis. For example, if you put two six-year-old children alone in a room together and give them fifty toys to play with, what is predictable? Eventually they will probably fight over one toy. Why? I contend that the answer is hidden in the three laws of energy. At some intrinsic level, they will recognize each other as sources of energy. The toys themselves do not have energy. They are simply inanimate objects on the floor. Perhaps the two children will play alone for a while but eventually they'll play together (seeking energy). Sooner or later, conflict will probably arise when they want different outcomes and don't have the internal discipline to cooperate. So they will fight over one toy as a way of maintaining connection. It's easier to get negative energy than positive.

Suppose you have one child in a room with fifty toys. Where is the energy? Again, not in the toys. The energy is in the child. If the child is well socialized, the child will play quietly for a while, amusing him- or herself. Eventually though, the child will say, "Mummy, I'm bored. Come play with me." Gradually the child will become more and more insistent, until eventually mummy (or daddy or whomever) plays with the child (positive energy) or yells at the child to be quiet (negative energy.) Predictable.

2.3.2.3.1. Psychological Games

The Laws of Energy are so predictable that a type of therapy called Transactional Analysis has developed the concept of psychological games. By definition, psychological games are other-than-conscious processes with a predictable negative outcome. To put it simply, you are playing a psychological game if you ever say to yourself about someone else's behavior, "Here we go again" with the expectation of some kind of negative outcome. Likely the other person is a part of the game but you are also one of the players because you know the outcome in advance and you don't do anything to make apparent the details of the game in order to change the outcome.

The classic psychological game is called the drama triangle (or Karpman triangle.) It consists of three players: Blamer, Victim and Rescuer (see Figure 25.) To understand the dynamics of the game, pretend that each player starts off with one hundred units of energy. Blamer criticizes Victim, thereby giving him forty units of energy. Blamer now has sixty units and Victim has one hundred forty. Rescuer comes along and says to him- or herself, "Blamer should not be so critical." Rescuer gets in the middle by scolding Blamer and placating Victim and gives each of them thirty units energy, or sixty units in total. Blamer now has ninety units, Victim has one hundred seventy and Rescuer sixty. Who is winning? As the game continues, people change roles --- Rescuer becomes Victim ("I'm only trying to help!"), Victim become Blamer ("If you had minded your own business, …") and Blamer now becomes Rescuer ("Stop it, you two!") The game goes on.

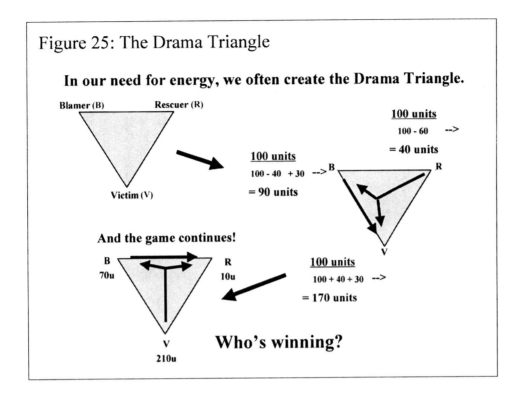

Figure 25: The Drama Triangle

In our need for energy, we often create the Drama Triangle.

The dynamics of the drama triangle are simple yet very powerful in their seductive qualities of energy exchange. The game does not require three people, only three roles. For example, an alcoholic comes home drunk and has an argument with his or her spouse. The alcoholic becomes the Victim (criticized by spouse) or Blamer (anger at spouse.) The spouse takes whatever is the opposite role. The next morning, the alcoholic complains of a headache (and is now Victim) while the spouse becomes Rescuer, "Oh, stay in bed and let me get you a cup of coffee. You had a bad night again."

You can even play the game with yourself. It's Friday; you've have had a bad day at the office (Victim), so you go out and get drunk (Rescuer.) The next day you have a hangover and call yourself stupid (Blamer.) You resolve never to get drunk again (Rescuer.) Next weekend, you go through the whole scenario all over again.

There is no resolution in psychological games, nor is resolution intended --- it would stop the energy exchange. In our current idiom, we frequently name this lack of resolution as co-dependence. We stay in such relationships because negative energy is better than no energy at all; and we do not resolve it because it is easier to get negative energy than positive energy. Positive energy would take us into effective choice where the whole nature of the relationship might change, likely for the better but probably only after much more work.

2.3.2.4. THE POINTING FINGER

In our society, we have so much opportunity to blame others. We only have to listen to the radio or watch TV to observe how we often teach children to appreciate the pervasiveness of blame in our culture. Blame is useful --- on one level, it is a great way to discharge energy. But rarely does it resolve issues, at least not in the long term.

The metaphor of "The Pointing Finger" illuminates many characteristics of blame (see Figure 26.) It is an emotional triangle: I have some power to change me; I have limited opportunity to change you and I create "stuckness" if I attempt to do so. The thumb of The Pointing Finger reminds me that there is always a trigger (an issue that is as much a part of me as it is of you), my index finger points at you in blame and three fingers point back at me. The three fingers pointing back at me remind me of the following:

1. It is easier for me to move energy by blaming you with my pointing finger than to examine myself,

2. What I critique in you is also true of me, perhaps more so. My filters are a major component of my criticisms.

3. If I change and act more effectively, the issue will also change and you will have to change too although how you do so is unpredictable.

The exercise outlined below demonstrates The Pointing Finger in action.

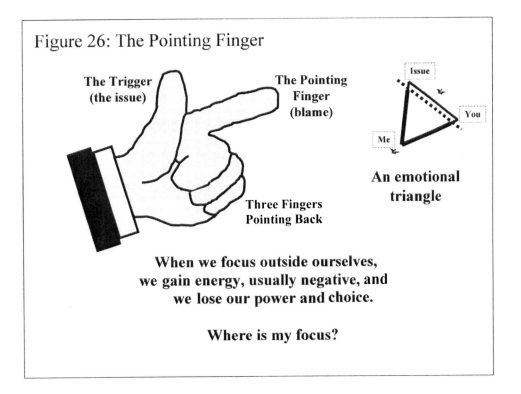

Figure 26: The Pointing Finger

The Trigger (the issue)

The Pointing Finger (blame)

Three Fingers Pointing Back

An emotional triangle

Issue

You

Me

When we focus outside ourselves, we gain energy, usually negative, and we lose our power and choice.

Where is my focus?

Skill: Where Is Your Focus?

Part A.

1. **Recall a specific situation when you have been in significant conflict with another person, one in which it ended up with you getting angry. Recall as many sensory details of the situation as possible. Initially just describe the experience. Resist the temptation in what follows to "analyze" what happened in the past or even what is happening as you recall the scene in the present.**

2. **Imagine the scene in a spot in the room outside of your**

body and see what you are doing in the memory (this is called the dissociated observer position.) Notice your current body sensations as you view this image.

3. **Now physically step into the spot in the room where you placed the scene and be in your body in the memory (associated observer position.) Re-experience the memory and notice where in your body you now have sensations.**

4. **After ten seconds or so (whatever time you need to gain awareness), step out of the scene (back to where you were) and see yourself again in the memory from the dissociated observer position. What happened in each of the two ways of viewing your memory? I imagine your body sensations were quite different in the two ways of experiencing, either dissociated from or associated within the memory.**

Part B.

5. **Now step into the memory again, this time focusing your energy on the other person in the scene and what they did that "made you angry" (the pointing finger.) Notice your body sensations this time. Step out of the memory. Shake off the experience.**

6. **Step into the memory again, this time focusing your energy on the situation and what actually happened — what rules were broken (the thumb.) Notice your**

body sensations this time. Step out of the memory. Shake off the experience.

7. Finally, step into the memory again, this time focusing on your self and what underlies your anger (the three fingers pointing back at you.) Notice your body sensations this time. Step out of the memory. Shake off the experience.

--- Author's Personal Commentary ---

My experience of these last three associated states is that my body sensations are different for each state. When I am focused on the other, I feel my anger in my face. When I am focused on the situation, I feel my anger just behind my face. When I am focused on myself, I feel most of my sensations in my neck and chest. Likely, you will have different experiences from mine.

After gathering the above information of yourself, think of various memories from your past in which you were angry; where do you usually keep your focus? Were you in a position of feeling authentically powerful within yourself or of feeling powerful over another person or the situation?

The metaphor of The Pointing Finger suggests that if you are focused on yourself, you are in the optimal position to access authentic power (although you may not yet know how to do so.) If you are focused on the other person or the situation, you are into the third limb of the triangle and hence definitely in a place where you are powerlessness (although, and ultimately

ineffectively, you may still be attempting to gain power over the other person or the situation.)

2.3.2.5. SOME IMPLICATIONS OF EMOTIONAL TRIANGLES

a. What happens when we focus on that which we are powerless to change? Generally we rage or stonewall. If the pointing finger were actually a gun rather than a finger, we could kill another person or, at the very least, threaten that person. Is this really how we want to live?

b. What happens when we focus on that which we can change? Generally we feel good, satisfied we have done something useful.

c. Personally speaking, I feel most honest and powerful when I am authentically living within the limits of emotional triangles (the Serenity Prayer.) Others tell me it is also true of themselves.

In the next chapter, the book will explore how the principles of Chapter Two can be implemented to allow effective management of our emotional life issues.

CHAPTER THREE --- THE BLOWING OUT! PROCESS

Summary

This chapter develops the Blowing Out! process in depth and gives a broad perspective on how life problems occur, including what tools can be used to resolve them. The model is thus intended as a very practical approach to finding peace within the problems that life offers; in later chapters, it will offer a philosophic perspective of emotional growth. This chapter begins with a detailed description of how we create our realities and discusses some of the possibilities of how we trap ourselves as full pots of energy.

The Blowing Out! process separates the four key areas of human problems — Conflict, Powerlessness, Full Pot and Lack of Safety — and offers specific skills for each area separately. Safety is first of all created by the management of time-outs with specific boundaries: private time for emotional processing, a commitment to return to the relationship within a negotiated amount of time, a commitment to safety, summarized by the phrase "No SAD" (no Scare, no Attack, no Destroy), and a commitment to ensure that everyone feels secure, activated by the word "STOP" (all activity stops if anyone is feeling unsafe.) Within this container of safety, an individual can discharge energy appropriately and return to being a relatively empty pot, now able to think more clearly, be safe with self and other people and able to distinguish what happened in the past versus what is presently occurring.

The discharge or release of energy may be either active and noisy or relatively quiet and seemingly passive. Many methods of release are explored in this chapter as well as the myths and dangers of active energy release.

In returning to an empty pot state, the individual can then separate the appropriateness of behaviors in the present from the issues of the past (the re-surfacing of Ghosts we carry from traumas of the past and which we are usually powerless to manage in the present.) If the issue is one of past Ghosts, attention can be given to resolution of these issues, perhaps requiring some form of therapy. These issues are generally changeable, once clearly recognized.

If the issue is that of inappropriate behavior in the present on the part of the person needing the time-out, an appropriate apology with a true commitment to change can be brought into the affected relationship. Alternatively, if the issue is that of a difficulty within the current relationship, the person who now has an empty pot (Person A) can choose to approach the other person in the relationship (Person B) with the intention of problem-solving in a cooperative manner. Since the energy of Person A is now managed (and can continue to be manageable into the future), the stance of cooperation can be maintained as long as necessary. If Person B chooses to cooperate, the problem can generally be resolved (often easily.) Some of the skills of cooperative problem-solving are developed in this chapter.

If, however, Person B chooses not to cooperate, a different skill set is necessary. It then becomes necessary to make a distinction between non-cooperation and true violation. The major need of Person A in a non-cooperative relationship is to manage his or her own energy in such a manner that he or she is not subject to the impact of the lack of cooperation. The powerful concepts of playful intervention are developed in this section. True violation, on the other hand, is unacceptable, not only because it represents inappropriate power dynamics but also because it is ultimately either ineffective or even dangerous in healthy relationships. The major need of Person A in managing violations is to ensure his or her own safety; this may require leaving the relationship and/or calling "911."

Ultimately the individual can live at peace if he or she manages his or her energy and lives into relationship effectively.

CHAPTER THREE --- BLOWING OUT!

Building on the concepts of the previous chapter on how to achieve emotional balance in life (the transrational), I will develop in this chapter the fundamentals of the Blowing Out! process (see Figure 27.) Again, I emphasize that while anger and rage are the emotions that create the greatest difficulties in our current society, the Blowing Out! process is applicable to every kind of emotional difficulty.

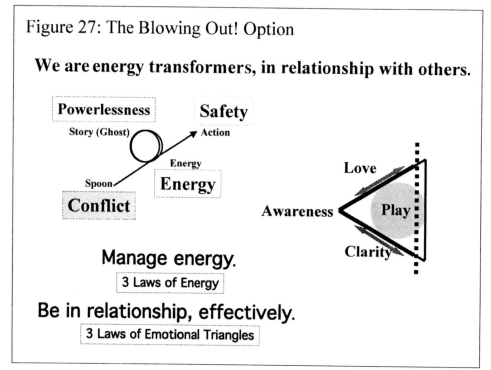

Figure 27: The Blowing Out! Option

We are energy transformers, in relationship with others.

Powerlessness   Safety

Story (Ghost)   Action

Energy

Spoon   **Energy**

Conflict

Love

Awareness   **Play**

Clarity

Manage energy.

3 Laws of Energy

Be in relationship, effectively.

3 Laws of Emotional Triangles

As human beings, we struggle with four key areas in our attempt to deal with the problems that our lives offer us. These are Conflict, Powerlessness, Energy and Safety. A major declaration of this book is that when we mash these four issues together, we create potential time-bombs in ourselves. We need to separate out these issues. When we do separate them, especially when we are able to think clearly about what is happening at the emotional level, we can have greater clarity as to what are the major components and what do we need to do to achieve resolution.

3.1. How We Create Our Experiences

So what actually happens when we process our life experiences? Imagine that you are sitting at a sidewalk café and you hear the sound of a vehicle driving by (see Figure 28.) You don't actually see the vehicle. All you do is hear the sound. How do you know it is a vehicle? How do you know what kind of vehicle it is (a car, a truck, or a motorcycle, etc.)? I suggest that a certain set of internal actions happen rapidly at an other-than-conscious level, supplying you with answers to these questions, even without you being aware of asking the questions. First, you hear the mysterious sound and compare it with sounds you have heard before. In so doing you draw on your faculty of memory, stored as sensory data, and for a brief moment you likely visualize a vehicle of a particular shape and color and with a certain number of passengers. Almost certainly, your experience, if you bring your memory to consciousness, will be vague and indistinct. Yet if you really pay attention, the sensory details will be there or, at the very least, you will create the memory with the sensory details.

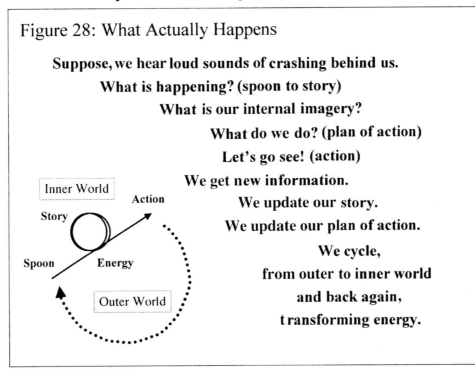

Figure 28: What Actually Happens

Suppose, we hear loud sounds of crashing behind us.
What is happening? (spoon to story)
What is our internal imagery?
What do we do? (plan of action)
Let's go see! (action)
We get new information.
We update our story.
We update our plan of action.
We cycle,
from outer to inner world
and back again,
transforming energy.

Inner World

Action

Story

Spoon   Energy

Outer World

Now imagine you want to have a conversation with a friend who also heard the same mysterious sound. You would probably assume that the two of you are visualizing the same type of vehicle as the source of the sound. You are not! You never are. Each of you will be talking about your own unique constructs of reality, based on your own unique memories of similar sounds, with subtle but important differences between them. If the topic of conversation has energy or emotional resonance for one or both of you, you may end up arguing about the type of vehicle as if there is a "right" answer to an argument about your subtle differences. I imagine that you've had a number of conversations in your life where you have started out neutrally and then unexpectedly ended as an argument. If you have ever wondered how, the above explanation is the most likely answer. You each had different constructs of "reality."

Usually, our unique constructs of reality create only minor issues, if any at all. A more problematic situation arises however if, continuing on with the same example as above, the original sound of the vehicle is followed by crashing sounds, perhaps with screams. Now you interpret the sounds as a "car accident" and likely you invest much more energy in this meaning. Very quickly (likely out-of-consciousness), you develop a "plan of action" ("go see what is happening"), energize yourself and move into action. Once you actually see what is happening, you gather new data from the environment (it doesn't matter if it matches your previous story or not.) You see two cars, three people staggering around, and one person lying on the road, obviously hurt. You update your story (meaning) and plan of action ("phone the police and ambulance; get out there and help.") You energize yourself and move into action. Perhaps you notice your own emotional experience (maybe you are anxious), but likely you give little attention to it. You are busy moving in response to the environment. You are busy transforming energy.

You continue in this fashion, cycling between your inner world of processing and your outer world of movement. Depending on your training and previous experience in accident situations, you will have a variety of internal reactions and display a variety of external skills. You will continue for as long as your energy is high, and you are doing whatever is necessary to correct the situation as you encounter it. Eventually the police and ambulance arrive and the situation settles down again. You are no longer be needed, and can go back to what you were doing previously. What are you most likely to think about? If you encounter someone else, what are you most likely to talk about? The car accident, of course. Although you stopped your external movement, you did not stop your internal processing. To my knowledge, there is only one way to stop the internal processing --- somehow to move it out into action. And one of the easiest ways to move the energy is by talking, perhaps to yourself, preferably to another person (as there is a greater energy exchange.)

3.1.1. The Reality We Hold Onto --- The Ghost

When we talk out our stories, we are not describing the events as they actually happened. We are describing what I name as the Ghost (see Figure 29) --- our story about the events contaminated by our values, beliefs, memories and expectations (our VBMEs.)

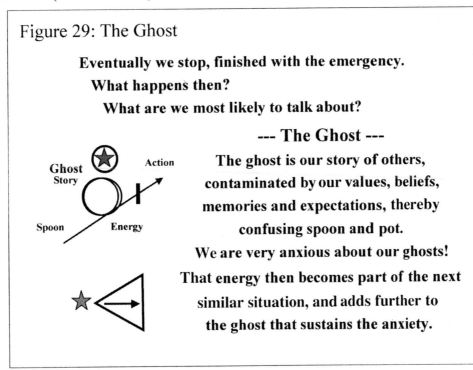

Figure 29: The Ghost

Eventually we stop, finished with the emergency.
What happens then?
What are we most likely to talk about?

--- The Ghost ---

Ghost
Story
Action
Spoon
Energy

The ghost is our story of others,
contaminated by our values, beliefs,
memories and expectations, thereby
confusing spoon and pot.
We are very anxious about our ghosts!
That energy then becomes part of the next
similar situation, and adds further to
the ghost that sustains the anxiety.

Our VBMEs are always present. They are the basic components by which we create meaning in and of our lives. As such, we invest much energy in them --- they are important to us. Because of our limited skills of awareness however, much of the time we do not make clear distinctions between the data that is occurring outside our bodies and the meaning we make of it inside our minds. When we confuse these two sources of information (outside data and inside meaning), we are very likely interacting with our Ghosts instead of the real people with whom we are engaging. This is especially true with the major relationships of our lives, our marital partners and closest family members, where we have much energy invested already.

I will first explain the process by which we create our Ghosts. What seems to happen is that, if we have an emotional experience that is not completed, the leftover energy of that experience is somehow stored in our bodies, ready to be activated into a next situation that is energetically similar to the incomplete experience. Our Ghosts carry the stored energy from one situation to another and trigger our state-dependent characteristics, or, to put it another way, they are part of the way in which our Sailors On A Ship manifest.

In some fashion, the emotional brain is outside of time; completion of an energetic (emotional) experience may take years. For instance, I can have the same emotional response to a situation when I am sixty-four years old as I did when I was two years old. If anxious, this energy then becomes the basis by which I draw myself into the third limb of an emotional triangle. What's more, I will continue to have this same emotional response as a seventy-four year old, an eighty-four year old, etc., at least until I resolve the original incomplete experience from the energetic perspective of the two-year-old that created the original Ghost.

****

<u>Skill: Distinguishing Ghost From Reality</u>

A useful skill is to be able to distinguish Ghost from "reality."

Awareness of self and the environment is the key to successfully distinguishing the two states (see Chapter Five — Essential Skills for further details.)

As an example, I will describe my own experience while having a conversation with another person. I notice that my visual focus is centered directly on the lines and shadows of that person's face. This indicates to me that I am dealing with the reality of that person. However, if I notice that my vision of the person is slightly fuzzy (perhaps I am focused about six inches in front of him or her), then I am likely attending to one of my Ghosts at that moment. Similarly, if my attention drifts from the person in any way, I have likely shifted to one of my Ghosts. I may or may not be aware of the details of my Ghost at this time, just that I have shifted my focus. This is a starting point to note what is actually happening inside of me. Having noticed the shift of focus, I now have choice as to what to do about it. I may need to give myself a red flag, that something is happening at an other-than-conscious level, especially if my energy is activated.

As the reader, please notice your own experience the next time you have a conversation with someone you know. Practice giving awareness to what is actually happening. Attempt to add details to what is actually present in your consciousness rather than what "should" be present at the time.

3.2. THE WAY OUT

Our present lives are complex; many difficult situations occur in our current society that we did not encounter even a hundred years ago. If our childhoods in particular were not safe, we bring much unresolved energy from our pasts into the present. Under these circumstances, we risk becoming relatively full pots, perhaps even pressure cookers. Many of us already are pressure cookers. Witness the frequency of road rage and family violations.

My assertion is that it is always possible to empty the pot, and it takes only about ten minutes. Resolving the conflict is what takes time and effort but is very possible if the pot is empty. I suggest that we are not biologically designed to be time bombs. We are meant to access all parts of ourselves that are appropriate to the situations in which we find ourselves. However, there are two fundamental problems that limit our integration as human beings:

Problem #1: Conflict with self. We have no Captain on the ship and our Sailors are in conflict. Generally, this can be considered as an internal emotional triangle with a third limb problem.

Problem #2: Conflict with others. We are caught in other people's anxiety about us or our own anxiety about them. Generally, this is an external emotional triangle with a third limb problem.

The process by which we create conflict within ourselves with other people generally follows a similar pattern each time (see Figure 30.) First, something happens. We feel threatened by it. We feel powerless to do anything about it; it reminds us of our childhood, our personal history. We call it conflict. Perhaps we feel stressed, angry, depressed or some other unpleasant emotion. But we tell ourselves that we shouldn't feel that way: "It's not such a big deal." This is our personal crab trap. We stop our actions, afraid of the consequences if we act into such a confusing morass of emotions. We stuff our energy and, over time, become a time bomb. We cycle through the various options of the pot and always do what we've always done, always getting what we've always gotten.

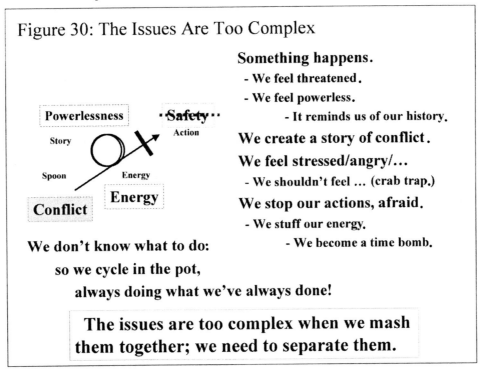

Figure 30: The Issues Are Too Complex

Something happens.
- We feel threatened.
- We feel powerless.
    - It reminds us of our history.
We create a story of conflict.
We feel stressed/angry/...
- We shouldn't feel ... (crab trap.)
We stop our actions, afraid.
- We stuff our energy.
    - We become a time bomb.

Powerlessness   ·Safety··
Story   Action
Spoon   Energy
    Energy
Conflict

We don't know what to do:
    so we cycle in the pot,
        always doing what we've always done!

The issues are too complex when we mash them together; we need to separate them.

My belief is that emotional issues are too complex when we mash their different components together. When we do so, we create a dynamic within ourselves wherein we cannot think clearly, we don't feel safe and we have difficulty distinguishing Ghosts from current experiences. No wonder we have troubles.

3.2.1. BLOWING OUT!

The Blowing Out! process is a process which I developed, over my years of practice as a therapist, to allow people to <u>safely</u> discharge their stuffed, pent-up energy in physical fashion (e.g. yelling into a pillow, hitting a punching bag), after which they can think much more clearly about the issues and then attempt to resolve the issues that caused their energy to build up in the first place. Other processes I have known over the years have tended to either discount the need for release of energy or discount the need for resolution. Initial safety (for all concerned), energy management and final resolution of difficulties (in any of a variety of ways) are all essential to the Blowing Out! process.

The Blowing Out! process honors this reality of what we actually do. It separates the issues (conflict, powerlessness, energy and safety) and deals with them in reverse sequence so as to maintain optimum choice, allowing options to be planned for predictable patterns. Four steps are involved. I remind the reader again that my emphasis is on anger and rage but that the principles of the Blowing Out! process are applicable to all emotional experience. Before I delve into each of the four steps in detail (in the next section of this chapter), I will briefly outline them here.

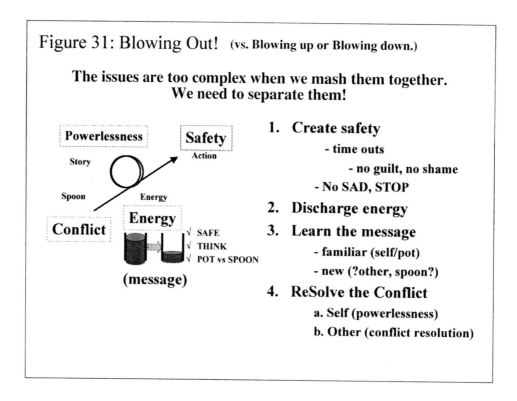

Let us say that you, as reader, are the person who is becoming overwhelmed with your energy. The first step, and unquestionably the most important, is CREATE SAFETY. This generally requires a time-out and the creation of a space (physical and/or psychological) where no one, especially yourself, will experience threat, shame, guilt or embarrassment. It does not necessarily mean that you will be alone --- you can be with others who are safe with your energetic processing, for example, a therapist, a good friend, your spouse, etc.

Two commands become important in this context: "No SAD" and "STOP." No SAD means you commit yourself to:

    a. having no intention to "Scare" another human being;

    b. nor will you "Attack" another biologic creature;

    c. and you will not "Destroy" with your energy that which you would not destroy if you were peaceful.

If others are present, you also commit to "STOP" all action if anyone "feels" unsafe, at least until the feeling of security is restored.

The second step of the Blowing Out! process is DISCHARGE THE ENERGY. Within parameters of safety, you release your energy and move from confusion and terror to feeling secure, able to think and make choices and distinguish your Ghosts from current experiences.

The third step is to LEARN THE MESSAGE of the energy. Generally the message is fairly clear. The energy is either familiar (powerlessness or a Ghost, for example that of fighting with a parent in teen years) or the energy has arisen from some unexpected behavior on another person's part (conflict where, for example, you loaned your friend five hundred dollars; he said he would pay you back yesterday --- you haven't seen the money yet.)

The fourth and final step of the Blowing Out! process is to RESOLVE THE CONFLICT. The message of the energy usually consists of more than one layer of meaning and each component of the message requires a different skill set for management. Since you have discharged your energy, you have time to think and plan responses that will be effective for you. You also have time to mobilize your resources. If your energy builds again, you can repeat the steps of emptying your pot so as to return to an emotional space of having choice.

If the energy of the conflict is familiar (powerlessness), likely you need some form of therapy to resolve it. As I indicated in the Introduction, I dislike the connotations of the word "therapy" for it implies that you are sick or helpless. This is not true for me --- it simply means you do not have the necessary tools to resolve the problem at this time. Are they available? ... Likely but you may have to search for a good therapist so that you can learn how to use the tools.

If the energy represents some unexpected behavior (conflict) --- a problem between you and another person --- two basic options present themselves. In both, you can manage your energy and thus stay present to resolving the problem. In the first option, you can approach the other person and say, "We have a problem to solve. Are you willing to cooperate?" If the other person is cooperative, you will resolve the conflict. For, as human beings, we are generally not stupid in our behaviors, only habitual. Resolving the conflict may require a number of attempts on the part of yourself and the other person but, assuming that you both manage your energy, you will resolve it.

If the other person does not wish to cooperate, you could end the relationship but this is often not practical or possible --- the other person might be a family member, a close friend or a colleague, currently stuck with his or her own issues. The second option in resolving the difficulty is to find a solution that does not violate the other person and yet places you in a position wherein you are not subject to his or her choices. For you are not a doormat upon whom the other person can dump his or her current life difficulties without your permission. If the other continues to behave in a way that is not acceptable to you, particularly if it impacts your choices, then you can act in such a way that blocks the other person's behaviors from influencing you. You may leave; you may say "No" the next time he or she asks for a favor; or you may even act in such a way that he or she feels confused or restricted by how the situation has evolved (I will discuss this last situation in more detail later in the book.)

3.3. THE COMPONENTS OF BLOWING OUT!

I will now explore in greater depth the individual components of the Blowing Out! process before returning to a general discussion of the process at the end of the chapter. Again, the individual components are: Create Safety; Discharge The Energy; Learn The Message; and Resolve The Conflict.

3.3.1. CREATE SAFETY

Safety is mandatory! For many reasons, safety is the first step during the Blowing Out! process to allow all persons present (yourself and others) to be free from violation. By violation, I mean "the restriction of any individual's choice without his or her permission." For example, I violate you when I tell you how you must behave or when I block your actions other than in the interest of public safety. Here, language becomes very important in distinguishing between safety and security. As example, suppose you are standing within a restaurant high in a tall building, looking out a window onto the city far below. You fantasize what would happen if you fell out the window. Assuming no earthquake or other environmental issues that would precipitate such an event, you are safe but you do not feel secure. The *Webster New World Dictionary*[1] defines "safety" as the "quality or condition of being safe, of being free from danger, injury or damage" and "security" as "something about which there is no need to feel apprehension." I define safety as the absence of conditions that pose long-term negative consequences, especially at the physical level. If there is no danger or I believe myself to have many choices in the presence of danger, it generally means that I am safe; there can still be minor risk of danger. Nevertheless I may not feel secure in my perception of what the danger represents to me. Hence security is the feeling associated with believing myself to be safe, not only in actuality being safe. Thus, when an innocuous event reminds me of past danger, I may not feel secure while I am actually safe. As a species, we are terrified of feeling insecure; we often do not "feel" safe. It is the principle reason we dissociate from

1. Webster's New World Dictionary: College edition (Toronto: Nelson, Foster, Scott Ltd, 1959).

the present. Indeed, fear is a basic definition of biological function: organisms respond to their environments with movement towards pleasure and away from pain.

In dealing with emotional issues when you do not feel secure, your ability to think is generally compromised in a particular fashion. You will probably act from an other-than-conscious state and your need for protection will be high. Your responses may be less than desirable or even inappropriate. For when the danger is more perceived than real, you will likely confuse Ghost with reality in your inability to think. If you do not feel secure and have grown up with significant family violations as your norm, especially physical violations, then in your profound need to create safety, you may even violate another person in this state.

In addition, if you do not feel secure, it is highly unlikely that you will explore your emotional issues at this time. For, as human beings, we are pain avoiders and want to get away from our pain. In wanting to get away from our pain, we hide, avoid, escape, get drunk, etc. --- all words to describe the same process of avoidance or, more accurately, dissociation. Eventually when we get back to a state of feeling secure, distanced from the emotionality of the issue, we may look back on the problem from this dissociated position and analyze what happened, not re-experience it.

Unfortunately, the ability to analyze, especially to understand "why," is not generally a useful exercise in the resolution of emotional issues. When we approach the problem from a dissociated position, we gain only a small amount of the information that is available. While there is nothing wrong with the dissociated position, it simply is not all, or usually not even most of, the available information. Much more useful information is generally available in an associated position. In therapy, as people become more able to tolerate insecurity, a pattern of avoidance can change to a pattern of choosing to stay with the painful emotional dynamics so as to explore what actually is happening at an experiential level. Once you recognize that you are safe in dealing with your emotional issues (even though you may feel insecure), your emotional brain can recognize that you may not be thinking clearly --- you are in trouble psychologically. Only then can you initiate options for either the release of energy (so as to gain further choices by accessing your human brain) and/or to achieve resolution of the conflict, thereby cycling back to long-term safety and satisfactory relationships. Because the actuality of safety is mandatory, and processing from an associated position is usually necessary for problem solving, how then do we create safety in dealing with our emotional issues? Fortunately, the answer is fairly simple. If it were not simple, we would have to access our skills of emotionality in complex ways and thus would be in an even greater Catch-22 than we already are.

3.3.1.1. TIME OUTS

To create safety, first you need to create a "time-out" (see Figure 32.) In practice, a time-out means that if you get into a heated conflict with someone and start to feel overwhelmed (usually from your Ghosts), you have the right to ask for a time-out to re-establish yourself into safety. You ask for a time-out so that both parties involved are safe, not just yourself. The other person has the same options.

Ideally, the two of you have a pre-arranged agreement that time-outs are permissible (if not, you may need to negotiate the parameters of the time-out on the spot.) A request for a time-out consists of your stating that you need a time-out and you will be back within a designated time period (whatever is appropriate to your needs, hopefully brief.) I usually suggest twenty minutes. Ten minutes is generally enough time for most people to manage their energy while twenty minutes allows them some time to process what they have learned from their energy. As well, this time period is generally brief enough for the other person that they are willing to wait in anticipation of conflict resolution. If you make the time-out too long (for example, hours or days), likely both of you will spin into conflict again. Also, a limit on your time-out is mandatory so that the other person knows when you will be back. Most importantly, you need to keep your

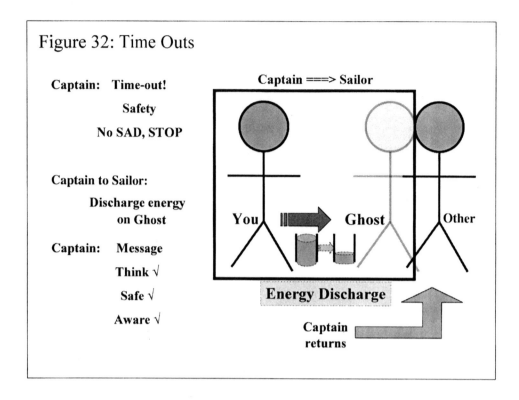

word and return in the agreed time or sooner. Most people can wait a brief period of time, at least once they have learned that you will return after the time-out to continue the conflict in a problem-solving manner. Otherwise the other person is likely to get caught in his or her own emotional distress of the conflict and possibly spin into his or her own personal Ghosts. Both of your difficulties will then escalate.

Typically though, most people, when they take a time-out go, for a walk or sit quietly and reflect on the situation. My concern with this kind of behavior is that action is either minimal or absent. The musculature used may not even be the musculature activated by the conflict (see below, Section 3.3.2.1. How Energy Is Stored for more information.) Under these circumstances, the energy is usually stuffed back into the pot, ready for the next event.

Instead, during your time-out, you will want to release the energy that has become trapped. For this, you will need privacy or at least the company of others who feel safe with whatever you choose to do with your energy. Therefore, choose a space where you can be as noisy or as quiet as is appropriate to your needs, one where the boundaries of safety and security are easy to maintain. When you return from your time-out, you can now return to interacting with the other person in a manner that encourages cooperative conflict resolution. Ultimately, this is your goal --- to go on feeling good about the relationship while resolving any major differences.

Suppose the other person is not willing to allow you a time-out (presumably he or she is caught in his or her own issues at this point.) What then? First, you need to realize that you are in an emotional triangle: you, the other person and the issue. You need to remember that your connection to the conflict is not the same as your relationship with the other person. The conflict and the relationship are separate issues. When the other person is not willing to allow you a time-out, you can separate somewhat from the other person for a moment (energetically, emotionally or physically) and create a zone of safety within yourself while quietly discharging energy in some fashion that does not threaten the other person or anyone else who may be present (see below for examples.) Once you have learned to manage your own energy and have an effective Captain, it is fairly easy to discharge your energy safely, even in the presence of someone who is easily threatened. Nevertheless, dealing with your energy in this manner is not ideal and, in the long-term, may require negotiation between you and the other person as to how to resolve the problem of your collective energy dynamics, let alone the problem itself.

3.3.1.2. No SAD And STOP

The commands of "No SAD" and "STOP" allow for the safety and security of all concerned during the Blowing Out! process. Considering again the metaphor of Sailors On A Ship, when you are caught in your own energy, one or more of your Sailors are likely caught at this point. Ideally there is (and eventually can be) a Captain on your ship. It is the Captain's job to declare a time-out and institute the rules of No SAD and STOP (see Figure 33.) The Captain can then say to the appropriate Sailors: "Discharge your energy within the container of these rules in any way that works, but you as the Sailor do not have permission to step outside of this container!"

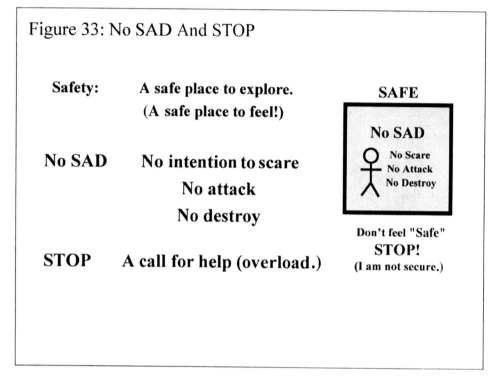

Figure 33: No SAD And STOP

Safety:	**A safe place to explore.** **(A safe place to feel!)**	**SAFE**
No SAD	**No intention to scare** **No attack** **No destroy**	**No SAD** No Scare No Attack No Destroy
STOP	**A call for help (overload.)**	Don't feel "Safe" **STOP!** (I am not secure.)

Specifically, No SAD means that you do not intend threat with your behaviors. You will not intentionally Scare another human being, you will not Attack another biologic creature (person, dog or tree) and you will not Destroy with your energy that which is not acceptable to be destroyed when you are peaceful. In this manner, you and any other persons around are totally safe at the physical level, barring any unintended accidents. This does not mean that the other person will feel safe --- his or her security may be threatened by your actions, but not his or her actual safety. Again, this is a subtle but important distinction between being safe and feeling safe. Your actions (without your intention) may remind the other person of actions in his or her past that were truly issues of safety. As such, the other person's Ghosts may come to the surface and he or she could feel scared, unbeknownst to you, the one who is doing the action. If the other person's security is compromised, the word STOP is meant to take this scenario into account. If anyone says STOP, then all actions stop, at least until "security" can be re-established.

3.3.2. DISCHARGE THE ENERGY

The second step of the Blowing Out! process is to manage your energy. As stated in the Introduction, I define energy as the ability to initiate movement (internally and externally.) Because as a species, we are orientated to action, we generally give our energy an emotional name such as anger or joy, dependent on meaning and direction. Recall that emotion is "a biologically useful action tendency" which we learned to name so as to communicate to ourselves and others that which was happening within us energetically.

3.3.2.1. HOW ENERGY IS STORED

In seeking understanding of energy, I am convinced that the energy is stored selectively in two locations: in certain muscles of the body and, in some fashion created by the mind, within the story in a state-dependent fashion. For example, depending on the situations where the individual learned to name his or her emotional experiences as a child, most people store anger as an upper body experience, especially arms and neck; sometimes the energy is stored in legs and pelvis.

Practically speaking, energy is stored in (or at least accessible from) two locations: story and muscle. First (and often less important), energy is stored in the story --- the meaning you give to the circumstances: the Ghost that carries your values, beliefs, memories and expectations. Story often is "I am right; you are wrong." To which I usually respond, "Would you rather be right or in relationship?" If you are to problem solve, you both need to be validated in your individual perspectives.

Story is generally held by one of the Sailors and can usually be discharged by verbal or written expression. The expression does not need to be directed at the person with whom you are having the conflict --- doing so at this time will often escalate the conflict and/or the energy. Instead you need to find a friend or colleague who will authentically listen to your story of the Ghost; or you may need to explore privately using journal writing or expressive muscular work.

The muscular body experience of energy is generally more important than the story. You can be rationally aware of your story, its craziness and its traps, and still be caught in the energy of your body. From personal experience, I've learned that the standard musculature we exercise in gymnasiums or learn about at the doctor's office isn't the musculature that holds emotional energy. In my office, I have two posters hanging on the wall, one poster labeled "Human Musculature," a standard set of medical drawings of human anatomy showing the muscular system; and the other poster showing a man holding a picture of a cow. The second poster is entitled "This is not a cow." This title is accurate --- the man is holding a picture of a cow. He is not holding a cow. The muscle poster is less accurate in its title --- it is only someone's idea of the musculature of the human body.

My belief is that the muscle poster shows the standard muscles that are responsible for movement, for example, when I am walking or reaching for an object. I call them the muscles of mobility. However, the poster does not indicate the vast number of muscles that are too small to be seen at the scale of the poster size. These smaller muscles are responsible for holding the body together. I call them the muscles of stability; and they provide the muscles of mobility with the necessary stable base for movement to occur. Nor does the poster include much of what is generally called the myofascia, the complex network of fibrous tissues that hold all the muscles intact and together so that they can function properly. For simplicity's sake, I include the myofascia within my discussion of the muscles of stability. In my personal experience, emotional energy is stored in the muscles of stability, not the muscles of mobility. It is the stability component of the muscular system that our brains access in our complex mind-body creation of our emotions. And it is this component wherein lies the interplay between our story and our energy.

Practically speaking, this means that I need to access my muscles of stability if I am to discharge the energy. When I am associated in an experience, for example, angry, sad or joyous, the connections to my muscles of stability are automatic --- they are my experience. When I am dissociated from an experience, usually observing it from an out-of-body stance, the connections to my muscles of stability are likely broken. The energy is unavailable for movement into action.

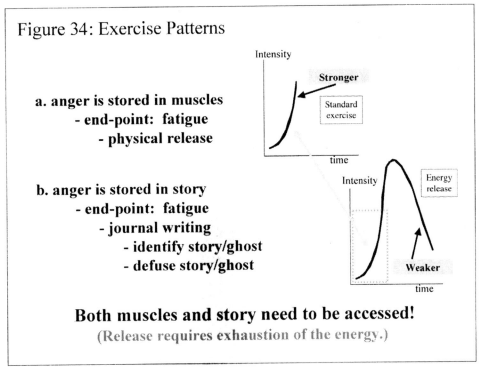

Figure 34: Exercise Patterns

a. anger is stored in muscles
  - end-point: fatigue
    - physical release

Intensity

Stronger

Standard exercise

time

b. anger is stored in story
  - end-point: fatigue
    - journal writing
      - identify story/ghost
      - defuse story/ghost

Intensity

Energy release

Weaker

time

Both muscles and story need to be accessed!
(Release requires exhaustion of the energy.)

The question here is that if energy is stored in muscle (and story), and if I need to move into action to discharge the energy, does it get more intense when I do so (see Figure 34)? The answer is yes and no. To illustrate, when I go to the gym to work out, my muscles get stronger and tighter within the limits of a sub-maximal range of exercise. However, if I exceed the sub-maximum range, the muscles get weaker --- they are "spent." Similarly in emotional physiology, if I tell a friend my story in complaint, the energy often gets more intense. But if I authentically tell my story and am authentically heard, the energy is perhaps permanently discharged. I say perhaps because the pot of energy may fill up again for many reasons. When I discharge the energy in my muscles of mobility without shifting my story, the deep underlying energy has not been changed. A residue exists which can build up again over time and presumably be triggered by interactions within a similar environment.

My experience as a therapist is that, if a client can shift his or her story to a meaning that has a felt sense of authentic power, that which I call an "authentic feel-good" experience, the residue of energy is likely dissipated in its final form. The client's rational memory of difficulty may remain, but his or her energetic involvement with it is gone. This shifting of story seems to be most effective when the energy has been accessed through the muscles of stability. I will explore further in this chapter and Chapter Four some of the ways in which this final resolution can be achieved.

3.3.2.2. ACTIVE ENERGY RELEASE

There are many ways to discharge the energy. The essential need is action, moving energy while maintaining a stance of safety. In my experience, I have three rapid ways of consciously choosing to discharge the energy (see Figure 35.) I will explore each of these methods in detail shortly but list them here to emphasize the wide range of options available:

1. Safe physical release after associating into the emotional experience (perhaps with much noise.)

2. Specifically targeting the musculature holding the energy and using it actively (perhaps quiet.)

3. Using the skills of hatha yoga, especially targeting the specific musculature (usually quiet.)

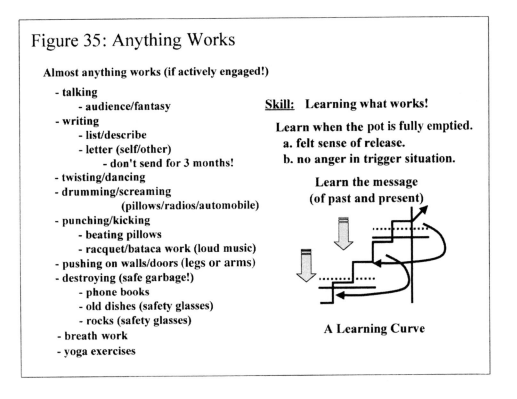

Figure 35: Anything Works

Almost anything works (if actively engaged!)

- talking
    - audience/fantasy
- writing
    - list/describe
    - letter (self/other)
        - don't send for 3 months!
- twisting/dancing
- drumming/screaming
            (pillows/radios/automobile)
- punching/kicking
    - beating pillows
    - racquet/bataca work (loud music)
- pushing on walls/doors (legs or arms)
- destroying (safe garbage!)
    - phone books
    - old dishes (safety glasses)
    - rocks (safety glasses)
- breath work
- yoga exercises

Skill: **Learning what works!**

Learn when the pot is fully emptied.
a. felt sense of release.
b. no anger in trigger situation.

Learn the message
(of past and present)

A Learning Curve

My first method of energy release is to move into an associated position of actively feeling my emotional state, immersed in my story, and moving the energy out of my musculature (within the boundaries of safety.) This method may necessitate active exercise such as screaming or pounding on a heavy bag. It is the most reliable and most useful method in the early stages of learning to manage energy, especially since the individual needing release is often strongly associated into the problem, even if he or she is not conscious of the musculature. For example, I may talk with a friend who will actively listen without suggestions or criticisms; I may vigorously write in my journal; I may push quietly against a doorframe; I may scream into a pillow; or I may pound on a coach with a tennis racquet. Often, I do not even need to access the story at a conscious level; the energy is so intense that the story automatically comes to the surface once I start active muscular release. Some of these methods of energy release are quiet. Some generate much noise. If I am in a circumstance where noise would be misinterpreted, I retire to another room and push quietly on a doorframe or I write in my journal. If safe to do so and my energy is intense, I might scream or chop wood or pound on a couch with a tennis racquet. The absolute limits are the safety and security of myself and those around me.

The second method I have to release energy is to identify the musculature that is currently holding the energy and target this area specifically. My best illustration of this method is when someone physically manages the shortness of breath (generally due to hyperventilation) that often accompanies the emotional difficulty. Shortness of breath is a symptom of a full pot, this time with a loose lid, and is what people often call anxiety or panic. A specific breathing exercise that I use at these times is described in the accompanying skill insert.

****

Skill: Management of Anxiety

If possible, identify any feelings of anxiety within yourself at this time. Likely you will feel tightness in the chest, with a variable sense of being unable to take a deep breath.

What is happening here? Psychologically, anxiety stems from the gap between the present and the future as we anticipate catastrophic consequences from our current circumstances and possible actions. Physiologically what happens is that we restrict our breath in order to hold back energy for this possible catastrophic future (see Figure 36.) We do this by tightening the musculature of our chest wall, thus sustaining the tension in a way that restricts our ability to take a deep breath.

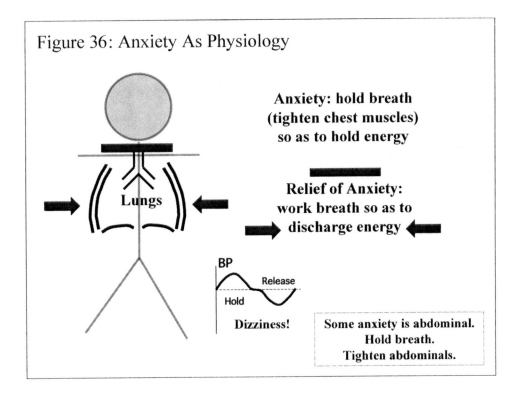

Figure 36: Anxiety As Physiology

Anxiety: hold breath
(tighten chest muscles)
so as to hold energy

Lungs

Relief of Anxiety:
work breath so as to
discharge energy

BP

Release

Hold

Dizziness!

Some anxiety is abdominal.
Hold breath.
Tighten abdominals.

Because our muscles are attempting to do work and it is difficult to work our musculature against our open breathing system, the skill of managing anxiety is to give the musculature something more to do. (The following exercise is optional: be cautious the first time you do it, especially if you are not in good health; read through the whole exercise before your first attempt; sit down for the first few attempts until you become aware of what the activity entails.)

If you are in good health, take as deep a breath as possible and hold it. Now, without letting your breath escape (closing your throat on your breath), forcefully attempt to exhale against your closed windpipe. Do this hard for about ten seconds and then release your breath. Let the dizziness pass (usually within five to ten seconds.) The dizziness is a transient consequence

of the high pressure created in your chest, which momentarily decreases blood flow from the heart to your head and is usually of no consequence (but can be unsettling, so again be careful the first time you attempt this exercise.)

After the dizziness has passed, note what has happened to your anxiety. What happened? Most likely your anxiety is gone. You performed the work the muscles were attempting to do so that they could then relax. The result is no tight muscles, and no anxiety.

The above maneuver is called a Valsalva maneuver and is a very rapid way of dealing with anxiety. It can also be easily done while standing if you are in good health and are aware that the dizziness will occur briefly. If necessary, the maneuver can be repeated after a minute or so if your anxiety returns.

****

The third way I have of discharging energy is through Hatha Yoga, the type of yoga that is practiced by most Westerners. I will discuss here some of the subtle but important distinctions between our Western understanding and application of yoga and its original intent. Contrary to the popular myth that exists, yoga is not about flexibility. Flexibility is an important component, essential only for some of the more advanced postures. Rather, yoga is a study in awareness. The postures are more accurately called "act-ures" --- studies in quiet action.

When I enter a yoga posture, I stretch (without compressing my opposing muscles.) Perhaps I reach my arm outwards to the limits of my stretch. In so doing, some parts of my arm feel alive, tingling with vibration. Other parts, though, have no sensation. At this point in my stretch, I am engaging my muscles of mobility --- the tingling acknowledges their activation. My muscles of mobility are generally more easily brought to conscious awareness. In contrast, my muscles of stability are only partially activated and for the most part silent. Now, without compressing my opposing muscles, can I bring a sense of awareness and aliveness into those areas of my body that are currently silent? When I do so, I am likely activating the muscles of stability in contrast to those of mobility. In so activating my muscles of stability, I access and release emotional energy. To the outside observer, when I access these components, the movement of my body is not apparent. Nonetheless, at the end of a yoga session, even when I'm not aware of the details of the practice, I feel both very alive and relaxed. This feeling is generally the appeal of yoga.

The above three methods of discharging energy give me a spectrum of ways in which I can access emotional energy, some of which are potentially noisy and active (accessing the emotion directly) and some that are seemingly quiet and passive (yoga and its variations.) Almost anything works to discharge energy, if actively engaged. The essential skill is learning what works. My criteria for "learning what works" is, first, to ask myself if I have a felt sense of release of the stuffed energy and, second, do I have reduced energy in the trigger situation? Am I able to access the meaning of the energy, either of past patterns or present difficulties? Learning what works for you, the reader, requires that you enter the learning curve of actively releasing your energy in a variety of ways and exploring what outcomes develop. Every few months in my therapy groups, a client says to me: "It's time for me to do some release work." He or she may have joined the group six months previously and said at that time: "But I'm not ever going to do that energy release stuff." This time however, after a few minutes of release work, the client usually says: "I never knew I could feel like this," referring to the sense of release and peacefulness that follows authentically experiencing energy, without guilt or shame. Hopefully, he or she will now be more aware of his or her energy in future. As the client does further release work, he or she will train his or her awareness to be sensitive to the subtle shifts of experience that occur when energy is being stuffed in the pot, especially when a lid is clamped on it.

As the reader, once you have created a space for a time-out, a space where you feel private and safe, you can release your energy in a number of different ways. Perhaps you access the Ghost, attacking your story of the other person, knowing that you am not attacking the other person in actuality, simply your contamination of the data as you attempt to go deeper into the mechanisms whereby you are caught. Hitting a heavy bag or pounding on an old sofa with a tennis racquet is often very useful. If you store energy in your legs or pelvis, pushing with the legs is a good release (push from the pelvis so as to be careful of your back). Over time, as most people's experience of energy release deepens, they become aware that the energy is often located deep in the thorax or abdomen, requiring even more selective activation of muscles. (This is where a more extensive knowledge of yoga becomes useful, as many yoga postures can activate this deeper energy.) If during your energy release, you are worried about noise, either drawing attention to yourself or scaring others, you can release the energy quietly or put on a loud radio and close all the windows in your home to muffle the sound. You can also scream in your car (preferably not in a moving car), lying on the seat with the windows closed and yelling into a pillow if necessary. If you are at a business meeting, you can excuse yourself to the bathroom as a way of creating a time-out. You can yell underwater in a pool or the ocean if you are on vacation; and no one will be able to hear you. If you journal write your story (using muscles and story together) and do not want others to misinterpret what you have written, you can immediately destroy the writings. Or you can write in a foreign language. You can also note early in the writings that this writing is filled with mistruths; therefore, let the reader beware.

Sometimes the release is inadequate and you need to move towards more intense tools. In the early stages of developing your awareness, you might have needed to destroy or release your energy intensely. In my experience, some people who have grown up in highly violent families need to destroy something so as to contact their energy (later as they are more aware of their energy, this need to destroy usually diminishes.) If this sounds like you, you can go to a garage sale, buy some old dishes and, while in your garage wearing safety glasses and other protective clothing, smash the dishes into an old garbage can. When finished, you can roll the can out to the roadside for the garbage workers to remove. Later, as your awareness becomes more sensitive, this need to destroy usually diminishes. You may only need to do some journal writing or occasionally some intense release work.

You do need to remember that it has taken you years to stuff your energy; hence, it will not all come out immediately at once. With time and repeated releases of your energy, you will train yourself to be aware of subtle shifts in your energy, to know when your energy is accumulating in the pot and when you need to do something corrective to restore your internal balance. My experience is that when you release the energy of your emotions (in muscle release and fantasizing using the Ghost), you release the possibility of being trapped by your fantasy. You stop acting out in a devious fashion. You stop being sneaky, manipulative, passive-aggressive or inappropriately aggressive. More importantly, you generally know what step to take next. My experience is that when you are thinking clearly, you are aware of the parameters of the Pointing Finger (see previous, Section 2.3.2.4. The Pointing Finger.) If necessary, you can describe the parameters in detail to yourself and the other person. You can note your own internal experience --- your body sensations and emotions and your own behaviors in sensory-grounded descriptions. You can also describe the other person's behaviors and the situation in a more neutral fashion using sensory-grounded descriptions. As such, you can recognize the assumptions you are bringing into the meanings that you are currently creating of the conflict.

If you are thinking with clarity, you can proceed to explore what issues exist: either you have become aware of your own powerlessness (and what it represents, perhaps stemming from your family of origin) or you are aware of your relationship difficulties with the other person and your options of responding within the relationship. Sometimes the issues are mixed and, if so, you generally need to clear up your own powerlessness as much as feasible before proceeding to the relationship difficulties.

In summary, to the extent that you are not able to take account of your behavior and the situation in the above manner is the extent to which you are not thinking clearly. And if you are not thinking clearly, your ability to separate spoon from pot and resolve conflict is compromised. Therefore, you need to manage your energy in order to negotiate your relationships with other people.

3.3.2.3. DANGERS OF ACTIVE RELEASE WORK

If you are to engage in Active Energy Release, you need to be aware that there are dangers even here. Some of these dangers are listed in the insert (see Figure 37.)

Figure 37: Dangers Of Active Release Work

Physiologic (NB These are the risks of any high intensity exercise)

High pressure in body systems:
a. high blood pressure (??)
b. hernias and haemorrhoids
c. glaucoma (acute or poorly controlled)
d. high intracranial pressure (aneurysm)

Unstable cardiovascular system:
a. unstable angina
b. exercise induced angina
c. anxiety induced angina (??)
d. recent heart attack (6 months)
e. recent stroke (6 months)

Psychologic
a. Forgetting the basic rule of No SAD (self and other!)
- using energy release as a subtle threat
b. Risking exposure to the craziness of others
- police mandates

Active Energy Release work is potentially a vigorous exercise. (I have known big, strong men who have engaged in this process and later said that they did not know how vigorous it would be.) Therefore, you need to be in reasonably good physical shape. You also need to be aware that body cavity pressures will increase during Active Energy Release, and that there is a significant cardiovascular stress during the process. The dangers do not preclude the use of Active Energy Release, but rather invite care on your part. Care is especially important if your health is already unstable. Positively, for some health dangers such as high blood pressure, stress likely plays a major role --- hence if you achieve long-term stress relief, you may actually benefit your body dysfunction.

There are also psychological dangers in Active Energy Release. Principally, these revolve around the inappropriate ways in which energy is manifest in our society. I have known the occasional client to use this process as a subtle form of threat within his or her relationships. I'm also aware that if anyone feels threatened and calls the police, there may be major misunderstanding, possibly even arrest by the police, regardless of your intentions.

Finally, please remember that up to this point we have only covered emptying the pot during the Blowing Out! process. The processes of how to diminish the pot from filling up again are still to be discussed.

****

Skill: Active Energy Release

The skill of Active Energy Release is to be able to be "out of control while in control." Initially, the process may seem hokey or embarrassing; acknowledge this to yourself and thank your other-than-conscious self for its concern.

First, pick something (a person or a situation) about which you know you are angry. Appoint a Captain to be responsible for safety (if you are unclear who is your Captain, pick one of your Sailors who is fairly reliable.) Your angry Sailor is responsible for energy. Next, make a written list of what it is that angers you; put a star

by the aspects that carry significant anger for you. Sometimes you will not be aware of being angry. If you want to explore what feelings may be present inside of yourself, write down any resentments of which you are intellectually aware. Then note any body experience associated with these resentments. During Active Energy Release, you will ideally engage these areas of your body in discharging energy onto the Ghost.

Create a safe place where you can explore, one where you are not likely to be disturbed and where it will be safe for you to make noise. Ensure that the appropriate people are aware of what you are doing, so that if you are heard, they will not interfere. Have on-hand an old tennis racket or baseball bat. As well, have available something that you can hit (the discharge object), such that only a minimum amount of dust will be created by the racket or bat. Additionally, ensure that if any object is damaged (accidentally or purposely), no harm is done. Take care that the bounce-back of the hit will not result in unexpected harm. Wear gloves to minimize blisters and have suitable protective clothing that are appropriate for whatever you choose to do (for example, safety glasses.) If you need to scream, create the sound with an open throat. If you are worried about noise, you can scream into a pillow tucked into a big bowl, play very loud music from the radio, and/or close doors and windows and cover them with pillows.

Now, visualizing the person or situation at which you are angry, place yourself before the discharge object and start to "imagine" the Ghost, getting as full a sensory experience of it as you can. Allow yourself to start expressing your energy towards the Ghost, either verbally or physically. Attempt to engage those areas of your body that earlier you noted as carrying significant energy. Experimentation may be necessary as you learn how to connect with your energy. Allow yourself to recognize the paradox that the Ghost is both real to you and also fictional. The goal is to get into a state where you experience a definite sense of honesty and authenticity while expressing what you have always wanted to do to the Ghost.

Continue the process of release (hitting, screaming, etc.) until you have a strong sense of physical fatigue. Stop and allow yourself to calm down for a few moments. Then, check if you feel an authentic sense of energy release (the pot will seem empty even though you may still have a sense of the problem intellectually.) If you are satisfied, stop and rest for a few minutes. You may find it helpful to journal write about what occurred during the release so that you have a written record for later review.

A common limitation of Active Energy Release is the participant's willingness to go into the painful parts of his or her life. If he or she is not willing to go very deep, it may be useful to seek the assistance of a therapist who can guide the participant through active release work.

3.3.3. LEARN THE MESSAGE

The third step of the Blowing Out! process is to learn the message of the energy that you carry about the problem you are experiencing. Up to this point, you have safely managed your energy through Active Energy Release and moved to a place where you feel safe. Generally you will be able to think more clearly and distinguish spoon from pot. You now need to assess what is the problem or, at the very least, its major components. Then you will know where to direct your next efforts.

Problems are always an overlap of what is happening in the environment (conflicts in your relationships) and your interpretation of what is happening based on your past experiences (powerlessness with your Ghosts.) Most of the time, one or the other --- relationship or Ghost --- stands out as the major component. Frequently, after the release of energy, your assessment comes automatically as a felt sense. Certainly it becomes easier with practice to make the distinction between environment and interpretation.

If the major component of the problem is the relationship, you will recognize that the behavior of the person with whom you are in conflict was inappropriate to your value system in a significant way. Perhaps the other person borrowed your lawnmower and brought it back in a broken state, without explanation or comment. Even if you carry energy from similar past problems (with this person or others), you have a current relationship problem. If you contaminate your current relationship problem with energy from the past, likely you will be critical and harsh with the other person, perhaps making a "mountain out of a mole hill." Having emptied your pot however, you can approach the other person and calmly and clearly state that there is a problem and request cooperation in resolution. For example, you can explain how you found the lawnmower and ask for an explanation. Or you can negotiate with the other person that you share responsibility for the repairs (as the lawnmower was an old one to begin with.)

The other person may or may not want to cooperate. I will discuss options for non-cooperation below in Section 3.3.4.3.2. Categories of Conflict Resolution.

If the major component of the problem is your Ghost, it will feel like you are fighting with a sibling or other significant person from your past rather than the person with whom you are currently in conflict. The felt sense of the energy will be familiar from your childhood or some other time in your personal history. With practice, as you search within yourself (usually quite spontaneously and quickly after Active Energy Release), you can find the memories or beliefs you are holding on to, perhaps at an other-than-conscious level, that are contributing to the present conflict. If you consciously recognize that you have focused on the other person as causing the problem, while the real problem is actually your Ghost, you may need to apologize to the other person. Ideally you will also indicate that you intend to resolve your own issues as you value the relationship with the other person. I will discuss options of how to deal with issues of powerlessness below in Section 3.3.4.2. Powerlessness.

3.3.4. RESOLVE THE CONFLICT

The fourth step of the Blowing Out! process is to resolve the conflict. Although you can achieve an empty pot by energy release, you also need to consider how your pot fills with energy. The message of the energy release gives you some indication of how your pot fills and the different skills that may be necessary for keeping it empty. Generally the message is fairly clear --- perhaps the energy of the conflict is familiar to you from another situation and hence, the major component is you (your Ghost.) Likely, the source of the conflict is that you are dissatisfied with yourself in some way and feel powerless to change. Much of our powerlessness as human beings comes from unresolved issues of childhood; much also arises from fundamental limitations of life. Even in the best of circumstances, there are painful aspects of life such as accident and illness. Alternatively, the energy of the conflict is somehow new and your relationship with the other person is where you need to focus your attention.

Likely, the source of your conflict is that you are dissatisfied with the other person's behaviors and want change in your relationship.

3.3.4.1. PERCEPTUAL POSITIONS

When the message of the energy is not clear to you, the ability to step into different perspectives of the conflict becomes important to gather data about the conflict (see Figure 38.) The exercise associated with this ability is called Perceptual Positions. It is a form of awareness based on the ability to step into the perspective of another person so as to guestimate their experience and is described below in detail.

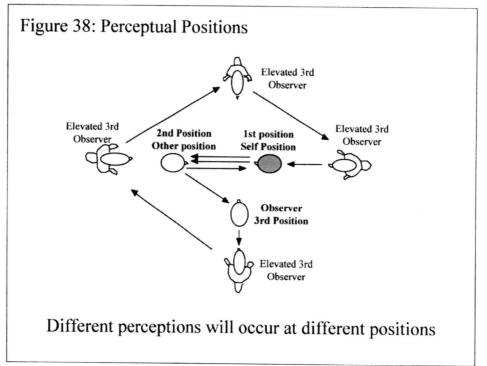

Figure 38: Perceptual Positions

Different perceptions will occur at different positions

****

<u>Skill: Perceptual Positions</u>

The purpose of this exercise is to gather information so as to explore the various contributions of yourself and other persons involved in the conflict. The process is only your best guess at the present time as to what is occurring within the conflict. It needs to

be taken as "truth for a while" as you explore what is happening in your life and then dropped as fantasy after you have gathered the data.

Imagine a conflict and step into the experience. Act it out from your own perspective, noting the behaviors of others. (Action, moving your body, generally allows much greater awareness of a conflict compared to sitting and thinking about the difficulty.) While you are re-enacting the experience of the conflict, notice what you learn about yourself. This is the 1st position, or "self" position.

Now shake off that experience and start to act out the scene again, this time from the perspective of the other person (or persons) involved in the conflict. Be that person as completely as possible, incorporating what you know about his or her values, beliefs, memories and expectations. This is the 2nd position. Notice what information you gather about that person — his or her thoughts, emotions and physiological reactions. (Repeat your enactment of the conflict from the 2nd position perspective of whomever else is significant to the experience.)

Now start your enactment again from an entirely new position. This time, consider yourself to be a fly on the wall, observing the behaviors of yourself and the other person (or persons) from a relatively neutral position. This is the 3rd position. Get a stool or chair in order to elevate your perspective of the situation — to give you an overview. Move the stool or chair around the scene

several times while keeping the scene fixed in its location. Very likely you will see different aspects of the conflict from different locations.

As a final step, return to the 1ˢᵗ position and consider all that you have learned from these other perspectives. Ask yourself: "What now do I need to do that I was not doing before?"

3.3.4.2. Powerlessness (Internal Conflict)

The sense of feeling powerless is an internal conflict. Similar to the issue of safety and security, there is a distinction between feeling powerless and bring powerless. Sometimes as human beings, we are authentically powerless and can be at peace with this experience. At other times we feel powerless because we do not recognize that we have skills and resources. The resolution of powerlessness can come through acceptance or through gaining skills and resources.

Resolving your feeling of powerlessness is appropriate when it is clear to you that the primary difficulty in your conflict with someone else is yourself. In order to shift your sense of powerlessness, there are two basic but complex requirements. First, gather data about your powerlessness. Second, know what to do with the data. As human beings, we are all pain avoiders; we have difficulty noting our own contributions to conflict. Or, if we note our own contributions, our awareness shifts so quickly that it is very difficult to catch ourselves in the act of avoidance. Once you have safely discharged your energy through the Blowing Out! process, you can think more effectively and start to examine what underlies your sense of powerlessness. Being an empty pot, you are much more prepared to do the work of data collection, even if it is painful. Given time (which you have gained through energy release), you can also explore what to do about your issues. Likely, you want long-term respite from your habitual difficulties.

Since most people's skills are limited here (otherwise we all would have resolved our problem long ago), there is a good probability that you will need other resources, such as a therapist who has previously handled such problems. Your need is not for someone to tell you what to do, but to aid you in finding a resolution that works for you. Here as the author at this point in the book, I will merely identify skills that are easily available to you. This may be enough to aid you. Other skills will be examined in Chapter Four.

3.3.4.2.1. Data Collection

The first requirement in shifting your sense of powerlessness is to collect enough data that you can find the predictability in your behavioral patterns. Simply writing brief descriptions of your conflicts is a good starting point (structured journal writing, to be discussed in detail in the next chapter, is probably the most useful tool you could have in this regard.) It allows you to collect written records of those transient yet emotionally painful moments or events in your life wherein you experience discomfort. Then, having collected the data over weeks or months, you can review your patterns and come to some understanding of how you create your own difficulties.

A second way to learn about your patterns is to study your family of origin[2]. This is where you gained most of your patterns, be they genetic or environmental. Some of the best data is your own and other family members' perceptions of each other. You can take the role of an investigative reporter, genuinely seeking information from them. It is important in this regard that you have no agenda to prove and that you do not blame anyone. Interviewing family members can be an invaluable resource; and, if approached well, most people will be cooperative. Most people want to tell their story --- to be heard, not criticized, and to have another person truly listen to them. The basic interviewing tool is a set of questions about how the interviewee experienced life in its many different facets

---

2. Many books are available in this subject area. See Monica McGoldrick, Randy Gerson and Sylvia Shellenberger , Genograms: Assessment and Intervention (New York: W. W. Norton, 1999) and Augustus Napier and Carl Whitaker, The Family Crucible: The Intense Experience of Family Therapy (New York: Perennial Library, 1988).

and what conclusions he or she came to in his or her own struggles. Since you both are members of the same family, likely you both have been exposed to the same influences. Different perceptions between individuals like yourselves can then simply become a place to explore how you each have arrived at your interpretations, not a place of judgment.

A third way to get at your patterns is to truly accept the criticisms of others as having some accuracy. When my wife or some other person gives me feedback, especially feedback I do not like, it is seldom their intention to hurt me. So, as soon as I am able, I ask myself: "What is the pearl of wisdom hidden in the information?" There are really only two possibilities. Either there is some truth in the other person's statement, truth that is valuable to me if only I find it. Or there is no truth, in which case, I need to discard that person's statement --- but only after careful examination.

Although this data collection may sound very easy, most human beings are expert at avoiding the truth. We generally do not know how to find our own truthfulness. Such a skill will be developed in the next chapter.

3.3.4.2.2. What To Do With The Data?

The second requirement in shifting your sense of powerlessness is to figure out what to do with the data you have collected about your behavioral patterns. For the most part, this is the true realm of therapy --- the development of skills that aid others in shifting their sense of powerlessness, being a guide to others as they struggle to find their way through the swamp in which they find themselves. Hopefully, their struggle will result in them finding their way out of the swamp, perhaps to a vastly better place.

If you choose to see a therapist for help with shifting your sense of powerlessness, two things are required from you. First, you need a vision of what you as a client want. Second, you need an examination of your present status that explores what are your strengths and limitations. One way to do this is with a sociological model called The Lewin Force Field (see Figure 39.) Using this model, you can recognize your present status as a balance of forward (usually positive) forces that are moving you towards your vision versus backward (often negative) forces that prevent you from reaching your desired state. Any shift in these forces will shift the balance in your life, moving you either towards or away from your goal.

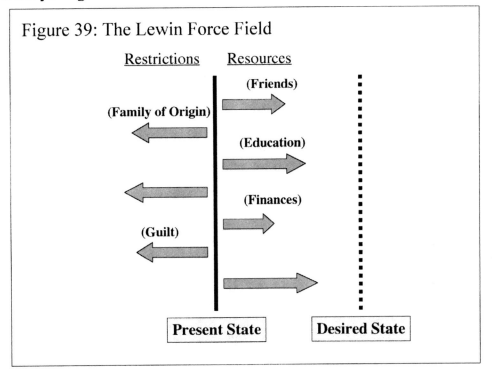

Figure 39: The Lewin Force Field

For movement towards your goal, you need to improve the positives or diminish the negatives in your life. Generally, reducing the backward forces is more effective than augmenting the forward forces. For this reason, a large component of therapy focuses on negative experience as compared to enhancing positive skills. As a therapist, I find The Lewin Force Field model to be a good starting point for my clients to organize their strengths and limitations. From there, I need to proceed to the underlying emotional issues of my clients. For most people, this next step requires a guide, someone who has been over the territory before. Please see Chapters Four and Five for further discussion on how to address underlying emotional issues.

3.3.4.3. CONFLICT (EXTERNAL RELATIONSHIPS)

In contrast to internal conflict, external conflict occurs between you and another person with whom you are in relationship (whether it be romantic, family, neighborly, etc.) When you interact with someone, you both have choice and you both have Ghosts. It (your relationship and your issues) has become a party with several uninvited guests. You need to check that you do not have any Ghosts in this particular situation or have already clarified them prior to seeking conflict resolution with the other person. Choosing to move towards conflict resolution is appropriate for external conflict when it is clear to you that the primary issue is the relationship, not your Ghosts.

Conflict necessitates an exchange of energy. As stated earlier, we are energy transformers; our energy is meant to circulate. At this point, the Laws of Energy and the Laws of Emotional Triangles are especially pertinent.

To repeat, the Laws of Energy are:

1. We want positive energy.

2. Negative energy is easier to get than positive energy.

3. Negative energy is better than no energy.

The Laws of Emotional Triangles are:

1. Within any one triangle, we can change only the limbs to which we are directly connected.

2. If we ourselves change, others must change; we are all connected.

3. Change requires we stay connected.

The exchange of energy in conflict can be cooperative, non-cooperative or actively restrictive (violation.) My contention is that a healthy exchange of energy is a direct exchange of energy (see Figure 40.) The direct expression of energy is experienced as truthfulness; likely it has the underlying message of cooperation. To illustrate, when one person honestly tells someone else his or her experience, without coercion, he or she directly exchanges energy with that other person. The energy might be excitement or it might be anger; but it is directly stated, and it is not intended that the other person change in response to that energy.

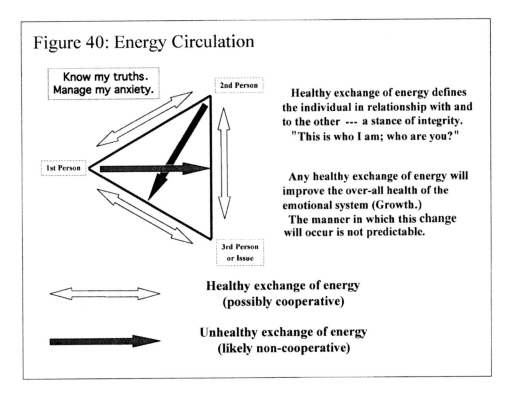

Figure 40: Energy Circulation

Know my truths.
Manage my anxiety.

2nd Person

1st Person

3rd Person
or Issue

Healthy exchange of energy defines the individual in relationship with and to the other --- a stance of integrity.
"This is who I am; who are you?"

Any healthy exchange of energy will improve the over-all health of the emotional system (Growth.)
The manner in which this change will occur is not predictable.

Healthy exchange of energy
(possibly cooperative)

Unhealthy exchange of energy
(likely non-cooperative)

Secondly, I claim that any healthy exchange of energy will improve the over-all health of an emotional system in the long term. The manner in which this change will occur is not predictable. An unhealthy exchange of energy, on the other hand, crosses over into the third limb of the triangle. It is likely non-cooperative (for example, swearing at the other person) and may even be non-communicative (for example, stone-walling.) Usually though, the message of the non-cooperation is clear: "I'm not interested in cooperating!" Finally, in conflict if someone truly restricts another person's behavioral choices, he or she violates that other person and is potentially dangerous. The major difference between non-cooperation and violation is that if someone is not intending to restrict the other person (he or she simply wants the other person's behaviors to stop), the other person still has freedom of choice to continue. The party wanting change may not like the other person's choice and may be very angry, but he or she is not dangerous.

Thus, when seeking to resolve a conflict, a major consideration is to ask yourself: "Am I truly safe (as opposed to feeling unsafe)?" or "Does the other person truly threaten me?" Your ability to assess and contribute to your safety, to manage your energy and to explore your powerlessness is one hundred percent dependent on your own choices. Safety and energy management may take ten minutes. Management of powerlessness may take weeks, months or perhaps years. But if you are limited in these areas, it is because you are limited by the lack of resources.

3.3.4.3.1. Violation --- The Dangerous Option

Before I further discuss conflict resolution in relationships that are cooperative or non-cooperative, I will address the issue of true violations in relationships, as it constitutes an entirely different approach. Violations exist when one person truly restricts another person's freedom without his or her permission. The only time that this is allowable is in the interests of public safety. We call this "the law." When violations are present in a relationship, the participants of the conflict are not demonstrating conflict-management skills (see Figure 41.) If the participants desire that the relationship continue, the first pre-requisite is to establish safety. Then someone with skills at negotiation (a third party) is required to step in and aid the work of healing the rifts.

If repeated violations exist within a relationship, the choices are limited. My best advice as a psychotherapist is for the client to leave the relationship, at least temporarily. If there are issues of safety, call "911" as soon as safe. Calling "911" is expensive --- emotionally and financially (approximately five to ten thousand dollars by my estimate --- for legal fees, change of residency, etc.) The major difficulty in not calling "911" is that if one participant continues to tolerate the other's violations, eventually the victim is likely to become a violator. And

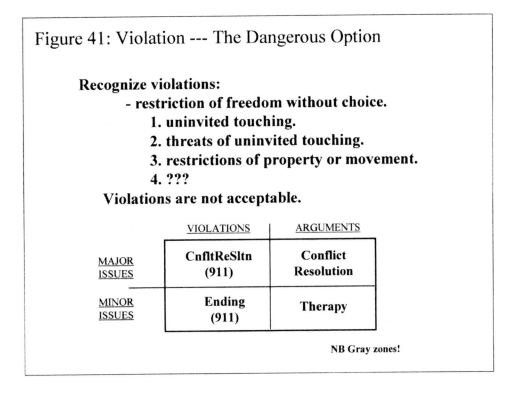

Figure 41: Violation --- The Dangerous Option

Recognize violations:
    - restriction of freedom without choice.
        1. uninvited touching.
        2. threats of uninvited touching.
        3. restrictions of property or movement.
        4. ???
Violations are not acceptable.

	VIOLATIONS	ARGUMENTS
MAJOR ISSUES	**CnfltReSltn (911)**	**Conflict Resolution**
MINOR ISSUES	**Ending (911)**	**Therapy**

NB Gray zones!

then someone will call "911" on that person. The other major danger here if the violations go unchecked, then there is the possibility of murder-suicide within the relationship dynamics.

3.3.4.3.2. Categories of Conflict Resolution

In relationships that do not involve true violations, three general categories of conflict resolution emerge (see Figure 42.) I will outline them briefly here and then discuss options in relationship in more detail in the next section.

The first category of conflict resolution is to take a stance of forgiveness. What would happen if you simply let go of the energy and moved to forgiveness? Is this issue of sufficient importance to you that you need resolution with the other person? My rule of thumb is the following: if in all circumstances the issue is not going to bother me in a year or so, and it simply represents difference between me and another person, often I let it go. I am not interested in wasting my energy needlessly.

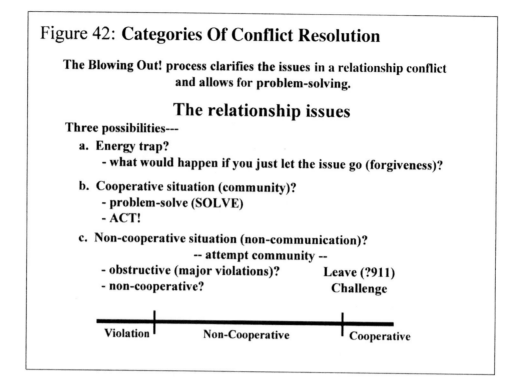

Figure 42: **Categories Of Conflict Resolution**

The Blowing Out! process clarifies the issues in a relationship conflict and allows for problem-solving.

The relationship issues

Three possibilities---
 a. Energy trap?
   - what would happen if you just let the issue go (forgiveness)?

 b. Cooperative situation (community)?
   - problem-solve (SOLVE)
   - ACT!

 c. Non-cooperative situation (non-communication)?
        -- attempt community --
   - obstructive (major violations)?   **Leave (?911)**
   - non-cooperative?   **Challenge**

Violation | Non-Cooperative | Cooperative

The second category of conflict resolution applies in the case when you and the other person are both willing to cooperate. However, this must be true cooperativeness on both of your parts. If you go to the other person and he or she agrees to cooperate but somehow indicates that you need to do all the work (or all the compromise), this is not cooperation. Nor is it cooperation if the other person agrees to do something and then doesn't keep his or her agreement spontaneously. If you have to chase the other person to keep his or her commitment, he or she is not being cooperative. Of course, the same rules apply to your behavior.

The third category of conflict resolution is applicable when the other person is non-cooperative. If the other person is not willing to cooperate, are you then to absolve yourself of all responsibility in the conflict? Perhaps you can, falling back to forgiveness. Most likely though, you cannot forgive at this time, having considered this possibility in the first place. Your next step then depends on whether or not the issue is simply non-cooperative or a true violation. If violations are not present and the non-cooperation of the other person simply takes the form of an argument or stonewalling, for example, the basic question to ask yourself is to what extent are you willing to seek resolution for yourself without violating the other person. If the situation is non-cooperative on a repetitive basis and the consequences resulting from the non-cooperation are major, it is likely that a third party (someone with skill at conflict resolution) is necessary to step in --- for you and the other person are not demonstrating sufficient skill at this time. And if the consequences resulting are minor, one or both of you needs to be in therapy --- there are many Ghosts surfacing that need to be explored.

3.3.4.3.3. Options of Behavior In Relationship

In conflict resolution, the options of your responses at any one time, with any conflict, cooperative or non-cooperative, fall into six categories (see Figure 43.) They are applicable to all three of the general categories briefly outlined in Section 3.3.4.3.2.

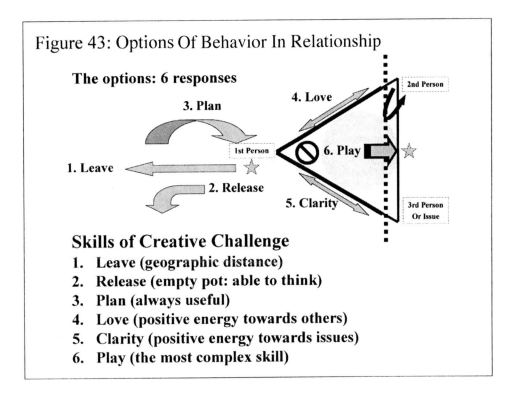

Figure 43: Options Of Behavior In Relationship

The options: 6 responses

3. Plan
4. Love
2nd Person
1st Person
6. Play
1. Leave
2. Release
5. Clarity
3rd Person Or Issue

Skills of Creative Challenge
1. **Leave (geographic distance)**
2. **Release (empty pot: able to think)**
3. **Plan (always useful)**
4. **Love (positive energy towards others)**
5. **Clarity (positive energy towards issues)**
6. **Play (the most complex skill)**

First, you can leave the relationship. Leaving is an appropriate resolution when you have truly come to terms with the issues and simply do not want to waste your energy anymore on a relationship that is not going forward. Leaving is not generally an easy solution; it is often filled with pain as you struggle to find resolution without success. Also, the major difficulty with leaving is that you risk taking with you any unresolved emotional residue of the issue to which you have contributed. Likely, you will then re-institute it elsewhere as you seek someone else to resolve the emotional turmoil you carry within yourself. For example, I have been married four times in total. I used to practice serial monogamy as my out-of-conscious method of dealing with my life problems in romantic relationships. I moved from relationship to relationship, seeking an external resolution to internal pain. (If I even could have found the perfect partner to resolve my pain, likely she herself would also have been seeking her perfect partner. Could I have lived up to that? Am I a perfect partner? Definitely not. No one is.)

Your second option is to safely release your energy anyway you can. This option forms the basis of the Blowing Out! process. It allows you to think more clearly, feel safe even when not feeling secure --- to distinguish pot from spoon and separate the other person from your Ghosts of the other person. It may even allow you to move to forgiveness and simply let the issue go. A third choice is to leave and plan what you can do when you return to the relationship and its emotional dynamics. This option is almost always useful if you choose healthy responses with which to return. This option may be coupled with the second option above --- release your energy, so that you are able to think as clearly as possible when you return to the relationship.

Fourth, you can extend healthy energy into any relationship through honesty and cooperation within the Laws of the Emotional Triangles. For lack of a better term, I call this "growth" or "love." Again, this option is almost always useful and can be totally independent of the nature of the conflict --- for there is an important distinction between the relationship as a whole and the conflict within the relationship. A fifth response in conflict resolution is to extend healthy energy into true understanding (not over-standing) of the issues involved. I call this "clarity" and define it as the ability to think at the emotional level. The questions to ask yourself are: "Can I get the perspective of the other?" and "What am I missing in my own values, beliefs, memories and expectations?" Again this exercise is almost always useful.

Play is the sixth option you can take as a response to conflict. In most relationships, there are often huge issues that remain unresolved. If you have authentically extended love and clarity into a relationship on at least two occasions (which is my personal standard) and no response occurs from the other person that is consistent with cooperation, you can assume that the other person somehow is not able to cooperate with you. The reasons are unimportant --- the result is that you have not achieved cooperation with the other person. The issue is now a third limb problem and needs to be handled non-cooperatively; otherwise, to insist upon cooperation becomes a place of resistance.

It is at this point that play becomes important. Play is the most complex of all conflict-resolution skills and will be explored in greater detail along with non-cooperative conflict later in the chapter. For now, let me note that the major difficulty with non-cooperative conflict is that it is non-cooperative. You first need to recognize that change requires you stay connected (and generally move closer to the other person.) You then need to understand that the more you challenge the other person by play, the more likely the relationship is to deteriorate or dissolve, although this is not your intention generally.

3.3.4.3.4. Cooperative Conflict

This section will explore in greater detail conflict resolution when both parties involved are cooperative. Cooperation has long-term impact. If both parties cooperate with each other, in finding a resolution that works for both of you, your relationship is not compromised; perhaps you become better friends or spouses or neighbors because of your ability to resolve the conflict.

Problem solving is most useful in cooperative situations (see Figure 44.) The essential needs are to monitor the energy, especially your own, and to have genuine interest in resolving the difficulties. From there, you and the other person cycle and recycle between energy management and trial solutions as necessary. The most important components of cooperative problem solving are to keep your word and define your needs (not your positions.) Positions refer to how you want your needs met (for example, "No smoking inside the house."); needs reflect your underlying values ("I have asthma --- I want clear air to breath.") The next step is to define what you both can agree upon before discussing what you disagree about (for example, you both agree that you will talk quietly with each other before talking about why one of you needs to smoke inside the house.)

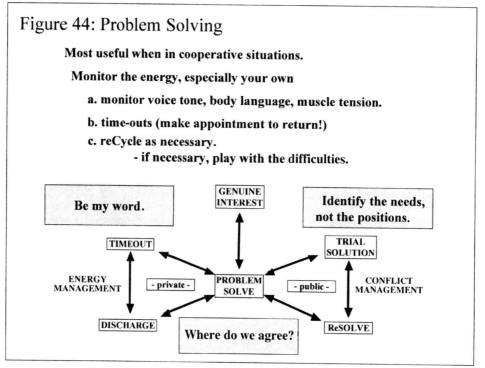

Figure 44: Problem Solving

Most useful when in cooperative situations.

Monitor the energy, especially your own

    a. monitor voice tone, body language, muscle tension.

    b. time-outs (make appointment to return!)

    c. reCycle as necessary.

      - if necessary, play with the difficulties.

Two acronyms are very useful in cooperative conflict: SOLVE and ACT! (see Figure 45.)

There are many layers of the acronym SOLVE. First, there is the truism that the problem stated is never the problem actualized. It is the first approximation of the problem. If the problem stated were complete, it would have already been solved. For we are not stupid as human beings, only habitual. Second, the following common saying applies to conflict resolution: "You're either part of the solution or

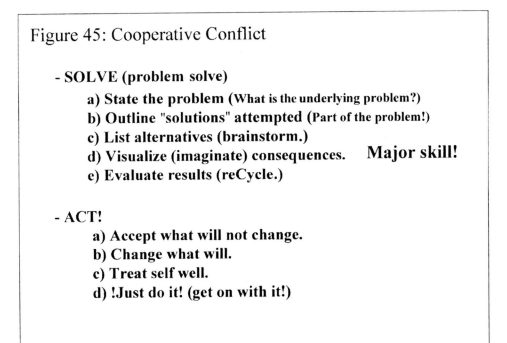

Figure 45: Cooperative Conflict

- **SOLVE (problem solve)**
  - **a) State the problem** (What is the underlying problem?)
  - **b) Outline "solutions" attempted** (Part of the problem!)
  - **c) List alternatives (brainstorm.)**
  - **d) Visualize (imaginate) consequences.** **Major skill!**
  - **e) Evaluate results (reCycle.)**

- **ACT!**
  - **a) Accept what will not change.**
  - **b) Change what will.**
  - **c) Treat self well.**
  - **d) !Just do it! (get on with it!)**

you're part of the problem.[3]" Generally in problem solving, the solutions that have not worked give you information about the boundaries of what is actually the problem. A third key component of cooperative problem solving is brainstorming. It is often used in business practices, but I seldom find people using it in their personal lives. Often the strangest solutions are the most successful. Fourth, visualizing (or, more accurately, "imaginating") the consequence of possible solutions is a very important skill. Imaginating is the ability to associate into the consequences "as if" they have already occurred, trusting one's own inner truth to reveal unexpected limitations not previously considered. Fifth and finally, most problems are not solved on the first attempt. Be prepared to recycle to other possible solutions, especially as you deal with the sabotage of the system that inevitably follows successful change. The sabotage is simply the attempt of the system to avoid change.

---

3. 1968 Eldridge Cleaver Speech in Eldridge Cleaver: Post-Prison Writings and Speeches, ed. by Robert Scheer (Random House, 1969), p. 32.

The second acronym, ACT!, is a restatement of the Serenity Prayer, with a twist. The first letter of ACT! refers to accepting what will not change. It is absolutely pointless to castigate yourself for "failure" or "falling down." What is the positive intention of castigating yourself --- does it make you more productive? Rather, look to the second letter of ACT! and change what you can. Times of failure or falling down are simply learning opportunities. Will you learn from them? The twist is to "treat yourself well." Ten minutes is usually enough time to sort out your energy and figure out whatever rules have been broken. Thereafter, feeling guilty is wasted energy. Finally, the exclamation point of ACT! refers to getting on with it! Get on with solving the problem! Appropriate action is necessary before change can occur.

To conclude the section on cooperative conflict resolution, remember that because the Blowing Out! process allows you to manage your energy, you can always choose to cooperate. Most people do not like conflict, including myself; but when it is a cooperative attempt at resolution, it often leads to surprisingly pleasant outcomes. In the long run, it is a more successful stance than a lack of cooperation. Nonetheless, in your attempt to cooperate, do not tolerate being violated by others nor choose to be a doormat in relationship. In cooperative conflict resolution, it is not required that you absorb the pain of others or be part of their crab trap. To complete the above example, in your need for clean air, you are not willing to let other people smoke in your house.

3.3.4.3.5. Non-Cooperative Conflict (No Violations)

Non-cooperative conflict requires an entirely different skill set than cooperative conflict. This section explores those situations where the other person gets caught in his or her own issues and is then not cooperative when you offer cooperation? (If you yourself are the one who is being non-cooperative, what is your intention in this stance? What need do you have that is keeping you in this psychological game?)

Non-cooperative situations are where most difficulties in relationships arise. Several questions surface here. When the other person is not cooperative, does this mean that you have to tolerate the other person or that the relationship has to end? What about when the conflict is between siblings? Or relationships that are semi-permanent but not necessarily cordial such as between divorced parents sharing child-care? In all of these cases, the lack of cooperation is a potential source of further problems. Within the skill set of non-cooperative conflict, it is generally entirely possible for you to be at peace in spite of the other person's lack of cooperation (assuming there are no violations.)

Your first approach in non-cooperation needs to be that of attempting cooperation. In the long term, it is more satisfactory for all concerned. Non-cooperative resolution may lead to the ending of the relationship. If your attempt at cooperation is met with resistance, management of non-cooperative conflict requires that you manage your own anxiety. When you want cooperation and the other is unwilling, you may have your own desire to get into the third limb and resolve the issues by means of using some "power over" dynamic on the other person. This is ineffective in the long term. Instead, you have the choice of using any or all of the six options of behavior listed above in Section 3.3.4.3.3. If you've already exhausted the first five options without success, this is when the use of play becomes important.

3.3.4.3.6. The Power Of Play

What is play? As stated previously, "play" is "an activity whose sole aim is diversion or amusement." A joke is illustrative of play. It is generally a build-up of tension followed by an appropriate but unexpected diversion, which then has the effect of releasing the tension. I invite you, the reader, to think about your response when someone says that they want to tell you a joke? I imagine you hold your breath somewhat in anticipation, knowing that the punch line is coming. For the joke to be successful, the punch line must take you by surprise; you then release your breath in laughter.

A playful intervention, sometimes called a paradoxical intervention, is something similar to a joke. Conflict-ridden situations are usually very tense, and a playful intervention ideally has the effect of lightening the mood without belittling the seriousness of the issues. Playful interventions are not intended to give solutions to problems; they are, instead, methods of changing emotional tension.

Below I give two stories of playful interventions that, even if they are fictitious, are emotionally true for me. The first story I received several years ago by email from a long-forgotten source. The second comes from the book Change[4]. In both stories, I interrupt the plot at various points to ask how you, the reader, would handle the situation.

British Airways

On a British Airways flight from Johannesburg, a middle-aged, well-off white South African woman finds herself sitting next to a black man.

She calls the cabin crew attendant over to complain about her seating.

"What seems to be the problem, Madam?" asks the attendant.

"Can't you see?" she says, "You've sat me next to a bloody kaffir. I can't possibly sit next to this disgusting man. Find me another seat!"

"Please calm down Madam." the attendant replies. "The flight is very full today, but I'll tell you what I'll do - I'll go and check to see if we have any seats available in club or first class."

The woman cocks a snooty look at the outraged black man be-

4. Paul Watzlawick, John H. Weakland and Richard Fisch, Change: Principles of Problem Formation and Problem Resolution (New York: W. W. Norton & Company, 1974), pp. 130-131.

side her (not to mention many of the surrounding passengers.)

[As the attendant, what would you, the reader, do in this situation?]

A few minutes later, the attendant returns with the good news, which she delivers to the woman: "Madam, as I suspected, economy is full. I've spoken to the cabin services director, and club is also full. However, we do have one seat in first class." The woman cannot help but look at the passengers around her with a smug and self-satisfied grin.

However, before the woman has a chance to get up, the attendant continues speaking: "It is most extraordinary to make this kind of upgrade; and I have had to get special permission from the captain. But given the circumstances, the captain felt that it was outrageous that someone be forced to sit next to such an obnoxious person."

At that point, the attendant turns to the black man sitting next to the woman, and says: "So, if you'd like to get your things, sir, I have your seat ready for you ..."

As the black guy walks up to the front of the plane, the surrounding passengers rise and give a standing ovation.

****

The Belloc Ploy

An experienced, intelligent executive assistant, accustomed to making her own decisions, was having difficulties with one of her bosses. Judging from her own description of the conflict, this man was apparently both annoyed and made to feel insecure by

145

her independent and rather forceful modus operandi, and in turn he missed few opportunities for putting her down, especially in the presence of third parties. She felt so offended by this that she tended to adopt an even more distant and condescending attitude towards him, to which he then reacted with more of the same belittling which had made her angry in the first place. The situation had escalated to the point where he apparently was about to recommend her transfer or dismissal, and she was considering outdoing him by handing in her resignation.

[The executive assistant has come to you, the reader, for advice?

What would you tell her in her situation?]

Without explaining to her the underlying reasons, we [the authors of Change] instructed her to wait for the next incident and then to utilize the first opportunity of taking her boss aside and telling him with an obvious show of embarrassment [fake it if she needs to] something to the effect that "I have wanted to tell you this for a long time, but I don't know how to tell you — it is a crazy thing, but when you treat me as you just did, it really turns me on; I don't know why — maybe it has something to do with my father," and then to leave the room quickly before he could say anything.

[What would be your reaction to the therapist's advice?

What do you think would happen at the workplace with this intervention?]

She was at first horrified, then intrigued, and finally she found the whole idea enormously funny. She said she could hardly wait

to try it out, but when she came back for her next appointment, she stated that the very next morning [before she had had any opportunity whatsoever to interact with her boss], her boss's behavior had somehow changed overnight, and that he had been polite and easy to get along with ever since.

[What do you think happened that she changed, and then he changed?

How do you explain it? Is this just coincidence?]

If proof were needed for the fact that reality is what we have come to call "reality," this form of change could help to supply it. Strictly and concretely speaking, nothing had "really" changed in the sense that no explicit communication or action had taken place between these two people. But what makes this form of problem solving effective is the knowledge that one can now deal differently with a previously threatening situation. This then brings about a change in one's behavior which is transmitted through the multiple and very subtle channels of human communication and which affects the interpersonal reality in the desired form, even if the actual behavior prescription is never resorted to.

****

Playful interventions have two major characteristics. First, they allow you, the playful person, to experience "wonder" (the feeling of surprise, admiration and awe aroused by something strange and exciting.) And when in a state of wonderment, you cannot be anxious --- the emotional brain cannot experience anxiety and playfulness at the same time. Since you are in a stance of wonder, you are also not available for the other person to dump energy on you; or, at the very least, you don't receive it in a customary manner.

The Belloc Ploy intervention is initially surprising and has many twists; the intervention illustrates the power of wonder. The executive assistant changed in the office of the therapist before ever applying the therapist's advice. She was somehow playfully empowered in what was previously a difficult situation. Change then occurred in the system. The outcome that would occur if the woman actually did the intervention is not predictable. Perhaps the boss would back off, afraid of the risk of a sexual harassment case in the future. However, the woman did not need to do the intervention.

The second major characteristic of playful interventions is that they are not necessarily experienced by the other person as playful, or even pleasant. Instead, they require the other person to confront his or her own anxiety and non-cooperation, not because they want to but because the strangeness of your response jars the other person. He or she is therefore likely faced with looking at his or her own actions in a new light. Because play does not have to be perceived by the other as playful, the danger in play is the possibility of your being sarcastic, that is, of actually intending (in subterfuge) to impact the third limb of the triangle. Sometimes there is a fine balance between impacting yourself in wonder and impacting the other person in a way that will be perceived as sarcastic. In my opinion, the British Airways story is a good intervention but not a clean intervention. The attendant's statement "But given the circumstances, the captain felt that it was outrageous that someone be forced to sit next to such an obnoxious person" is vague and not necessary to the intervention. It allows the recipient to focus on the possible sarcastic attack and has the intent to influence the third limb in a purposeful manner.

As an example of what I consider to be a clean intervention, I give the following story from my own experience. As you read the story, consider what you would have done as the reader if in the same circumstances.

I was returning to visit my extended family for my annual visit. I knew that I would be talking with a specific cousin of mine about the current events of my life. This cousin was slightly older than myself and frequently acted inappropriately as if he thought he was my father. Specifically, if I was anticipating any form of change in my life, he would say (in a serious voice tone): "David, are you sure you know what you are doing? You've got to be careful, you know." After fifteen years, this pattern was predictable for each visit, usually within twenty-four hours of homecoming. On each occasion, we would have a brief conflict and then somewhat avoid each other for the rest of the visit.

Prior to this particular visit, however, I had encountered the possibility of playful interventions. I was determined to respond this time with: "Yes, 'Dad,' you're right. I do need to be careful." My response I hoped would highlight my cousin's pattern of treating me like he was my father. Although I truly did not know what would happen if I did as planned, I was chuckling to myself at the possibilities.

As with the Belloc Ploy, I did not actually do the intervention. On the second day of my visit (approximately 24 hours into the visit), my cousin invited me out for a walk in the surrounding country. During that walk, he said to me that I had made better decisions in my life than he had in his. And never again did he ask me if I was sure I knew what I was doing or anything even close to it. Even though I didn't do the intervention, a change still occurred. Fascinating!

There are two major difficulties with playful interventions. First, you need to ask yourself if you have the right to expose the other person to his or her own foibles? I personally believe that, since the other person is already imposing on me his or her non-cooperative response to our conflict, I do have this right, assuming I do so safely and without violation. When I play in a clean and safe manner, the other person has choice as to how he or she responds.

The major limitation of play is further non-cooperation from the other person. The relationship may even end. This may be worth the risk; I refer to the following common saying as illustration. "If you loan a friend twenty dollars and it costs you the friendship in your attempt to get it back, it was worth it." The following personal story illustrates a "successful" playful intervention that was part of a deteriorating relationship.

--- Author's Personal Commentary ---

When I first learned of playful interventions, I was in relationship in which I did a lot of the cooking. I enjoy cooking and am a good cook. When I cook, I clean up as I go. I would plan a dinner party at our home and cook the meal in such a way that, by the time the guests arrived, the kitchen was clean except for the pots and pans. After dinner, I would invite the guests into the kitchen for conversation while I finished cleaning up. By the end of the evening, we had some good conversation and I had a clean kitchen.

However, when my partner at the time cooked, it hooked into my own issues around cleanliness. The kitchen was a "mess" (to me.) After dinner, we would sit in the living room talking. When the guests left, my partner would say she was tired and that she would clean up in the morning. However, somehow or other, this action did not occur. The next day, I would clean the kitchen, sometimes by nine a.m. in the morning, sometimes by noon. At first, I did this as a gift to my partner, not as criticism. As time went on, I got frustrated with the recurrent pattern and I shifted to resenting my need to clean the kitchen. My partner and I discussed options and made agreements. But nothing changed.

Eventually I decided to play with my own issues and to study my need for cleanliness. (I was very clear with myself that I did not intend my partner to change.) So one day, I copied her pattern and I left a mess in the kitchen, before and after supper --- to see what my anxieties were. Later that night, I told my partner I would clean it up in the morning, fully intending to get up at nine or ten and clean it up. Then next morning, she got up at seven in the morning and cleaned the kitchen. Thereafter, anytime I left the kitchen a mess, she would clean up. We never talked about the change in our pattern. To this day, I have no idea what her internal shifts were.

In the short term, my playful intervention was effective. In the long term however, the relationship ended. It ended not directly because of the kitchen but, from my perspective, because I could not make enough emotional contact with her to problem solve cooperatively and effectively. My own need for contact was highlighted by the playful intervention.

3.4. SUMMARIZING THE PROCESS OF BLOWING OUT!

Chapter Three lays out the fundamentals of the Blowing Out! process (see Figure 46.) It describes the four issues of emotional management: safety, energy, learn the message and resolve the conflict (internal powerlessness and external conflict.) In my experience, both personally and professionally, if these issues are mashed together, most people are overwhelmed and potentially become pressure cookers. The consequences are then either to blow up (rage) or blow down (stonewalling.) I generally call this emotional "stuckness."

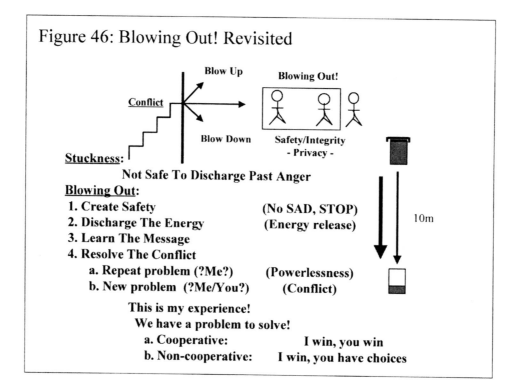

Figure 46: Blowing Out! Revisited

The Blowing Out! process separates these four issues of emotional management, with the intention of dealing with them individually and sequentially (and possibly in repetitive fashion), so as to allow for a person's ultimate resolution. In order, the four issues are listed here.

1. Establish safety (No SAD and STOP.)

2. Discharge the energy safely, anyway that works, in order to get to a place of being safe, able to think and distinguish spoon from pot.

3. Learn the message of the energy.

4. Resolve the conflict by separating the components of powerlessness and external conflict. Deal with the powerlessness in some form of growth process. Manage the conflict (internal or external) within the Laws of Energy and the Laws of Emotional Triangles (see Figure 47.)

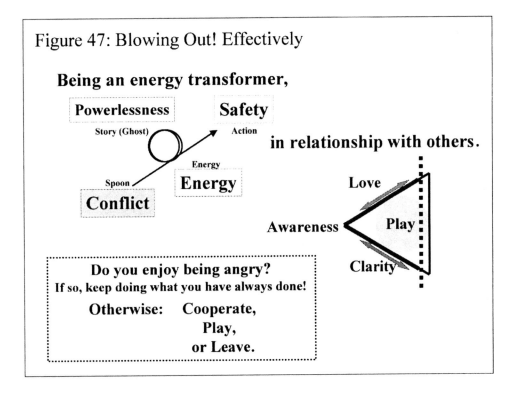

Figure 47: Blowing Out! Effectively

The next chapter will focus on certain skills that are essential if you are to be effective in utilizing the Blowing Out! process.

CHAPTER FOUR --- ESSENTIAL SKILLS

Summary

Even if clients can identify their problems, they seldom come to a therapist with sufficient skill to resolve their difficulties. If they had the skills, likely they would have already resolved the difficulties. This chapter outlines several different skills that can help clients resolve their issues. These skills underlie effective application of the Blowing Out! process; and while the skills may seem relatively simple, I frequently suggest to my clients that if they will practice any one of these skills faithfully every day for six months, they will totally change the orientation of their life for the better.

Of all the skills examined in Chapter Four, the primary skill is awareness. Awareness is not the same as what is generally called thinking. Rather, awareness is attention to the spontaneously emerging perceptions (sensations and the interpretations of these sensations) as they are presented to consciousness. It is the act of witnessing one's thoughts, watching oneself in action in sufficient detail as to be able to interrupt the process when necessary for more effective action.

After awareness, the next most important skill is one's precision of language which then allows for one's clarity of mind. As illustration, take the metaphor of fish swimming in water; if the water is clean, it sustains the fish. If the water is murky, it hides the fish from enemies. Our human equivalent to the fish's water is language. Language can either keep us healthy or can hide us from our enemies. Some of the ways in which we are murky with our language will be explored in this chapter, especially the linguistic distinctions between violence and violation and between data and story.

Some important immediately-practical skills will be developed in this chapter. The ability to know one's own truth and to use body-mind-heart-soul-spirit as a resonator of experiential truthfulness will be explored. The complexity of the "Sailors On A Ship" metaphor will be expanded, including tools for accessing a Captain. Lastly, the ability to collect sufficient data to predict emotional patterns will be expanded.

CHAPTER FOUR --- ESSENTIAL SKILLS

Clients seldom come to a therapist with any sense of the basic therapeutic concepts presented earlier in this book nor do they usually have the skills necessary for resolving their difficulties. Even if they do understand the skills (or more commonly, "overstand" them), they seldom have enough experience about how to apply these skills to their everyday lives.

The essential skills of therapy involve developing your ability to predict and plan for the various emotional responses of yourself and other people (see Figure 48.) This chapter will explore the minimum skills I believe are required to do just that, especially those skills that you can learn on your own after adequate practice. More refined skills will be explored in Chapter Five.

Figure 48: Essential Skills

For any emotional problems:

❖ I need to have precise knowledge of what the mechanisms of emotional issues are. I need precision of language and clarity of issues so as to study the predictable patterns.

❖ I need to know what assumptions I bring to emotional issues. I need to know my contribution, especially how my values, beliefs, memories and expectations contaminate the issues.

❖ I need to practice and hone my emotional skills on real-time issues. There is a learning curve to all skills.

I wish to state a caution here. The development of skills for managing emotional issues is not easy. The process may open up pain that cannot quickly be reversed --- it certainly did for me. The journey has been fully worth it but I did not realize at the beginning into what I was getting myself.

4.1. THE PROCESS OF SKILL DEVELOPMENT

In developing the skills of emotional management, a useful metaphor to keep in mind is that of learning to drive a car. When you first learn drive, you will need to learn many skills. Optimally you would go to driving school. There you will receive some classroom instructions and perhaps some parking-lot experiences where you can learn to maneuver around fake objects, causing little harm if you make a mistake as you learn. You do not learn to drive a car by sitting in the classroom or even sitting in a car with someone else driving. Human beings learn best by experience something for themselves, then reflecting on how that experience went, especially how they contributed to their outcomes achieved. After the classroom and the test lot, you could go out driving on quiet streets with an instructor. As you learn to navigate the vehicle safely according to the rules of the road, you could venture onto busier streets and eventually onto major highways. Soon enough, you will get your license and be able to drive about freely.

You must never forget, though, that other drivers may not know how to drive well; they may be poorly skilled; they may be drunk; or they may not have a valid license to drive. Defensive driving is necessary. You must also never forget that the more care you give both to how you handle the car and the other driver, the better outcomes you generally will get. After you've been driving a while, you may find you want more skills. Maybe you want to drive heavy trucks or be a better winter driver or even enter car races. New and different sets of skills are needed for each of these possibilities. Moreover, your skill set works best if your car is regularly serviced --- which is yet another set of skills. Occasionally, your car will break down and need to be repaired. If you know a lot about cars, perhaps you can take it into your own garage to fix it. Or maybe you will need the help of a mechanic who knows more about cars than you do. Ideally you'll learn from the mechanic about how to repair your own car in the future, gaining more skills along the way.

In all of the above scenarios, you could learn the various skills by yourself. However, the learning curve would be costly, likely with you making numerous incorrect guesses, causing accidents and missing turns in the road. It makes sense in this light to learn from others what they have already learned, although you must never forget that what they tell you is only what they themselves have learned. If they tell you what they should have learned, they are simply giving you their best guess as to a better direction (but it is not their own experience.)

All of the above steps in learning to drive a car are applicable to learning the skills of the Blowing Out! process, and of the processes called therapy. Therapy is both about searching within yourself at greater depth and learning the skills of living (caring for our bio-socio-psycho-spiritual selves we call human beings.) Fundamentally, therapy is a relationship between two or more people who are committed to growth as human beings. In other words, it is one or several emotional triangle(s) in which the principle issue is growth of self. Ideally, the therapist's own growth of self means he or she has been to driving school and also has kept adding skills to learn more and more about driving cars (i.e. the growth of human beings.) Most of all, therapy is a symbolic place where two or more people meet to explore and offer up how each has integrated the skills of living with the difficulties of life. At its best, therapy is a place where one person (the therapist) supports and challenges a second person (the client) to do the essential work of learning the skills of emotional living that are particular to that client in order to live authentically in relationship with others. At its worst, therapy is a place where one person (the therapist) tells another person (the client) how he or she should or must live his or her life.

Therapy is not necessarily easy; often it is extremely painful. It is not necessary if all you want is to drive your car from point A to point B. But if your intention is to become a good driver and especially if your intention is to become a great driver, more advanced skills (of emotional living) are necessary. This chapter will examine in considerable detail some of these essential skills and, in the later sections of the chapter, will suggest tools for how to develop these skills.

4.2. Awareness --- The Primary Skill

This chapter will repeatedly emphasize awareness as a primary skill as well as explore how to develop the skill of awareness. The developer of Gestalt Therapy[1], Fritz Perls, once said: "Awareness by and of itself can be curative." After being a therapist for more than twenty years, I am in utter awe as to how profound this statement is. Each year, my awe increases. So what does this word "awareness" mean? The Gestalt Therapy definition is "attention to one's spontaneously emerging perceptions." Awareness is not what is generally called thinking; awareness is attention to the spontaneously emerging perceptions (sensations and the interpretations of these sensations) as they are presented to your consciousness (see Figure 49.) It is the act of witnessing one's thoughts, watching yourself in action in sufficient detail as to be able to interrupt the process when necessary for more effective action. The primary skill of awareness is that of noting sensory-grounded data (observations in which the visual, auditory and other sensory features are predominant and separated from assumptions about their meaning.)

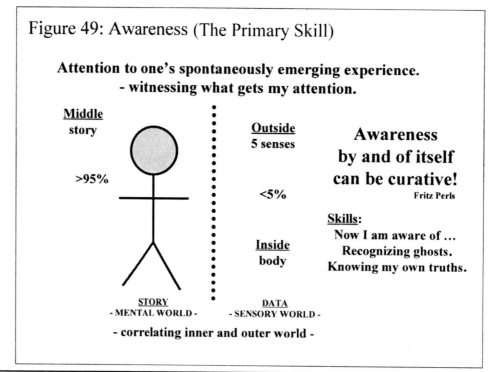

Figure 49: Awareness (The Primary Skill)

Attention to one's spontaneously emerging experience.
- witnessing what gets my attention.

Middle story

>95%

Outside 5 senses

<5%

Inside body

STORY
- MENTAL WORLD -

DATA
- SENSORY WORLD -

- correlating inner and outer world -

Awareness by and of itself can be curative!
Fritz Perls

Skills:
Now I am aware of ...
Recognizing ghosts.
Knowing my own truths.

1. Gestalt Therapy is a therapy developed in the 1940s based on the principles of awareness, emotional contact and personal responsibility. It is my principle philosophic stance in my own life.

To illustrate the power of the skill of awareness, I use a story from the book *Dancing With A Ghost*[2]. In this book, the author Rupert Ross reflects on the skill set of members of the Native North American hunter-gatherer societies prior to European interaction. In the following story, he describes his own developing awareness while working in a fishing camp where the guides were principally Native. Over an eleven-year period, his own skills of awareness gradually improved and approached those of the Native guides.

****

Dancing With A Ghost

(by Rupert Ross)

I can recall one particular day when I realized that my own perception skills had shifted onto a new level. I was guiding a man and his young son one beautiful August morning. We were some twenty miles from camp, fishing the very exposed north shore of a large body of open water. The sun was shining, there wasn't a cloud in the sky and the light southwest breeze gave us the small waves that are perfect for walleye fishing. The fish were biting, and all was as it should be. Around eleven o'clock, however, I began to feel uneasy. That particular shore is a dangerous place to be if a storm comes up from the south, for there is little shelter and lots of room for heavy waves to build. Over the next half hour or so I watched the sky carefully for any signs of change to justify my concern, but there were none. Still, my uneasiness grew, my sense that something was coming. I finally told my guests that

2. Rupert Ross, *Dancing With A Ghost: Exploring Indian Reality* (Markham, Ontario: Reed Books, 1992), pp. 75-76.

the air "didn't feel right" and that we had better get ourselves back across the open water to the south, into the shelter of a string of islands.

They were not happy, for the fish were biting and, as I readily conceded, there was no visible threat on any horizon. I was insistent, however, and they reluctantly reeled in.

It took us over half an hour to cross the open water, and during that time nothing visible changed. The sky was still absolutely clear and the breeze remained light. When we stopped to fish on the north side of an island I again took stock of things. The air "felt" worse still. After half an hour (with no bites, I should add), I suggested we head still closer to camp. It is accurate to say that my guests were becoming increasingly grumpy, convinced that they had a guide who was determined to be in early.

When we rounded that island and broke into the channel heading south, their unhappiness turned quickly into fear. Ahead of us was the most threatening storm cloud I had ever seen. Its leading edges curled up high and then back in towards the centre, and it was green and black in color. It was not large, but it completely blocked our route home. I headed back to the north side of the island and pulled the boat in close under a large cliff. We waited there for about fifteen minutes. During that time we felt the temperature drop a good twenty degrees. The storm cloud carried its own winds, and when they raced up the channel they churned the water into large, white-capped waves advancing in a solid front. Within minutes we were battered by quarter-inch hailstones that forced us to put our seat-cushions over our heads. The storm only lasted some fifteen minutes, then left us once again under the same sunny skies and light breezes we'd had before.

Needless to say, my guests declared their heartfelt gratitude; they also declared their willingness to follow my hunches from then on without complaint. They knew that we'd have been in considerable difficulty had we stayed on that exposed north shore. It remains a strange event to me. I do not know, to this day, what signs I was reading, what patterns I was feeling. I suspect that the uneasiness I felt had something to do with barometric changes, but there was not, in my own mind, any question of having guessed. I knew there was danger approaching, and felt it so strongly that I was ready to risk the displeasure of my guests.

I mention this event for several reasons. First, if I could predict a severe, though very localized, change in weather with my amateur's skills, then the skilled hunter-gatherer would be able to read much more subtle changes, probably down to things I would not be able to recognize as changes even when they were upon me.

Second, it illustrates something seldom recognized about human survival in the wilds; the essential skill is accurate prediction and it is a mental skill, not a physical one.

****

I invite the reader to practice the following skill for developing awareness for a few moments. Although it is a very simple exercise, I contend that if you will do this activity for twenty minutes every day for six months, you will totally change your life. The impact of this skill will be immense and can be profound even when developed to a limited extent.

****

Skill: Development Of Awareness

To develop the skill of awareness, I generally suggest a simple sensory awareness exercise. The primary skill is the ability to notice your experience and not get caught in making a story about it. First, complete the sentence "Now I am aware of ....." with a simple sensory experience. For example, "Now I am aware of dryness of my upper lip." Then repeat the statement with another sensory experience — whatever comes spontaneously to your attention in the moment. Perhaps it is the same as the previous sensory experience. Perhaps it is different. Finally, do this repeatedly for about twenty minutes a day.

While doing this exercise, recognize that you can experience "outside" sensory data (visual, auditory, olfactory, etc.) as well as "inside" sensory data (the position of your hands, the temperature of your feet, the beat of your heart, etc.) You can also have complex relationships of sensory data, such as "that chair is about to fall.") This is generally simple story-making. Or you can notice internal sensory data occurring, such as seeing visual pictures on your mental screen or the perceiving of an auditory voice talking to you (perhaps your own voice, perhaps that of someone else's.)

Be aware that the more complex the data you notice, the more likely you are close to story-making. If you find yourself in story, simply label it "story" and let it go. Come back to the basic "Now I am aware of ....." as you continue to develop your skill of awareness.

If desired, after you have developed the basic practice of awareness, you can learn to focus on individual areas of sensory information. As an illustration, perhaps you could track only what you see visually in your current location. What gets your attention spontaneously?

Alternatively, you could focus inwards on what flashes briefly in your internal visual field or hear how you talk to yourself. Often this latter option is much harder to note, but is ultimately more rewarding.

Taken to an advanced degree, the development of the skill of awareness is the practice of such meditation techniques as Buddhist Vipassana Meditation. However, no belief system need be attached to the exercise; it is simply what you experience.

4.2.1. Domains Of Awareness

Awareness can be characterized as residing in three domains: outside (i.e. the so-called five senses although there may be several more, for example, seeing forms of energy such as auras), inside (body sensations of position, tension, temperature, etc.) and middle (interpretation; story; meaning assigned to the interplay of these outside and inside sensations by neurological mechanisms.) As human beings, we are story-makers; it is one of our great strengths. We create meaning out of chaos. We fill in the details where gaps exist in our understanding of the world. Sometimes we fill in the details with amazing accuracy; sometimes we do not. Story-making is our weakness when we fill in the details and then wonder why our story does not match the data. Although it is likely impossible as humans to totally avoid making up stories about the data around and within us, awareness is the ability to stay as close as possible to our sensory experience, thus dealing with the data as cleanly as possible. In my training as psychotherapist, I heard the estimate that most people spend more than ninety-five percent of their lives "in story" and less than five percent directly with sensory experience. After being a therapist for many years, I myself can now attest to the accuracy of this estimate.

4.3. The Need For Precision of Language And Clarity

In my experience, the next most essential skill after awareness is precision of language. As a culture, we are very sloppy with our language. Take, for example, the number of times we qualify our action statements with words such as "maybe," "perhaps" or "someday." By using such qualifiers, we do not make an emotional investment in our action statements and hence have no compelling reason to revisit them.

A metaphor of fish swimming in water is useful in understanding the importance of precision of language. Imagine yourself as a fish, swimming about in a lake. Food is plentiful; but predators are also around --- sometimes you are the food! What function does the water serve for you as a fish? For one, it sustains you. It allows you to float and move around; it makes it possible for you to get food and to avoid predators. What happens when the water is dirty? At one level, dirty water makes it easier for you to hide from predators as they can't see as clearly. But neither can you see clearly to find your own food. Plus, dirty water is likely to compromise your health in the long term.

As human beings, we swim in language. When our language is sloppy and imprecise, it is like swimming in dirty water. It makes it easier for us to hide from our emotional pain and the hurtfulness of others; but it also makes it more difficult for us to be emotionally healthy in the long run. And as with dirty water, there are several difficulties with sloppy language. The major difficulty is that our primary experience of language, especially the emotional meaning we give to words, arises from our experiences as infants, observing and responding to the behaviors of others; these experiences were uniquely ours. If we do not recognize each other's unique experiences associated with the words that we use, we run into trouble communicating. To explain further, I will first remind the reader that our primary experience of language translated actions, not concepts. We first learned words that taught us to "stop" and "share" and to have words for our internal beginnings of action (e.g. "anger.") When it comes to these basic words that we use, each one of us has had similar-enough experiences associated with these words that we can share meaning with each other and still make sense of what the other person is saying. However, when we explore the actual experience of each other's basic words, we are very different indeed. Your experience of your "anger" is very different from someone else's experience of "anger."

Because, in our sloppiness of language, we generally think that each other's use of basic words are the same, we make assumptions that, if stressed, land us in an argument. I imagine you, as reader, have had many experiences where you were in a conversation that seemed to be going well. Unexpectedly, there was a shift in the tone --- a conflict about some small point. Most of the time, the conflict centered on the minor differences of meaning you each attributed to the words you were using. You argued, not because the connotations were slightly different, but because the slightly different connotations were important to you. They carry energy from your past experiences. Nor are dictionaries much help when it comes to resolving the subtle subjective experiences we each have regarding these words.

4.3.1. CLARITY

Ironically, even the verb "to clarify" has its own difficulties of sloppy language. Yet "to clarify" and its counterpart "clarity" are vital words in understanding the processes of emotional health. The *Webster New World Dictionary* defines "to clarify" as "to make or become clear and free of impurities" and "clarity" as "clearness (in various senses.)" The word "clear" takes up half a page in the dictionary but essentially suggests freedom from cloudiness, haziness, muddiness, etc. --- either literally or figuratively. The official definition of each word is rather circular, typical of most dictionaries.

In the context of this book, I will define and use "clarity" as "the ability to think accurately at the emotional level;" that is, without internal conflict at the emotional level. This ability directly translates into the ability to deal effectively with emotional energy so as to integrate safety, energy and choice. Other words that are important in this book include the following: "emotion," "feeling," "feeling judgments," "anger," "rage" and "violation." To my knowledge, there is no consistent interpretation to these words, certainly none that are satisfactory to the development of ideas in this book. For the purposes of this book, and at the risk of repetition, I will therefore give the precise meanings that I intend for the use of the words listed above (see also Appendix A for my definitions of these and other words.)

4.3.2. EMOTIONS

The best definition of emotion I have found comes from an article in *American Psychologist*[3] wherein the authors of the article, in attempting to develop a precise definition of emotions, state one possibility of "emotions" as being "biologically adaptive action tendencies" (see Figure 50.) Biologically adaptive means that emotions play a positive role in helping us to survive as human beings. You do not have to like emotions for them to be purposeful or helpful. Emotions are also "action tendencies;" in other words, the "beginning of action."

---

3. L. Greenberg and J. Safran, "Emotion in Psychotherapy," American Psychologist, 44:1 (1989), 19-29.

The very spelling of the word "emotion" emphasizes its inherent quality of motion. I define emotions similarly as "energy to which I give meaning and direction." To illustrate, if I want to move towards you, I call this action tendency "excited" or "joyous;" if I want to push you away or push against you, I call it "anger." However, if I want to move away from you, I call it "fear;" and if I want to collapse down, I say I am "sad." If the energy occurs in the context of my feeling overwhelmed or powerless, the energy feels "bigger" and I name "joy" as "ecstasy," "anger" as "rage," "fear" as "terror" and "sadness" as "despair." These "emotions" are our inherent biological mechanisms for assessing the impact of the environment upon us at any given moment. It is likely that, if we had to rely only on conscious processes to assess the environment, then our responses to safety, pain and pleasure would be much slower. We would also frequently be overwhelmed with too much unfiltered data. Emotions therefore have a positive intention to protect us.

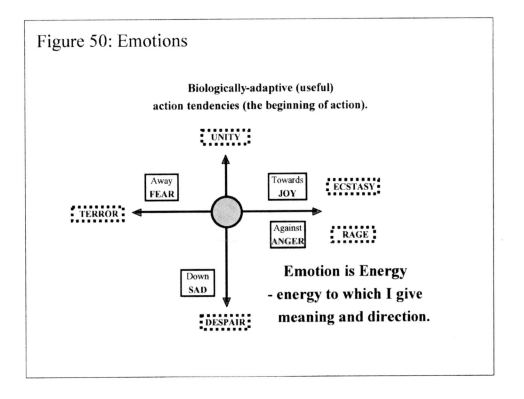

Figure 50: Emotions

4.3.2.1. THE POSITIVE INTENTION OF EMOTIONS

Because emotions are purposeful, one of the most important skills to learn in emotional living is the answer to the following question: "What is the positive intention of what I am experiencing?" (This question is equally applicable to any feeling, thought or behavior that I am experiencing.) Most people are not able to answer the question immediately and often say of their "negative" experiences that there is no positive intention. While it is true that there may rarely (and I emphasize rarely) be no current positive intention, the pattern of response in your behavior was learned in the past with a positive intention. Moreover, some component of this positive intention almost certainly persists in the present, even if it is not part of your present conscious awareness. A major skill of emotional change work (therapy by another name) is to accurately identify this positive intention in your awareness and find another way to accomplish what the emotion intends.

--- Author's Personal Commentary ---

To illustrate the impact of identifying positive intentions, consider the following story of my own journey. During my own explorations about fifteen years ago, I found that I was having twelve to fourteen hours of despair each week. It was a very familiar emotion and had probably been with me for years. A therapist I knew asked me "What is the positive intention of your despair?" I couldn't give a good answer to the therapist but I stayed with the question. It was quickly apparent to me that my despair occurred anytime I had more that one emotional experience: sadness and anger, joy and pain, excitement about something and curiosity about another. The quality of emotion did not seem to matter, only the quantity.

As I studied my pattern of despair further, with much writing in my journal, the despair persisted, week after week, twelve to fourteen hours per week. Then, after about six months, sitting quietly by myself one evening, I spontaneously spoke two words: "Search Mode." With these words, I recognized that, in the confusing double messages of my childhood, I had not felt safe and I would go into this specific emotional state (which as an adult I learned to call despair) in my attempt to respond to what was happening around me. Despair became my mode of searching within myself --- my entry point into exploring emotional issues --- a very important process and a survival issue for a small child. The positive intention of my despair was to search for resolution.

To my amazement, with the recognition of these two words "Search Mode," my despair instantly disappeared. Instantly! And for the next a year and a half, other than a brief ten-minute period at around the four-month mark, I had zero despair in total. As an adult, I already had many other skills for searching within to find resolution.

****

Skill: Identification of Positive Intentions

The skill here is to repeatedly explore (most usefully through journal writing) examples of what has actually happened to you at a behavioral level (your repeated thoughts, emotions or behaviors.) You are seeking the purpose underlying this particular behavior. (The questions developed later with the Skill of Journal Writing are very useful in this regard.)

If the positive intention is still not clear after exploring a few examples in your present life, consider how you learned the behavior in the first place. For example, perhaps you learned it from your mother — it was her pattern and you simply copied it. So if the positive intention of your behavior was somehow to please your mother, do you still need to do so?

****

Recognizing the positive intention of your negative experiences may have profound positive impacts on who you are. At the very least, if you wish to create change in your life, you need to take into account the positive intentions of your now-ineffective actions. You also need to recognize that, given your available resources at the time, you are making your best attempt at achieving this positive intention with your ineffective actions. What you need is a different approach to get this positive intention. What you need is more resources. The resources will either aid you in achieving what you want or will convince you that what you are seeking is not truly in your best interest. I will reiterate: it is very important to realize that you are always doing the best you can with the resources that are available to you at the present time. Most people respond to a situation in the present with the expectation of a good outcome. When this outcome does not occur, the usual pattern that we demonstrate is to blame ourselves as if we had made a bad decision in the original situation. If this were true, that would mean we could have predicted the future outcome of our behaviors with perfect accuracy. No one can do that. The most we can do is learn from our difficulties in not getting what we originally wanted. And then get on with our lives.

4.3.2.2. Emotions Are Action Tendencies

Emotions attempt to inform you of your basic biologic responses, based on your values, beliefs, memories and expectations. Emotions are generally describable by single words (such as angry, sad or excited) and have some connection to what is happening in your current environment. Breaking down the process of how emotions work, the first stage is that something happens in your environment. You take in the information neurologically and process it rapidly at the other-than-conscious level for safety and energy, i.e. "Am I safe?" and "Is the environment pleasant or unpleasant to me?" If either answer is significant, your body starts to respond before the information reaches your conscious awareness --- your human brain. Your other-than-conscious body response is detected by your neurology and then rises to your consciousness where it is given a name based on familiarity (for example, "I am angry") although you seldom recognize the complexity of the feedback loops involved. Perhaps you name the body response as it was originally named from your early childhood experiences, not presently recognizing the details, yet it feels vaguely familiar. Perhaps you even consciously know that it is somehow connected to that part of your early life.

Thus, emotions are the interpretation or label you give to certain body experiences that occur right here, right now in your body (see Figure 51.) This label is principally based upon early childhood experiences wherein certain of your behaviors and external body responses were given names by your parents and significant others as if they could accurately describe your internal experiences. In your early childhood need to learn language, you accepted these words so as to be able to communicate with others and within yourself.

4.3.2.3. FEELINGS AND FEELING JUDGMENTS

What then are feelings, and how do they differ from emotions? There is, to my knowledge, no consistent definition of feelings. Rather, there exists a variety of definitions, ranging from feelings as sensations (skin and internal body tensions) to feelings as internal states prior to the beginning of actions (emotions) to feelings as complex emotions such as betrayal. In this book, I will refer to the word "feeling" as the act of giving focus to my emotions (see Figure 51), for example, such words as feeling threatened, feeling included, feeling involved. To clarify, feelings are, like emotions, usually single words, describing your "here

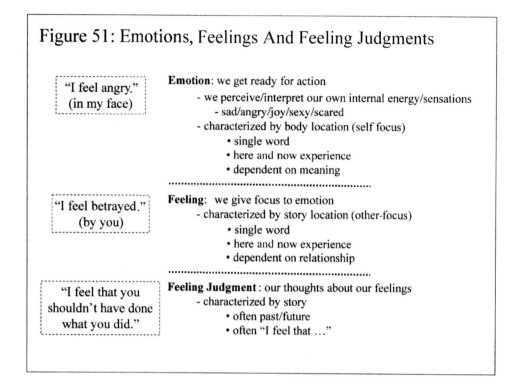

Figure 51: Emotions, Feelings And Feeling Judgments

and now" experience. However, they point to your relationship with others, not to your own bodily experiences. They focus on the relationship between you and the other person (or persons) rather than your intrinsic reaction to your environment.

Another group of feeling statements --- so-called feeling judgments --- are confusing in that they are not feelings. They are your thoughts about your feelings. They are thus even more complex. They are characterized by multiple words and usually speak of the past or the future. Statements such as "I feel we should go to the movie tonight" or "I feel that you are wrong" are not feelings. They are your judgments or your thoughts about your environment or your relationship with others, likely with an underlying feeling or emotional experience.

It is important to pay attention to these distinctions between emotions, feelings and feeling judgments because the content of emotional words, feeling words and statements of feeling judgments give different information. The more accurately the information is defined, the more likely you can resolve an emotional difficulty, if so desired. Again, I will use the metaphor of driving my car to illustrate important differences between all these ways in which we label our emotional world. Say, for instance, your car is not working. You go to your mechanic and say, "My car is not working. Please fix it." Basically you have given the mechanic no information as to what is going on inside your car, expecting somehow for the mechanic to know what to do. This is the equivalent of a feeling judgment, and there is not much detail in your statement. However, if you say to the mechanic, "When I put the key in the ignition and turn it, nothing happens," the mechanic will have additional information and likely think there is something wrong with the electrical system. This is the equivalent of a feeling and contains more detailed information. If you then say further to the mechanic, "I left the lights on while I parked overnight," the problem with your car is much more obvious and, as a result, possibly easier to solve. Most likely the battery is dead and needs charging. This last scenario is equivalent to naming an emotion with clarity as to what happened. You are in a much better position to evaluate your next step --- what underlies your emotion.

4.3.2.4. BELIEFS UNDERLIE EMOTIONS

Near the beginning of my weekend workshops, I invite two strangers to stand facing each other, four or five feet apart without any obstructions between them. They are instructed to be silent during the activity. One person is requested to walk towards the other person while the other person remains still. As reader, what would happen if you were to do the activity yourself in my workshop, either from the perspective of the person moving or the person being still. Almost invariably in my workshop, the moving person stops a predictable distance from the stationary person, often about eighteen inches apart. Why? Because they have gotten close to each other's boundaries --- their personal spaces. Each has signaled to the other, with both conscious and out-of-conscious signals, as to his or her level of comfort. Fundamentally, personal space is a culturally determined belief about what is a comfortable space between people, as highlighted by body language and facial expression. In North America, this cultural belief is translated into action, usually at a distance about eighteen to twenty-four inches apart for most people. When I ask the participants afterwards, "What was your emotional reaction during this experiment," usually it is some form of fear: anxiety, apprehension, uneasiness, etc. Seldom is their reaction a form of anger. Why fear, not anger --- because this experiment was voluntary; it was invited. My suggestion is that every belief has a physical or emotional space (and energy) attached to it. In the above activity of two people moving towards each other, the belief is quite literally attached to the physical space around each person. When people get upset about what their government is doing, for example, about childcare, it is not their physical space that is affected but their emotional space.

Skill: Beliefs Underlying Emotional Experience

For any emotional experience, explore (most usefully by journal writing) what is preceding your emotion by examining what is the underlying belief that is present. What is the purpose (positive intention) to your belief? How, and perhaps from whom, was it learned?

Now list some of your beliefs, ones about which you have some energy. For example, some people believe that "Men shouldn't cry" or "Women are responsible for keeping the family together." After listing your beliefs, explore what physical or emotional space they create for you. Ask yourself: "In what ways do they sustain me? In what ways do they limit me?"

Finally, explore through journal writing, what emotions are

likely to arise if your beliefs are somehow challenged. What happens to the "space" around these beliefs when they are challenged?

4.3.2.5. ANGER AND RAGE

Anger and rage are emotions that represent the energy of difference between people in relationship. Relationships are "spaces" that are relatively permanent or "closed spaces." Anger is an emotion that occurs when there is an uninvited or imposed disruption of personal boundaries (see Figure 52.) Common phrases associated with anger are: "You shouldn't be here" or "You shouldn't be doing that!" Moreover, we are complex being with very complex boundaries. Suppose you meet a stranger on the street (person #1) who is doing something that you believe inappropriate to a second stranger (person #2), yet these strangers are still safe. You probably would not get angry. More likely, you would leave the scene, perhaps in confusion or disgust. Why would you not get angry? Because in this context, the actions of the other people are not very important to you; they don't impact you directly. Why then would you waste your energy being angry? However, if this second person were important to you (for example, your sibling or your child or your close friend) and was being impacted by the first person on the street, you likely would get angry at the first person because you now have a relationship with this first person. His or her actions right now are going to affect you in the future, even though you may never see this person again. This person's actions will impact the existing relationship you have with the second person.

Anger is often a Catch-22, especially in relationship with people you know well. It is a Catch-22 because you want to have your relationship with that other person and yet you want to have your belief that you are right --- that the other person's behavior is inappropriate. As a result, you have an internal conflict with yourself that you call "anger." And it is easier to focus outwards on the

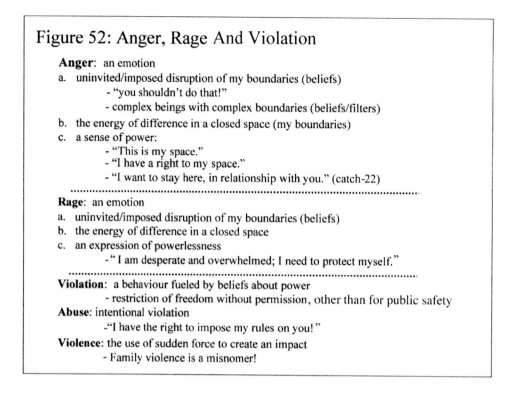

Figure 52: Anger, Rage And Violation

Anger: an emotion
a. uninvited/imposed disruption of my boundaries (beliefs)
- "you shouldn't do that!"
- complex beings with complex boundaries (beliefs/filters)
b. the energy of difference in a closed space (my boundaries)
c. a sense of power:
- "This is my space."
- "I have a right to my space."
- "I want to stay here, in relationship with you." (catch-22)

Rage: an emotion
a. uninvited/imposed disruption of my boundaries (beliefs)
b. the energy of difference in a closed space
c. an expression of powerlessness
- "I am desperate and overwhelmed; I need to protect myself."

Violation: a behaviour fueled by beliefs about power
- restriction of freedom without permission, other than for public safety
Abuse: intentional violation
- "I have the right to impose my rules on you!"
Violence: the use of sudden force to create an impact
- Family violence is a misnomer!

behavior of others than inwards on your own internal conflict. Focusing outwards is a place in which you may feel powerful, potentially able to influence your environment (albeit in a third limb manner.) In this sense, a useful question to ask yourself is, "Would I rather be right or would I rather be in relationship?" It is frequently not possible to be both right and in relationship at the same time (unless you both can be right.)

Similar to anger, rage is also an emotion, where there is an uninvited energy of difference in a closed space. However, it is a stance of feeling powerlessness --- initially feeling overwhelmed by your circumstances, with diminished ability to think and potentially not feeling safe. In rage, your biology mobilizes to get you back to a place of feeling powerful, but rage is not usually a place where you can have clarity. Sometimes perhaps, this mobilization of energy by rage is not effective and you feel trapped and threatened by this powerlessness; as author, I name this state "raging" and regard it as a dangerous "space" where one human being is highly likely to violate another.

4.3.3. Violations

Violation is an interesting word (see Figure 52.) It is not an emotion; rather, it is a behavior fueled by inappropriate beliefs about power. In other words, violation is an intention on the part of one person to impose his or her beliefs on another person, restricting that other person's right to act on his or her own behalf. Please note that I have not written "violence" or "family violence." In the workshops I demonstrate the difference between violation and violence by walking over to the entrance doorway, locking it and standing there before the locked door. In so doing, I am violating the workshop participants by restricting their freedom (to leave the workshop) without their permission. However, I am not being violent. To talk about violence, I give the example of taking a hammer and nail so as to hang a clock on the wall of my office by the process of banging the nail into the wall. Here, I am being violent --- I am using sudden force so as to create an impact. But I am not violating!

A second example will illustrate the difference between violation and violence as it applies to the Blowing Out! process. Say, for instance, I am deeply angry and I slap my hand down on the table. In this case, I am being violent. But am I violating anyone else in the room? In slapping my hand down, if my intention (conscious or otherwise) is simply to release my energy, I suggest that I am not violating anyone else. All people in the room are safe within the rules of No SAD. Perhaps we have previously agreed that such release of energy is entirely acceptable; perhaps I am just being spontaneously passionate and have no intention to threaten. However, in the situation where I am being spontaneously passionate, there is the very real possibility that my actions will be perceived as threatening. If this is a pattern of my behavior, I need to be aware that my passion can be misinterpreted by others. On the other hand, if my intention is to scare another person by my physical display, then I am violating that other person. I have breached safety for all concerned, specifically for the other person to whom I was directing my energy. If any person in the room says STOP and I continue with my slapping of the table, even simply to release my energy, I am violating that other person who has indicated that he or she does not feel secure and, in fact, feels threatened. For me to continue my actions would constitute an attempt to scare that other person, even if I do not consciously recognize this intention.

I suggest that the reason why North American culture focuses on violence as a major problem of our society, rather than violation, is because it is easier (although less accurate) to focus on the act of violence rather than the intent of violation. The act of violence is far easier to identify. From my perspective as psychotherapist however, if we as a society do not allow safe violence, we risk becoming pressure cookers, individually and at the societal level. The challenge therefore it to negotiate parameters of safety in which to practice safe violence. I believe this is possible.

Similar to our society's use of the word "violence," the designation "family violence" is a misnomer for me. It plays only a small part in what is more accurately called family violation. I believe the name "family violence" is sloppy language and, as a result, is part to the problem rather than part of the solution.

As stated above, my definition of violation is one person's "intentional restriction of (another person's) freedom without permission." In families with a long history of abuse, there is often a gray area to violation, especially emotional violation. Violations can result either from present or past actions --- for past actions imply the possibility of present or future actions. For example, if the violator has previously threatened or hit the victim (true abuse), and then the violator tells the victim that he or she is very angry, the violator may well be abusing the victim with words (one form of emotional abuse) because of the implication of further hitting.

Violation depends on the violator's intention to threaten, not on the victim's interpretation. The victim's interpretation may not be accurate to the actual events nor to the intentions of the other person (the person named as violator.) This can be especially true in cases of emotional abuse; emotional abuse exists in the intention of the action, not the interpretation of the action. Similar to what is noted above, it is easier to focus on the interpretation of the victim rather than the violator's intent to violate. It is not abuse if two people are in relationship and one person tells the second person that he or she is very angry that the second person is going out alone with friends on Friday night. It is one person telling the second person of his or her experience. However, if the person who is angry tells the person who is going out that he or she cannot go, then the person who is angry is abusing the person going out by restricting that person's freedom without his or her permission. If, in reality, someone (whether a family member or not) is violating another person, the victim has the right to resist. The victim does not however have the right to escalate by violating in return.

4.3.3.1. MYTHS AND HALF-TRUTHS ABOUT VIOLATIONS

There are many myths and half-truths as to what goes on in violation. The truth often depends on who is talking. The insert shows some of the most common inaccuracies (see Figure 53.) The left-hand column of the insert lists what I consider true dangers of acting out emotional energy. For example, when people go to a coffee shop and complain to each other about how life is unfair, I have no doubt that they frequently come away feeling more aroused in their anger. Alternatively, if people can resolve their anger in a satisfactory manner through talking and thinking about it, I have no disagreement with them.

However the Blowing Out! process is not applicable to the statements contained in the left-hand column, for these statements do not make a distinction between violation and violence. The two can be quite separate in emotional process. The Blowing Out! process insists on no violations as a standard and that violence can be very safe. It also suggests that this separation is key to achieving emotional aliveness. In addition, in working as a psychotherapist with people who have been in extreme circumstances where emotional suppression has been extremely important, for example, wartime military snipers, I have generally found them to be emotionally flat in their lives when the extreme circumstances have ended;

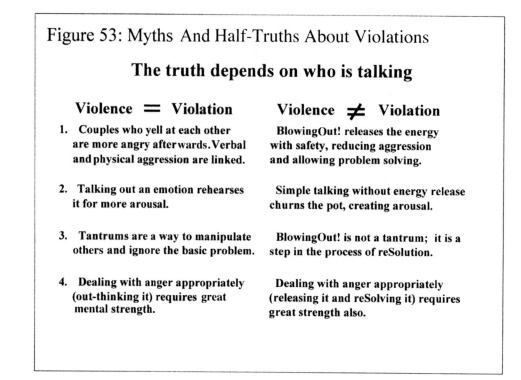

Figure 53: Myths And Half-Truths About Violations

The truth depends on who is talking

Violence = Violation

1. **Couples who yell at each other are more angry afterwards. Verbal and physical aggression are linked.**

2. **Talking out an emotion rehearses it for more arousal.**

3. **Tantrums are a way to manipulate others and ignore the basic problem.**

4. **Dealing with anger appropriately (out-thinking it) requires great mental strength.**

Violence ≠ Violation

BlowingOut! releases the energy with safety, reducing aggression and allowing problem solving.

Simple talking without energy release churns the pot, creating arousal.

BlowingOut! is not a tantrum; it is a step in the process of reSolution.

Dealing with anger appropriately (releasing it and reSolving it) requires great strength also.

they themselves have been fairly content with this but others have complained of their flatness. This is not the way I personally wish to live my life. The price of emotional aliveness is experiencing emotions at both ends of the spectrum: pain and pleasure, positive and negative. There is no morality in having these feelings, only in the actions I take as a result of these feelings.

4.3.3.2. VIOLENCE --- THE PERCEIVED RISK

As outlined in the previous section, the most common objection to the Blowing Out! process is that it is violent. In this section, I will discuss in greater detail how the Blowing Out! process can indeed be violent but that its quality of violence can lead to a richer emotional life. For one, we are a violent species and need to come to terms with this truth about ourselves as human beings. This inherent quality of our violence is not the same as violation. Similarly, we often confuse anger and rage with violation, even though they are quite different. I invite the reader to explore within yourself as to how much violence --- sudden force so as to create an impact --- you are exposed within your life on a daily basis. If you stop to think about it, violence is a reality in our lives. Some of it (but not all of it) is violation.

I contend the real challenge for healthy emotional living is to practice violence in a safe manner without violating anyone else's boundaries. I further contend that when a client authentically recognizes and discharge his or her violent energy, usually with some form of active release and fantasy work with his or her Ghost, the client releases the possibility of being trapped by his or her fantasy and ceases acting out at a later time in a devious fashion and also ceases to violate. My clients, many of whom say they have attempted other methods of resolving their emotional issues, tell me that what I offer them in the Blowing Out! process is effective. Without question, there is some risk to active release work but, in my experience, the risk is mostly physical (accidentally straining your muscles, for example.) The risk is not typically emotional. In fact, the opposite is more likely to occur. Rather than increase the risk of your acting out, the energy and the story are discharged through the Blowing Out! process and you stop acting out!

There are people who can use active release work as an excuse for violation. I recall one client who went home and tore the built-in vacuum system off the wall of his house, claiming to his wife that I had said this was an appropriate way for him to release his rage. People who choose to violate (consciously and unconsciously) can justify their actions any way they want. I cannot prevent this (third limb) application of my therapy work; I can however challenge it. In response, I now routinely say to my clients: "Please do not use my health as an excuse for your insanity!"

4.3.3.3. EXPOSING CHILDREN TO VIOLENCE WITHOUT VIOLATION

Clients often approach me to ask about dealing with the anger of their children, especially when the parents themselves have demonstrated inappropriate behaviors in the past. The Blowing Out! process can be a healing process for the whole family and teach everyone how to be safe with their anger and rage.

It further emphasizes the distinctions between violence and violation. My belief is that, in our North American society, we already expose our children to horrendous violence with violation (witness some of the cartoons on TV.) Given the distinction I make between violation and violence, I generally ask parents to explain and demonstrate this distinction (in age-appropriate language) so that children can come to terms with their own violence safely, and practice No SAD and STOP when they themselves need release of their intense energies.

--- Author's Personal Commentary ---

I received the following example from one family I know as to how the parents have incorporated the Blowing Out! process into their lives. I have added no modification.

"Our family has worked with Dave MacQuarrie for a lot of years, and so many of the tools and practices that Dave advocates have become part of our normal way of interacting. Both our children are quite familiar with the sound of a tennis racket connecting with a mattress. Our eldest was introduced to using a tennis racket to dump energy fairly early on: although its efficacy was rather lost on her when on the second or third stroke the racket slipped out of her hand, and bounced back up and connected with her forehead. Her younger sister was very adept at recognizing the signs of anger and would readily tell us that she was 'angee' too. The self awareness, and the acceptance that being angry is just as ok as being happy, or sad, etc. have flowed from the fact that we have chosen to deal with emotional content and the energy it creates openly and appropriately. When the four year old told us her sister was 'angee' and needed a racket we were prepared to

deal with both children's needs in a safe and loving manner. At 10 and

16 both still have times when their emotions create a lot of energy, but

they have each found ways to discharge that energy in ways that are

safe and satisfying. (Not just pounding the mattress: but through dance,

music, drumming.)

> *"MG, 2005 October 29th"*

Teaching safe anger to children has been overall very successful with the families I encounter (whose members have practiced the Blowing Out! process.) The only time difficulties arise is when the parents themselves do not manage their own energy, yet expect their children to do so.

4.3.4. ASSUMPTIONS AND HOW WE FUNCTION

Returning to the discussion of the need for precision and clarity in our language, we now need to look at how we create our stories by filling in the gaps between sensory data and the meaning we give the data through our assumptions. As human beings, we are exposed to vast amounts of data occurring around us, all at the same time --- the weather, loud noises, other people's voices, our own internal voices, etc. Neurologically and psychologically, we modify this data so as to simplify it and make it more manageable, both at the other-than-conscious and the conscious level. We do this by generalizing, deleting and distorting our experience so as to cope with its vastness. We have to --- we quite literally could not function otherwise. Unfortunately we pay a price for maintaining our sanity. The next few sections will explore how we do this and what it costs us.

4.3.4.1. PERSPECTIVE

Look at the diagram in Figure 54 and become aware of your first impression of the figure. What is it? Now turn the page ninety degrees to the left and notice what the figure looks like now. Turn the page another ninety degrees to the left. And another. Presumably you will notice a different figure each time: an "M," a "3," a "W" and an "E," as well as many other possibilities. Which of these possible interpretations is the right designation? They all are, of course. Where you might get into trouble is if you believe that any one of these possible interpretations is more right than the others, especially if you try to impose your sense of rightness on another person.

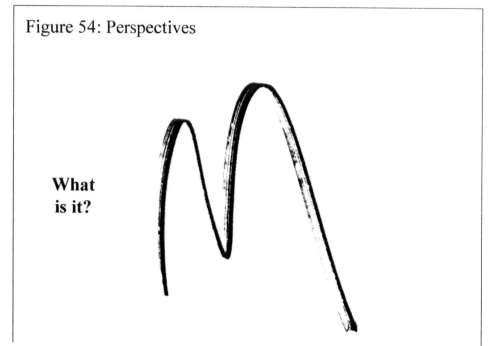

Figure 54: Perspectives

What is it?

I contend that ninety-five percent of conflict follows a similar pattern of stating one's interpretations of the data and then getting trapped in one's self-righteousness about these interpretations, unwilling or unable to step out of one's own story to get the other person's view of the world. One of the fundamental skills of successful emotional living is your ability to step into the worldview of another person and (for a while) accept that the other person is right in his or her interpretations. The other person does not have to be wrong for you to be right, and vice versa. You simply need to get that the other person is also right (from his or her perspective.)

4.3.4.1.1. The Story

The nature of our assumptions is even more complicated than simply getting trapped in our interpretations of the raw data. In the above exercise, there is no emotional investment in getting the "right" answer to what interpretation is intended by the diagram. In other real life situations, however, there is a lot more at stake. The more people become convinced in these situations that they are right, the more argumentative they become when alternative interpretations are proposed.

Before I explain further, please read "The Story [4]" and check off your responses to the True/False/Not Sure statements following "The Story."

****

The Story

"A businessman had just turned off the lights in the store when a man appeared and demanded money. The owner opened the cash register. The contents of the cash register were scooped up and the man sped away. A member of the police force was notified promptly."

Indicate for each of the following statements if you believe it to be true, false or if you are not sure of the answer.

T/F/NS **1. A man appeared after the owner had turned off the lights.**

T/F/NS **2. The robber was a man.**

T/F/NS **3. The man who opened the cash register was the owner.**

T/F/NS **4. After the man had scooped up the contents of the cash register, he ran away.**

T/F/NS **5. While the cash register contained money, the story does not state how much.**

T/F/NS **6. The story concerns a series of events in which only three persons are referred to: the owner of the store, a man who**

---

4. Source unknown. "The Story" came from a workshop I attended several years ago.

demanded money and a member of the police force.

****

Once you have checked off all your responses to the statements, let us consider what assumptions you have brought to the data. As I list my own responses, please note your tendency to agree or disagree with my interpretation. Please also note your tendency to criticize yourself for not getting the "right" answer. For there really are no absolutely right answers --- we all fill in details in the gaps; and these details will vary from person to person. The answers I supply are only my best interpretations of the data as given, given my beliefs about the distinctions between data and interpretation.

1. "A man appeared after the owner had turned off the lights." My best answer: not sure. Where does it say that the owner and the businessman are the same person?

2. "The robber was a man." Answer: not sure. Where does it say a robbery took place? Suppose you loan someone five hundred dollars and he or she agreed to pay you back the next day. Two days later, you haven't received the money. You go and demand the money from the other person. Is this a robbery? No. And Yes, a member of the police force was notified, but are there not other possible reasons for notifying the police?

3. "The man who opened the cash register was the owner." Answer: not sure. Where does it say the gender of the owner?

4. "After the man had scooped up the contents of the cash register, he ran away." Answer: not sure. Who exactly scooped up the contents? Also, "sped away" can mean either "ran away quickly" or "got into a car and drove away quickly" amongst other meanings. How can you be sure which one the man did?

5. "While the cash register contained money, the story does not state how much." Answer: not sure. Where does it say that the cash register contained money. Although cash registers are called cash registers because they

normally contain money, they often contain items, other than money, such as receipts, coupons, etc.

6. "The story concerns a series of events in which only three persons are referred to: the owner of the store, a man who demanded money and a member of the police force." Answer: false. The number of people who appear in the story is ambiguous; there could be three people, or four, or some other number. But this statement says "only three" and the "only" limits the answer to "three."

As you can imagine, if the above story were "a real-life situation," the stakes would be very high indeed. It could mean the difference between the right and wrong person going to jail, or even anyone going to jail at all. Consider the following example where I fill in the blanks so that there is no robbery committed.

"The (Possible) **Story: A business man had just turned off the lights in the store when a man** (a credit collector) **appeared and demanded money** (owed for outstanding purchases.) **The owner** (a woman, also in the store for closing) **opened the cash register** (to get the letter of receipts paid, the only remaining contents of the register, normally emptied for the night.) **The contents of the cash register were scooped up** (by the owner and handed to the man) **and the man sped away** (angrily, in his car.) **A member of the police force was notified promptly** (that the man appeared drunk and was driving dangerously.)**"**

✳✳✳✳✳✳✳✳✳✳✳✳✳✳✳✳✳✳✳✳✳✳✳✳✳✳✳✳✳✳✳✳✳✳

Skill: Noting Assumptions

Read any passage in a book about a specific event, preferably one that is emotion-laden. How does the author arrive at his or her conclusions of what happened?

What assumptions do you as the reader need to make in order to have clarity about what you think the author intends. To what extent is the passage an example of sloppy language?

Repeat this activity until you are confident that you can identify the distinction between data presented and the assumptions you need to make for clarity.

****

4.3.4.2. ASSUMPTIONS AND MIND-READING

A major way in which these assumptions we make trap us is called "mind-reading" and will be explored in this section. The above activities are meant to highlight the assumptions that you (and most people) bring to data as it is often presented and illustrate how easy it is to be caught in these assumptions. Most people do not notice the subtle sloppiness of other people's stories nor the additions they themselves make to the stories so as to create comprehensive meaning out of the stories. The human brain functions purposefully this way with the literally millions of details presented to us each moment of our lives; we have to generalize, delete and distort the primary data so as to keep our lives simple enough to be manageable.

How we make complete sense of the story of our lives is based on our assumptions that come from our values, beliefs, memories and expectations. And then we don't notice where the information has come from --- the world around us or from our own assumptions? This pattern of adding details that exist only in our minds is not right or wrong. Rather it is part of our basic design and is extremely useful in allowing us to "always do what we have always done (and always get what we have always gotten.)" However, if what we are getting is no longer what we want, we need to backtrack and examine our premises.

As stated earlier, I contend that ninety-five percent of conflict --- external and internal --- arises from our tendency to get stuck in our interpretations and our unwillingness to take the time to examine our premises. In my early university days, I studied Physics. I was exposed to the following engineering principle that I still hold to be true in my daily emotional life: "If it works, use it." There are two important corollaries: "If your conclusions are wrong, examine your premises." and "If your conclusions are right, don't trust your premises." These statements continue to guide me in my strong conviction that a major skill of emotional living is the ability to distinguish data from story.

Mind-reading is a specific form of this same pattern of filling in the details based on our assumptions; only, in this case, it is applied not just to a context but to the inner workings of another human being. Again, there is a positive intention to mind-reading. You can never know another person's inner world so mind-reading becomes a way for you to establish rapport with the other person and think you "understand" him or her. If the meaning you make of the other person's internal world is of only limited emotional significance, no harm is done. But it is not accurate --- if you make a significant emotional investment in your story of the other person's world and forget that it is only an assumption, sooner or later, you will get into difficulty.

4.3.4.3. Life Difficulties

Life difficulties occur for many reasons. The ease with which solutions or resolutions are available for your life difficulties is impacted by the assumptions you bring to the fore. Generally, life difficulties fall into three categories:

a. logical difficulties – the mechanism of correct function is known (by someone) and is somehow askew.

b. ethical difficulties --- a standard of comparison is not being upheld.

c. emotional difficulties --- we differ from each other in important ways but there is no standard upon which to make choices or agreements other than personal preferences.

In logical difficulties, there is some previously known verifiable data that can be identified and brought to bear on the solution to the difficulty. For example, when your car breaks down, the mechanism by which the car is not working can be identified. Because the mechanism is based on logical mechanical principles, you can recognize the logical difficulty and correct it.

There are, however, two other kinds of difficulties. Ethical difficulties have an agreed-upon standard to which you and other people can refer when having a disagreement. Often this agreed-upon ethical reference is dictated by society. For example, if you drive through a red light at an intersection and an accident results, you are "in the wrong." Driving through the red light is not necessarily wrong; rather, it is not safe! As a society, we have agreed that, for safety sake while driving a car, a red light means "stop." We incorporate this meaning at a societal level by calling it "the law." Standards are not necessarily logical. Consider the North American laws of driving on the right-hand side of the road versus the UK laws of driving on the left-hand side. Each is an important standard in order to keep order and safety on the roads, but there is no logic per se behind the choice of driving side that makes one choice inherently better than another choice.

Ethical standards also apply to personal agreed-upon standards. If you had an agreement to go somewhere with your friend on Friday night and your friend breaks his or her agreement with you, then you and your friend have an ethical difficulty. Generally, in relationship or as a society, we function best when we keep our agreements. We call this "fairness."

Finally, an emotional difficulty occurs where you and another person disagree, but you do not have an agreement (a standard) to which you can refer nor is there any logical data that you can agree to examine. The two of you have no basis to deal with your differences other than your personal beliefs. Conflict arises when one person takes the stance that his or her beliefs are more important than the other person's beliefs. It becomes violation when that first person imposes his or her beliefs on the other person.

4.3.4.3.1. Data Versus Story

Sorting out the different categories of life difficulties, as well as the conflict which occur within each category, requires two major skills:

1. The ability to separate out the data from the story.

2. The ability to check out your assumptions about the data once you have separated it from the story.

****

Skill: Data Versus Story

This exercise is a two-part exercise.

For the preliminary exercise, observe someone in whom you have no emotional investment performing an action that interests you. For example, observe someone standing up and walking out of a room. (If necessary, do so in your imagination or from memory.)

Describe in as much detail as possible what that person is actually doing, exclusively in terms of his or her behaviors (the data). Next, make up a story of what happened, including their internal thoughts and feelings. In the example mentioned, make up a story of why the person stood up and walked out of the room, including what you believed were his or her internal thoughts and feelings. Then make up two other stories of what happened that still account for all the data you listed, one that is positive in content and one that is negative. How did you arrive at each of your interpretations, especially your first one? What underlying belief (or other energy) did you have invested in your

first interpretation?

For the second part of the exercise, pick any disagreement in your life with another person, about which you have some stake in the outcome.

Take a blank piece of paper and put a line down the middle of it. On one side of the page, write down what happened at the behavioral level. Include your own thoughts, emotions and behaviors as well as the behaviors of the other person. Do not include his or her thoughts or emotions. On the other side, write down what you think were the thoughts and emotions of the other person. How did you arrive at this latter interpretation?

Finally, make up two more stories that could equally explain the available data at the behavioral level of the disagreement. Within each of these additional stories, write down what you think could have been the thoughts and emotions of the other person involved.

How do you know which story of he three stories to believe? What would have happened if you had started out the disagreement with one of your two other stories? Would it have changed the nature of your disagreement?

****

The first skill of sorting out life difficulties is the ability to distinguish your data from your story. In the preceding exercise "Data Versus Story," you were asked to take an example of a disagreement you have had and, using two columns on a piece of paper, write the actual data, and in the second column, the meaning you gave to these actions, including the thoughts and feeling of the other person.

You were then invited to write several other meanings that could also explain the available data. The only way to find out which of these versions is accurate is to use the second skill of sorting out life difficulties: check out the data. In this case, the easiest way is likely for you to ask the other person. However, either in our fear of criticism by others or in not recognizing that we have made assumptions, we seldom do this. And even if we do, we often don't believe the additional data --- because we believe we are "right." Much of the time when we do not check out the data, the consequences are minimal. We are close enough with our guesses to the truth or the difficulty resolves itself spontaneously. When this isn't the case, however, we are in trouble. As you may have found out in the above excerpt called "The Story" (Section 4.3.4.1.1. above), the process of communication can be so difficult when contaminated by our assumptions, especially those assumptions that carry a lot of emotional energy. Sometimes, as therapist, I feel amazed that we communicate at all as human beings.

4.4. ADDITIONAL IMPORTANT SKILLS

Awareness is the primary skill. The reason why awareness is so profound, even when developed to a limited extent, is that, you start to notice little details that you did not notice before. Slowly, you start to correlate these details with other details; and patterns emerge in your consciousness. Thereafter, similar to spontaneously going to get a drink of water when you become aware of your thirst, your behaviors change as your awareness develops.

--- Author's Personal Commentary ---

I will give an example of how I put to work the skill of awareness in

my own practice. As a therapist, I do not want to be emotionally caught

in attempting to change the third limb of the triangle involving myself,

a client and the client's issues (see previous, Section 2.3.2. Emotional

Triangles.) The third limb is a place of potentially being ineffective, especially when it involves telling other people how they should be. As a therapist, I am often making suggestions to clients, or exploring with clients how they interact with their own issues. But I have no investment in the client doing anything different than they are already doing ---- my work is simply to explore and bring to consciousness processes within the client so that the client can explore his or her own choices about the issues. I am being ineffective when emotionally caught in the third limb --- when I want the client to do something different besides what they are already doing. So how do I know when I am caught; how do I know to get out of the third limb at these times? The client is not likely to tell me.

After extended practice with the "Now I am aware of ..." exercise, I became conscious that the muscles of my eyebrows tightened when I was in this mode of being caught. So now that I am aware of this pattern within myself, I monitor it. If and when tension develops above my eyebrows, I remind myself that what I am doing is not being effective and then do something else. Alternatively, if I am working with a difficult client who says to me: "Don't push me, Dave!," I can check my eyebrow tension as a gauge. If my eyebrows are tense, I apologize to the client. If they are not tense, I may still apologize (in some fashion) so as to re-establish rapport but also wonder what is happening with the client that he or she is feeling pushed even though I am internally clear that I am not pushing. I may or may not bring this observation up to the client, but I do register it as potentially significant information about the client.

✶✶✶✶✶✶✶✶✶✶✶✶✶✶✶✶✶✶✶✶✶✶✶✶✶✶✶✶✶✶✶✶✶✶✶✶✶✶✶

Skill: Body Checking

A second exercise that is useful in developing the skill of awareness is learning to attend to my body reactions in common situations. If you pay attention, my personal experience is that you have a sensory response to every moment of "contact" with your environment. Before starting this exercise (and as good practice overall), do a body check of what sensory experience is available in your body at this time. Check your feet, your ankles, your calves ... through your entire body for detailed minor sensations. (Our tendency is to think there is no sensation present because we have accommodated and deleted most sensory experience as a response to its lack of prominence. Nevertheless, there is always sensation available.)

Once you have some skill at checking your entire body, stand near an object or person and notice your discrete body sensations (including your internal voice and internal visual experiences.) Scan your body and observe what is happening in as detailed a fashion as possible. Check if any of the sensations seem to relate to the object you have chosen to give your attention.

Now move a few inches closer to the object or person and note what shifts occur in your body experience. Move a few inches further away from the object or person and note again what

shifts in your internal processing. What do you experience? What meaning (story) do you give to these experiences, especially if you note shifts in your experience?

With practice it is easy to discover quite significant shifts in your experience with only minor changes in your orientation to the environment. Thus when someone does something in your presence or something changes in your environment, neurologically you can be responsive to what is occurring. This is a profound skill if you will develop it.

****

4.4.1. TRUTH-TESTING

Another key component of awareness is actually accepting your awareness as accurate. We have a truly incredible capacity for accurate assessment of situations, if only we trust it. More commonly we ignore it as being too subjective. I suggest that your capacity for accurate assessment is a trainable skill, one that as a culture we have lost in our overemphasis on intellectual analysis and our need to prove the objective basis of our decisions.

An important skill for accurate assessment is knowing your own truth signals. The concept of truth signals has been described in many fields. Examples include the use of Chevreul pendulums and idiodynamic signals in hypnotherapy[5], and applied kinesthesiology in naturopathy and other alternative health fields. Usually the act of determining one's truth signals has been set up so that the practitioner can test the client rather than teach him or her the direct skill development. The latter does not allow the client to develop his or her own skills of subjectivity. As a psychotherapist, the power of truth-testing is one of the best ways I know of helping clients make difficult decision in their lives.

---

5. Ernest L. Rossi and David B. Cheek, *Mind-Body Therapy: Methods of Ideodynamic Healing in Hypnosis* (New York: W.W. Norton & Company, 1988).

****

Skill: Truth-Testing

Generally I teach clients to know their own truth signals using the following exercise. The signals for any given individual are unique to that individual and hence I will describe it from my own experience for the purpose of explaining the exercise. I suggest that clients practice the skill daily until confident of the signals generated.

First, I speak aloud a simple statement of concrete fact. (Speaking aloud allows body-mind-heart-soul-spirit to resonate more effectively with the information spoken. Thinking often engages only the mind.) For example, I would say: "I am wearing a lime-green T-shirt," (which I am at the present time.) I pause and explore how I respond internally to this spoken truth — how I resonate with it. Next I speak my age: "I am sixty-four years old." Pause and explore. Now I speak how many children I have: "I have three adult children." Pause and explore. After stating aloud several more simple statements of fact, I check to see what is my common sensory experience of all these statements? For example, I notice that when I speak my truths, I get a sense of visual brightness above my eyes and a lifting of my chest as if I am standing taller. This "Yes" signal of mine happens every time I speak my truth.

Now, I do the equivalent training with what I know to be falsehoods. For example, I would say: "I own a green car" (which

I don't.) Pause and explore. "My wife is twenty-nine years old." Pause and explore. "My brother has sixteen children." Pause and explore. What is the common sensory experience here? I notice that when I speak a falsehood, there is a heaviness under my eyes and tightness in my throat. This set of sensations is my "No" signal and occurs every time I speak a falsehood.

As the reader, you will have your own unique set of sensations as you say such statements of concrete fact or falsehood. The tendency is to stop the exploration at the emotional response to these statements (for example, "Of course, It is obvious. I can see I am wearing a lime-green T-shirt.") I am inviting you, the reader, to go deeper and explore what is the sensory response that confirms your "truthfulness" (your "Yes" signal) has been spoken or that a falsehood (your "No" signal) has been spoken. In my experience, for most people, if they will step out of an analytic mode of conceptually wanting to understand these statements, they will find one or more sensations that are consistent throughout each category of statement and are independent of the content of the statement. Similar consistent bodily responses can also be obtained for such stances as "I truly do not know the answer" or "I don't want to know the answer — I am afraid."

****

--- Author's Personal Commentary ---

Truth-testing has been very important in my own life. For example, I was in a relationship a number of years ago with a woman who was Catholic. I am a deeply spiritual person but have little use for institutionalized belief systems. I had decided at that time that I wanted to re-enter Christianity as a way of exploring my spiritual and religious roots. I enrolled in the Roman Catholic Instruction for Adults (RCIA) program to become Catholic. As the time of my Confirmation came closer, my girlfriend and I started to argue more --- she kept telling me how I should act as a Catholic.

I didn't like this and started to question if I even wanted to complete the RCIA program. Despite much soul-searching over several weeks, I was unable to come to a conclusion. Finally, one evening while skiing, I simply said quietly out loud "I want to become Catholic." I got my "Yes" signal. Then I said "I don't want to become Catholic." I got my "No" signal. In this way, I found my answer in less than five seconds and simply let go of my internal struggle.

4.4.1.1. "As-If" Testing

Truth-testing can also be used as a method of assessing future options, for example, a new job. The skill is to step into a future experience "as if" the experience were real and at the present moment. In order to do so, you need to gather some preliminary experience of the new situation to be explored. Continuing the example of a new job, you might need to visit the new job location and talk with the people with whom you might be working in order to get a sense of what the future difficulties might be. In the process, you will actually gather much more information that you generally think you do.

****

<u>Skill: "As-If" Testing</u>

When you have a difficult decision to make, study the options carefully. Gather all the data you can. Analyze it in any way that is familiar to you. Determine possible options and outcomes.

Then give each option a physical place in the room and step into each option, one at a time, "as if" the possible future situation were true. Associate into each "reality" as fully as possible. Note your experience, especially your body sensations. Explore its meaning relative to what you are querying. (Note: give your body a shake after each possible future situation so as to shake off any residual energy.)

Finally, compare your responses obtained at each location. Stand somewhere in the middle between the options and sway your body, exploring what way your body wants to move. What information do you receive?

****

In my practice, I often use the skill of as-if testing as a means of truth-testing. Suppose a male client comes to me wanting resolution of a difficult decision in his life. In the job change example, the client might tell me how he has a good job but someone has offered me another very interesting job and he doesn't know what to do. He has written out the pros and cons, what he would gain and what he would lose, but he still doesn't know what to do.

At this point, I lead him through the very simple exercise describe above. I tell him to pick a spot in the room that represents his current job and another spot that represents the new job. As he stands in the spot that represents, for example, the new job, I ask him to imagine "as if" he have been working at this new job for a year or so. The client might say: "I feel bouncy in my feet, brightness in my face and also have some tension in my abdomen." The client then stands in the other spot, 'as if' he had kept his old job. He might respond: "My feet feel solid, I've a bit of a headache and my throat feels dry." Finally the client stands in the middle between the two spots, leaning each way and feeling how his body responds. Usually by this point, he already has a clear sense of what decision to make; it is confirmed by the sense of wanting to fall in the direction of the appropriate choice.

The most important component of "as-if " testing (and all truth-testing in general) is illustrated by the preceding example: the client has trusted his own awareness of the truth about what his life is currently offering. For all clients, the limitations of truth-testing are their willingness to trust themselves and their own truths. Of course, errors in judgment occur but I contend that the willingness to trust oneself provides a decision-making system that, in its scope, is incredibly accurate and sophisticated.

I have just finished reading the book *Blink* [6] that gives credibility to the above concept of truth-testing (albeit labeled differently.) *Blink* is about our ability to perform split-second decisions at an other-than-conscious level. Especially interesting is one of the stories in the book about a United States Marine Corp senior officer who was asked to act as the enemy in a staged combat situation involving a renegade Middle Eastern dictator. The Marine officer, who had had much combat experience and was known for his assertive and rapid decision-making, was in charge of a team who had vastly fewer resources than the USA team. However, the USA team lost despite having practically unlimited resources and a very sophisticated decision-planning strategy. The ability to make split-second decisions and incorporate highly unusual strategies in the real-time drama (both of which the Marine officer had) simply had not been incorporated in the USA team's predictions. Split-second awareness is often placed in the realm of "intuition" or "luck" and not given enough credence. As indicated above, I maintain that it is a trainable skill --- a skill for which I have profound awe.

---

6. Malcolm Caldwell, 2005, Little Brown

4.4.1.2. TRUTH-TESTING AS EXPLORATION OF POSSIBILITIES

Once you have the confidence in your ability to reliably know your own truths, the possibilities for exploration of life issues are profound. I will use an example from my own personal past as illustration.

--- Author's Personal Commentary ---

When something untoward happens to me, I often wonder as to the mechanism. If I can know the mechanism, I can more easily develop a tool to correct the experience. Approximately five years ago, I was having major difficulties with my health. I found that many common foods left me feeling ill and/or anxious for days after eating them. At the time, regular medical assessment was not helpful with my food sensitivities so I went to see a physician who specialized in alternative medicine. Following his advice on nutritional supplements, my health rapidly improved. Typical of the reception given by allopathic medicine, however, I could find few other physicians who believed the explanation for the advice he had given. I certainly accepted his explanation --- I had the results of better health to prove it.

Subsequent to my time with the alternative medicine, I use my truth signals to explore my "food sensitivities" and thus live a more comfortable life. My other-than-conscious signals can predict which particular foods are not a good choice for me at any given time. It astounds me --- even as a physician. I have no good explanation for how I do this. I am however very thankful as to how wise my other-than-conscious self is in knowing what is happening to me. It is this skill that has allowed me to sort out potential health difficulties, and hence bring

a corrective to them.

****

<u>Skill: Testing of Possibilities</u>

This skill requires a reliable method of truth-testing such as described above.

Pick any concern that troubles you, a concern for which you are unclear as to how it has arisen. Perhaps you have a skin rash that is persistent.

List any possibilities of which you are aware that could be causing the skin rash — both your own thoughts and those of other people's. Brainstorm as necessary, without censoring or analyzing the information that comes up. Examples for "skin rash" might include rubbing from your bedding while you were asleep, a food reaction or a stress reaction. Perhaps someone else queries if it is a form of cancer.

For each possibility, truth-test the possibility by speaking aloud the following types of statements: "Fifty percent of the rash is due to the rubbing of my bed clothes." Note your truth response. Then say, "Thirty percent of the rash is due to rubbing from my bed clothes." Again, note your truth response.

Hone your truth response for each possibility until you find out which statement has a body experience that feels closest to a "yes" signal. Also, note if you receive a negative signal from any statement you make. Usually you can get to within five

percentage points of accuracy for each possible cause if you are attentive. As you continue testing the other possibilities in similar fashion, take note of the percentage points you arrive at for each possible cause. Suppose your answers are: "Food: eighty percent; Rubbing: twenty-five; Stress: twenty percent; Cancer: zero." Obviously, in this case, you need to give more attention to what you are eating. If your top answer had been, "Rubbing: ninety percent," you would need to pay more attention to your bedding. Note that the numbers do not need to add up to one hundred percent; the various possibilities as named may overlap in their effect. For example, perhaps your skin is sensitized by the food you are eating but the rash requires rubbing by your bedclothes for it to become symptomatic.

****

In my personal and professional experience, any issue may be explored using the above exercise. The sorting of the possibilities is remarkably useful in directing how you need to approach a problem. It also consistently leads to a resolution of the issue with great reliability. Note that if I suggest a possibility to yourself, it comes from your other-than-consciousness; hence there is likely some truth to it. If someone else suggests a possibility, I allow that there may be no truth to it at all. In the above example, the possibility of cancer as the cause of the rash had zero percent truthfulness.

The limitation of truth-testing that I have encountered is that it is dependent on personal experience stored in my past by my other-than-consciousness. If I have not had any personal experience with a particular issue that I am truth-testing, my other-than-consciousness has no direct information to test. Hence, my truth signals give a clean signal of "don't know." (My "I don't know" signal is another sensory signal separate from the "yes" signal and the "no" signal.) Appropriately so, for truth signals appear to arise from the body-mind-heart-soul-spirit, not the rational mind.

4.4.2. THE FELT SENSE OF EXPERIENCE --- FOCUS

As discussed above, a key component of the skills of awareness and truth-testing is that of being attuned to the sensory shifts that occur when you make associated contact in your body, as if an experience were happening. The sensory shifts may consist of body sensations, internal visual shifts or images or internal auditory shifts or sounds. I name this ability to be aware as "the felt sense of experience." With practice, as you make repeated associated contact with your environment and with other people, you can become aware of how these shifts are generally quite consistent over time.

Earlier in the book (The Pointing Finger, Section 2.3.2.4.), I had asked you to recall a situation where you had been in significant conflict with another person in a specific situation, one in which you ended up feeling angry. I invited you to notice the difference between a dissociated and an associated experience. I also invited you to explore how you usually focus your energy, either on the other person, the situation or on yourself. The metaphor of The Pointing Finger consists of a conflict situation (your thumb), another person with whom you are in conflict (your index finger) and a place of resources (three fingers pointing back to you.) When you focus on the other person with whom you are in conflict, you might feel anger in our face. When you focus on the situation, you might feel anger in your head, somewhat back from your face. And when you focus on yourself, you might feel your emotional pain in your chest, a sensation that is not quite anger but something more subtle.

This exercise demonstrates how your focus shifts, and thus how your experience depends on where you focus your attention. Generally each of us has a preferred pattern of response, perhaps focusing on the other, perhaps on the situation, perhaps on ourselves. Although knowing where you typically focus may not correct the conflict, you have true power to shift the conflict only when your focus is on yourself. Focus on yourself is the starting point of conflict resolution.

4.4.2.1. THE FELT SENSE OF WORDS

There are other ways in which the ability to have a felt sense of experience can be very powerful. The book *Focusing*[7] by Eugene Gendlin describes the skill of taking an experience and finding just the right word that resonates with the client for that experience. When successful, the client often has a profound sense of relief and perhaps a resolution of any dilemma associated with the experience.

Such is the power of words. To explore for yourself, take any word, especially a concept word, and speak it out loud. With enough attention to awareness, you will have a sensory experience connected to this word that is congruent with your meaning of the word. For example, if I say "responsibility," I get an excited sensation of moving outwards from my chest, my body core. If I say "accountability," I have a slightly shameful sense of someone in front of me looking down upon me. These two words, often confused in sloppy language, create very different experiences inside my body. Being "responsible" actually means being "able to respond --- to make choices about and act on the choices." Being "accountable" actually means "the ability to give satisfactory results according to other people's standards." Because my sensory experiences of each word are consistent with these dictionary definitions, more likely I will be precise in my usage of them. Conversely, often parents will say that they are responsible for their children when they mean they are accountable for their children's actions --- if the children are troublesome, someone will blame the parents. The parent's sloppy word choice may confuse their experience of being parents and make it more difficult than necessary. The remedial skill is to know your experience of the words you are choosing and the use of the most congruent one --- the skill of awareness.

---

7. Eugene Gendlin, 1981, Bantam

4.4.3. A Sensory-Based Energy Transformer --- Energy Storage

As human beings, we are all sensory-based energy transformers. Energy storage, or where we store the energy associated with sensory data, is another key component in developing the skill of awareness. As the reader right now, imagine the experience of your pet, one of your parents or some other component of your experience that exists outside of yourself. Pick one of these experiences on which to focus your attention. Where and how do you actually experience these external events as you imagine them? For myself, if I imagine my dog, I conceive of her wandering around a room. Principally I see her, in my mind's eye, about six feet in front of me on the ground. Now, in your imagination, move your chosen external experience into a situation where there is some difficulty. For example, I would move my dog outdoors, where unattended, she might wander onto the road outside the front of my house and possibly be struck by a high-speed truck. As you shift your imagination, notice the other experiences that quite spontaneously occur inside of yourself.

Several aspects are important to highlight in the above exercise. First, humans process data at a sensory level, even when that data is imaginary. If you are really attentive, you process data as complete sensory representations. At a minimum, your experience has a visual, auditory and kinesthetic manifestation. Moreover, processing data at the sensory level, my imagination is not restricted to the physical limits of your body --- you experience data as both inside and outside of your body.

Secondly, humans surprisingly store much sensory data outside our bodies; and, at some level, everything we store is sensory, including our values, beliefs, memories and expectations (VBMEs.) If you are attentive, you can be aware of where you store your VBMEs, sometimes in quite unexpected places. Your language frequently manifests where you store your energy. I invite you to say aloud, at this moment, the words "my past" and explore where you keep your past at the sensory experiential level. Now recall the truism: "Put your past behind you." Do you? Or do you store your past somewhere where you are repeatedly caught in its dysfunctions. Many people store their past just within their physical bodies, for example, as a weight pulling on their shoulders. Experiment for a moment as to what happens if you move your past behind you into some kind of floating container so that your past has no weight. You may be surprised by the impact of this simple shift (or, in some cases, the difficulty of creating the shift.) A note of caution here: energy shifts can be magical and powerful. They can also be overwhelming and frightening if you are not ready for them. Fortunately as human beings, we have many built-in safety measures that prevent us from accessing too much change, at least not until we are ready for the shift.

--- Author's Personal Commentary ---

I keep my past behind me (I put it there intentionally a few years ago.) It feels to me like the tail of a dragon costume at a Chinese New Year's parade. When necessary, I can access my past. Most of the time however, it simply floats weightlessly in space behind me, moving as I move. Because I carefully planned this shift and was aware of my intentions within the shift, the change has been permanent for me. Rarely do I now think of my past unless I need to explore if my present responses are stemming from my Ghosts.

When you shift your experience, other aspects within you shift also --- you are a complete unit. This shift can be a permanent shift, one that you do not need to maintain consciously. One of the places of growth and awe for me, both personally and professionally, has been to realize that if I can find an "authentic feel-good" shift of experience, I can rapidly and spontaneously shift other aspects of who I am as a result of this initial shift. If I can assist a client to have an "authentic feel-good" shift of experience within himself or herself, further powerful shifts can occur for my clients.

Awareness is about recognizing your patterns of behavior. A major source of information and a possible source of change work is to study the structure of your own family of origin, as this is where your patterns began. In other words, your family of origin is the original source of your Sailors On A Ship.

--- Author's Personal Commentary ---

As part of my Master's degree in Applied Behavioral Sciences, I was required to interview as many members of my own family as possible and then explore the family patterns that I encountered. In my case, the major issues to uncover were: who was consistently angry, who was depressed and who was addicted. From my research, I recognized the high frequency of alcoholics in my maternal family. My definition of alcoholism is: "the use of alcohol as a means of avoiding life's pain." So what happened in my family dynamics that could explain this occurrence? Although no one really knows the mechanism of alcoholism, a truism in therapy is that, at the emotional level, alcoholism represents high anxiety.

One story I repeatedly heard as a young child became important to my own growth (see Figure 55) ; it explained a possible source of anxiety on my mother's side of my family. I heard this family story repeated many times (at least eight to ten times during my childhood.) The story concerned events that had occurred over eighty years previously. Of the hundreds of events in the lives of my family members, why would one specific story be perpetuated? For a story to survive eighty years, it must have some significance. To address my own growth, I will tell you different versions of the family story --- the story as it was told to me as a child and the story as it feels more authentic to me.

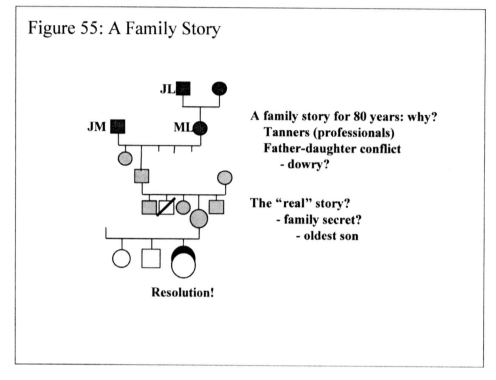

Figure 55: A Family Story

JL

JM   ML

A family story for 80 years: why?
Tanners (professionals)
Father-daughter conflict
- dowry?

The "real" story?
- family secret?
- oldest son

Resolution!

The story as told to me was that my great-grandmother (Mary L) had been in perpetual conflict with her father (John L) for much of her adult life. John L (my great-great-grandfather) was a tanner in a small town in Nova Scotia in the 1860s. At that time, tanners were considered upper class, the equivalent social status of physicians. Mary L was his only child. Then along came James M, Mary L's future husband and my great-grandfather. He was from another town and also a tanner. He moved into the same town as John L and set up a second tannery.

Subsequently, James M and Mary L got married. John L gave his daughter Mary L a dowry of $10,000 (which was a huge amount of *money in the 1860s.) Unfortunately the leather industry was declining due to changes in technology. John L asked for the dowry money back and then lost it. Thereafter, John L and Mary L fought with each other for the rest of their lives.*

Remembering this story as an adult, I found it interesting but it did not touch me at the emotional level. Yet this story survived for eighty years. It must have significance, perhaps to the alcoholism in the family. So I made up a new version of the story, one that satisfied my need to understand why there was so much alcoholism in my family. The story I made up is that before Mary L and James M get married, Mary L gets pregnant. This is a shameful state of affairs for an upper-class family and Mary L is a disgrace to the family; but being the upper-class family it is, the members won't talk aloud about such events. The topic is like a dead elephant in the middle of the room. It smells really bad but everyone just walks around it because they don't want to deal with the actual problem of how to remove the dead elephant.

So my family's pain and anxiety --- that everyone knows but nobody talks about --- becomes a family secret, thereby increasing the anxiety around the whole affair. This anxiety gets handed down through the generations, especially to the oldest or the most accountable child, in this case, my grandfather. As it gets handed down, the family anxiety becomes a source of shame, and the members of my family use alcohol to avoid the shame.

Is my version of the story true? Probably not; certainly it is not factual. But it is an emotionally true story for me. The significance of my version of the story is that it was a major step in my being able to reduce the family pressure to indulge in alcohol. I could say "Yes, of course. This is likely what happened. And I do not need to drink because of something that happened five generations ago."

Such is the power of story, albeit fictional in this case.

4.6. COMPLEXITY --- SAILORS ON A SHIP

If your family of origin is where you learned your Sailors On A Ship, how then do you learn exactly who the Sailors are, let alone who is the Captain. Again, awareness plays a major role in sorting out the complex relationships between your Sailors.

The metaphor of Sailors On A Ship occurs in most designated therapies, although they have assigned different names to the various Sailors. In most therapies, the Sailors are pre-assigned with specific characteristics, such as energy, beliefs and behavioral patterns that most people are easily able to identify. Transactional Analysis, for example, describes five common Sailors: Nurturing Parent, Critical Parent, Adult, Adapted Child and Natural Child[8]. Even the original Freudian Psychoanalysis had its Sailors: ego, id and super-ego. They were simply concepts phrased as metaphors that were useful at the time of the early twentieth century.

In working with the metaphor of Sailors On A Ship, my preference with most clients (and for you, as the reader) is to encourage individuals to explore and designate their own Sailors. Generally, one of several things will happen when you explore in this way. First, you might be embarrassed; you might think that

---

8. Nurturing Parent is the Sailor who takes care of others, perhaps because they are helpless. Critical Parent is the Sailor who criticizes self and others when they are helpless and "shouldn't" be. Adult evaluates on the basis of what is happening in the present. Natural Child represents our playful or authentically emotional self, sometimes angry, sometimes joyous. And Adapted Child is our manipulative sulky side.

doing this activity is silly. Embarrassment is often one of the ways we use to escape awareness; the life difficulty you are encountering may be uncomfortable for you. The skill is simply the tool at getting at this life difficulty. A second response that you may have in exploring your Sailors is to get quite different and unexpected perspectives on yourself --- new learnings from within. Third, you are likely to start discovering your own contribution, your own internal conflict that keeps you trapped in the external conflict. Fourth, you may get stuck and feel anxious and fearful. You may blame others, or you may just be confused.

If you are at this latter point, a therapist becomes useful. One of the major roles of a therapist is to safely guide you where you are afraid to go.

****

Skill: Sailors On A Ship

This exercise involves a lot of imaginary play. If you are embarrassed, do it alone so that others cannot criticize you.

Part A.

Write down several consistent ways that you behave with other people in your life, for example, your children, your parents when they are upset with you, your life partner, your colleagues at work, your boss. Also, write down how you consistently behave when you are in different states, for example, when you are relaxed versus when you are being criticized. Chances are that each of your behaviors has different energies, involve different beliefs about how people should function and even triggers different memories of significance. Often, these behaviors are associated with different internal voices. Although they talk to each other in your head, they somehow stay separate to their particular

environments.

Next, set up as many chairs in a room as number of voices you have discovered, one chair for each voice. I will call each internal voice a character. This designation is your first attempt to define your Sailors. For each character, write its name on a piece of paper and put the piece of paper on the chair (for further notations to be added as you proceed.) Now take a life difficulty that you have been experiencing recently. Choose one that still bothers you. Sit in one of the chairs and take on the attributes of this character of yours, the one sitting in this specific chair. Speak aloud to the other characters in the other chairs, as if you were an individual having a conversation with each one of them about your difficulty. Move to another chair when you have the sense that the character in the other chair needs to speak. Move back to your first chair if you wish to respond. Keep moving around to all the other characters in the other chairs until each of your characters has had a chance to speak.

As needed, take a moment to write (on the piece of paper assigned to this chair) some of the attributes of each of these characters (behaviors, voice tone, beliefs, sense of energy, etc.) As you practice this exercise over a number of life difficulties, the attributes of each character likely will become more consistent to this character. As this occurs, you can consider these characters to be your Sailors On A Ship.

Part B.

To identify other Sailors of yours, use the following guided meditation that I adapted from an exercise I was led through myself a number of years ago.

"Close your eyes, take a few slow deep breaths and relax.

"Imagine you are walking outdoors on a beautiful day in a country valley, in a field near some woods, with hills surrounding. As you walk, enjoy the scenery.

"Now notice that there seems to be a path leading into the woods. You decide to explore the path and follow it into the woods. Notice the trees, the leaves, the sounds, the smells and whatever else attracts you attention. Notice also the path is gradually going up the edge of the valley.

"As you walk, you begin to hear the sounds of voices and, in the distance, see a house in the woods. As you approach the house, three people come out of the front door and greet you.

"Stop and have a conversation with these three people. Note their characteristics, what attracts you about them and perhaps what might irritate you. Ask them any questions you wish and note their responses.

"After a while, take your leave of them and continue your walk in the woods.

"Gradually the woods begin to clear. In a fairly open spot, you see someone sitting, someone who somehow seems quite wise and knowledgeable of the world. Stop and chat with this person, asking any questions you might have. Somehow you know that

this person will give you wise and honest answers to the questions that trouble you.

"Shortly thereafter, this person reaches down to his or her side and picks up an object. The person hands you the object, while saying the following: "You will need this on your journey." Note what the object is and thank the wise person as you leave to continue your walk.

"Slowly the path leads down into the valley again and you find yourself in the original field where you started your walk. At this point, return to your present state."

The four individuals identified in the meditation, the three at the house and the wise person in the clearing, are likely to be Sailors on your Ship. Give them names and explore how they might relate to your life and your behaviors with others. Make up other meditations that allow you to create characters in your head who will be guides to your Sailors. As these characters evolve, some of them are likely to contribute to developing a Captain on your Ship, especially the wise person in the woods.

****

4.6.1. THE CAPTAIN OF THE SHIP

As you study your internal conflicts, you begin to recognize your patterns of behavior in which you get repeatedly stuck. As you defuse and reorganize your patterns of "stuckness" into more functional patterns, with more effective outcomes, gradually you gain the sense that some part of yourself is your Captain, in charge of your ship. He or she is the one who makes decisions in your life effectively. You also get to know your Navigator; he or she is the one who ensures that these life decisions are maintained. As time goes on, you develop a trust of this blended part of yourself that is able to make effective decisions and keep important commitments. My own experience has been that a separation of Captain and Navigator is not necessary (like most people, they developed simultaneously in me.) However, I can well imagine that, for some people, the distinction between the two would be useful. For instance, if you have trouble being decisive before moving into action, the Captain component needs further development; if you are very decisive but bog down in a lack of completion, your Navigator self needs further development. For simplicity's sake however, in the rest of the book, I will refer only to the Captain when I mean both the Captain and the Navigator.

So, exactly who is your Captain. Most people have a critic voice and you might assume that this is your Captain. Usually, the critic voice is not your Captain. Rather it's the part of you that has attempted to force the other Sailors into submission, claiming to be your Captain but easily manipulated by another Sailor who uses some pattern of irresponsibility.

Fundamentally, your Captain is that part of yourself who is willing to live by a value system of clarity, is accountable for your actions and able to respond effectively, with personal authority, to the many options that life presents. If your Captain is truly in charge, you will have a sense of inner peace and satisfaction that you are doing enough with your life and contributing to your relationships in a meaningful way.

4.6.1.2. ACCEPTANCE AND DISCIPLINE

The Captain is generally characterized by at least two words: acceptance and discipline. I invite the reader to explore what component of yourself is capable of acceptance and discipline. I suggest that this exploration will aid markedly in the naming and training of your Captain[9].

---

9. For further exploration in naming and training your Captain, one of the most important tools is the development of your beliefs and values (see Appendix C ?Truths? for a partial list of mine.)

To explain further, I refer to the Fourth Noble Truth of the Buddha which proposes acceptance and discipline as a way of dealing with life's difficulties. (The concept of The Noble Truths of the Buddha will be explored in greater detail in Section 5.2.4.) These two words, acceptance and discipline, are essential skills of the life journey. Yet these words are also poorly understood in our society. Using the exercise described in Section 4.4.2.1 (The Felt Sense of Words), I invite you to feel the words when you speak them aloud.

For myself, acceptance does not mean being a passive doormat. It is a very peaceful and active process of responding to what cannot be changed in its entirety. For example, I cannot change that I will get sick periodically. Within this unchanging state however, there is much that I can improve: changing my activities that contribute to my periodic illnesses, shifting my dietary patterns, moving to a new climate or altitude, etc.. I can also look at how I take care of myself when I get ill: do I overextend myself with work, do I criticize myself for getting ill, do I treat myself well?

As for discipline, it usually involves some action that, on one level, I don't want to do. But it is not what I or someone else makes me do. Discipline is doing what I want to do, even when I don't want to do it.

--- Author's Personal Commentary ---

To give an example of discipline in my life, I will discuss the role of exercise in my life. My Captain wants me to exercise daily. One of my Sailors doesn't want to. I do it anyway for the long-term benefits to my health.

However, I set up my system for exercising so as to be successful.

For example, I do a daily yoga practice, usually about thirty minutes per day. Most days I don't want to do it. So I set my commitment to myself, my discipline, to do two minutes per day.

Two minutes is not a lot of time. It is enough time, however, to get me from the place of not wanting to do my yoga to the sense that I feel good doing my yoga, more energized, and want to do more. Most days, I end up doing half an hour. If I am ill or anxious about having too many plans that day, I can choose to stop after two minutes or ten minutes or fifteen minutes, knowing I have kept my commitments.

There are three categories of disciplines that appear to have a major positive impact on people's life patterns.

1. The first one is exercising the muscles of stability. This activity has the dual impact of discharging your built-up energy and conditioning of the body to have awareness. To my knowledge, the most effective exploration of the muscles of stability occurs with Hatha Yoga. It is highly likely that other Eastern forms of exercise such as Chi Gong, Tai Chi and Eastern Martial Arts will also give good benefits.

2. The second major category of discipline is meditation. This tool trains the mind to develop awareness, witnessing experience without story-making. Mediation has the joint impact of teaching you to witness emotional experience without engagement and training you to hold a focus when it is necessary to engage at the emotional level, for example, in the face of sleepiness or uncomfortable physical sensations that might distract you from the process of meditating. You simply note these distractions and get on with the process.

3. The third major tool of discipline is journal writing as a way to train

your mind to observe and record data for future study. Journal writing is potentially the easiest of the three disciplines to apply. Great complexity of data collection and understanding can be developed with good journaling skills. The best journal process of which I am aware is the Progoff Journal[10], a very sophisticated recording and processing tool.

All three categories of disciplines require some skill and frequently a long learning curve, perhaps years, especially yoga and meditation. These tools, however, form a solid foundation for your life journey.

4.7. PREDICTABILITY OF PATTERNS

One of the major components of awareness is learning to predict your behavioral patterns. One of the major skills that helps you achieve this level of awareness is journal writing. For anyone who is serious about being effective as a human being, I strongly recommend learning this skill. This does not mean that you have to keep a journal all of your lives, simply that the skill is available to you whenever it is needed.

****

Skill: Changing Predictable Patterns

One way to change a pattern is simply to notice it (awareness can be therapeutic.) For example, you think you spend your money frivolously. To explore this, carry a small notebook and, every time you reach into your wallet for money, put a checkmark in the notebook. Once a day, take one of those times you reached into your wallet and describe in detail what happened. Do this exercise for three weeks in a row and your awareness of your

---

10. http://www.intensivejournal.org/

spending habits will dramatically improve.

Next, pick an emotion you want to change. For example, every time you have a twinge of guilt, put a checkmark in the notebook. Once a day, describe in detail one example of what happened in respect to one of those checkmarks. Do this for three weeks and your sense of guilt will dramatically shift. Perhaps it will resolve itself or perhaps it will be brought to the foreground such that you recognize that you have a major difficulty to deal with in your life.

****

Journal writing has three major advantages. First, it is a discharge of energy, in and of itself. You take the internal story that you carry, the Ghost, and move this energy through your body onto the piece of paper. Second, you can subsequently examine what you have written (immediately afterwards or at a later date) for differences between what actually happened and the Ghost you carry about the events. Third, you can re-examine what you have written on a much later occasion --- days, weeks or months later. In so doing, you will likely notice patterns emerging. Perhaps you get angry consistently at five in the afternoon or on Monday mornings. What is happening that this is your pattern? Once you begin to notice a pattern, you can dedicate a special section of your journal for gathering more data on your pattern.

Journal writing can either be stream-of-consciousness or a structured approach. There are advantages to both methods. Stream-of-consciousness writing necessitates that you simply start writing and don't stop, even if the writing seems to be nonsense. Usually you write whatever comes to your awareness with as little analysis or censorship as possible. This lack of censorship tends to reveal what is just below the surface of your consciousness and often gives you good clues as to what are the underlying issues. An interesting way to do stream-of-consciousness journaling is to write with your non-dominant hand. This change of your routine often accesses quite different components of your experience, sometimes more emotional or imaginative, which often give you fascinating insights.

Structured journal writing can take several forms. The Progoff Journal method I mentioned earlier is one example of a structured approach. Below, I describe another type that is useful for gathering data about your emotional patterns.

****

<u>Skill: Collecting Data of Anger Patterns</u>

For any given episode of emotional pain (anger, rage, etc.), the following questions can be answered to develop a structured assessment of what is actually happening within you at the emotional level. After examining a few examples, patterns will likely start to emerge as to what is predictable in your emotional behaviors.

1. **What was the problem? If you were to write a chapter in your autobiography on this problem, what would be the chapter title? This titling of the problem allows for quick comparison with other similar problems.**

2. **What happened first? What was the first clue of a problem?**

3. **What happened next?**

4. **What happened next?**

5. **How did it end?**

6. **How did I feel at the end? What emotions?**

7. **How was this feeling familiar (from your childhood or**

at least from earlier in your life)?

8. Where in your body did you feel the emotion?

9. Where was the focus of your story (the pointing finger)? How do you know this (what body sensations did you have)?

10. For how long did/do you maintain the energy? What did/do you do with it?

11. What would you like to be able to do with this problem (what is the positive intention of your problem)?

Next, you can gain further information about your patterns by exploring the problem from the perspective of an emotional triangle. Every problem has all three components of an emotional triangle — self, other and situation — even if it is an internal emotional triangle between two of your Sailors. Every problem also can be assessed in terms of the relationships between these components.

12. Regarding your problem, what can you change of yourself? What are you not willing to change?

13. What is it you would like to change about the other person? What can you not change?

14. What is it you would like to change about the situation? What can you not change?

15. What is your relationship to the other person? What could you change within this relationship that would add positive energy?

16. What is your relationship to the situation? What could you change within this relationship that would add positive energy?

17. What values, beliefs, memories and expectations of yours are being challenged by this problem? What is your anxiety?

18. Is the other person cooperative?

19. How can you play with your anxiety in a manner that creates wonder within yourself and yet challenges the emotional dynamics of the problem? What long-term outcome do you want for the problem that is consistent with healthy dynamics?

For a different approach to the above questions, they are shown in tabular fashion at the end of this chapter (slightly modified for the emotion of anger.) Your patterns are then often easier to spot. Also included at the bottom of the tables are further questions that will help you identify your emotional patterns.

****

Structured journal writing is especially useful in identifying your patterns that occur frequently. It gives you a format whereby data from one occurrence can readily be compared with data from other occurrences. At my weekend workshops, I ask the participants to explore their patterns of anger using two structured lists of questions in which they are asked to give a fair amount of detail. Once a pattern begins to reveal itself, it can then be studied in greater depth.

Fundamentally, this predictability of patterns is the basis of therapy. If you have a pattern of difficulty that is predictable, a tool can be developed to resolve the difficulty. Resolving the difficulty may take much time and effort but far less time and effort compared to how much most people waste with current ineffective management of life difficulties.

Further discussion of the possibility of changing your emotional responses will be left to the next chapter, including the possibility of bringing powerful shifts to the deeper issues of powerlessness.

What gets you angry? (a)

	Episode a	Episode b	Episode c
1. What was the problem?			
2. What happened first?			
3. What next?			
4. What next?			
5. How did it end?			
6. How did you feel at the end?			
7. How was this feeling familiar (from childhood or teens)?			

What are the rules that run you?

_____

What are your underlying emotions?

_____

Where/how did you learn all this?

_____

What gets you angry? (b)

	Episode a	Episode b	Episode c
8. Where in your body did you feel your anger?			
9. Where was the focus of your story (the pointing finger)? How do you know?			
10. For how long do you maintain our anger? What did/do you do with your anger?			
11. What would you like to be able to do (what is your positive intention)?			

Your general pattern of anger is:

_____

How are you attempting to change others?

_____

What do you need to do differently?

_____

With whom do you get angry (a)?

	a	b	c
12. What can you change of yourself?			
13. What can you not change?			
14. Where is the focus of your energy? How do you know?			
15. How are you stuck?			

What do you require to deal with these problems?

_____

_____

_____

With whom do you get angry (b)?

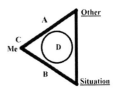

	a	b	c
16. What is your relationship A? What changes would help?			
17. What is your relationship B? What changes would help?			
18. What is your anxiety C? What VBMEs are challenged?			
19. How can you play with the middle D in a way that **a. tickles your fancy?** **b. challenges the patterns?**			

How can you change your anxiety (so as to be non-anxious)?

_____

_____

_____

Part C.
The Philosophical

CHAPTER FIVE --- INDIVIDUAL CONSIDERATIONS: THERAPY

Summary

The earlier chapters were designed to be practical in their immediate applications. Such immediate applications relied on the ability of the reader to do the necessary work of growth that likely lay within his or her current capabilities.

Therapy is about going deeper. Exploration of rapid and profound change will be explored in the second half of this chapter. There are two major limitations to going deeper: avoidance and lack of knowledge of the possibilities of change.

Early on in the journey of therapy, avoidance by the client is the most important issue to tackle — as human beings, we are pain avoiders. Almost certainly, we have all had life experiences that have been overwhelmingly painful, such that we do not want to deal with these experiences again. Unfortunately, the nature of being human is that our energies are trapped in these experiences. This energy then becomes the Ghost that creates major difficulties in later relationships.

In this chapter, the myths and illusions of the therapeutic journey will be explored. In essence, those myths and illusions are that we want life to be bountiful, and we hope we can bypass pain to live on the positive side of life only. I will explore my typical pattern of working with a client, which has the ultimate intention of developing awareness in that client and personal responsibility for choosing and living his or her own value system. The difficulties and traps of the therapeutic journey will also be explored.

Different styles of therapy will be briefly presented, contrasting deductive with inductive approaches. The latter will be emphasized as more powerful in the exploration of the subjective. Within that exploration, life issues generally fall into three categories: attending to the residue of childhood powerlessness, dealing with the inherent problems of life ("putting out the garbage") and dealing with the inherent pain of life (we all die eventually.) The most effective stance to all three of these issues results from acceptance and discipline. Change work itself can be easy with the right tools.

This chapter's suggestion is that all effective change is a change of perception at the subjective level. Some profoundly powerful skills will be described as they relate to change of perception. In particular, the emphasis will be on rapid and profound changes of emotional experience, changes which I would not have believed possible even ten years ago. Much of this type of change-work requires considerable development of the skills of the earlier chapters, especially that of awareness. Discussion of this rapid change-work is presented in an attempt to challenge the dominant models of therapeutic change that exist in mainstream therapy.

Finally, other rapid-change-state therapies known as Power Therapies are explored briefly in this chapter. One in particular, Emotional Freedom Technique (EFT), is explored in detail. Often profoundly useful, EFT is somewhat of a shotgun approach and easily learned; I routinely teach it to all my clients.

****

CHAPTER FIVE --- INDIVIDUAL CONSIDERATIONS: THERAPY

My first exposure to good therapy was an experiential workshop that I attended which allowed me to integrate the divergent influences of my life. At that point, I came to the conclusion that the therapeutic processes were (and still are) the only means in our current society that truly encourage ("bring courage to") growth of the human spirit.

Certain themes will be developed in this chapter. As an overview, I suggest that change in therapy arises from exploratory skills brought to the subjective (the product of internal processing of external and internal data by the mind.) As I indicated previously, I started out my adult life with the intention of becoming a theoretical astrophysicist, someone who studies the nature of the universe. I still have a mathematical bent and summarize this chapter with a formula that I developed a number of years ago (see Figure 56.)

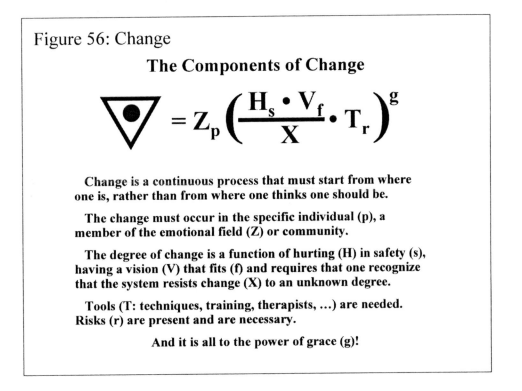

Figure 56: Change

The Components of Change

$$\nabla = Z_p \left(\frac{H_s \bullet V_f}{X} \bullet T_r \right)^g$$

Change is a continuous process that must start from where one is, rather than from where one thinks one should be.

The change must occur in the specific individual (p), a member of the emotional field (Z) or community.

The degree of change is a function of hurting (H) in safety (s), having a vision (V) that fits (f) and requires that one recognize that the system resists change (X) to an unknown degree.

Tools (T: techniques, training, therapists, ...) are needed. Risks (r) are present and are necessary.

And it is all to the power of grace (g)!

First, therapy is an exploration of self. At some level, who you are is always in flux. This flux is a continuous process, frequently with sudden turns in the road. Nonetheless, "you" as a whole continue onto the new road. A major paradox of growth is that you as client need to start from where you are rather than from where you think you should be. At some deep level, this means acceptance of yourself and your journey rather than being angry or frustrated with what is happening. It does not mean that you have to like where you are, nor does it mean that you have to stay where you are. You do however need to come to peaceful terms with where you are so that you can move to where you want to be. A brief summary of this paradox is contained in the truism "What I resist will persist."

The second theme that will be developed in this chapter is the idea of therapy as expansion of who you are. To fully know yourself is an illusionary lifetime goal, yet possible in the sense that you will eventually come to be at peace with your complexity. For me, this stance is best summed up in a passage from *Leaves Of Grass* by the American poet, Walt Whitman:

> *"Do I contradict myself?*
>
> *Very well then, I contradict myself.*
>
> *I am large; I contain multitudes[1]."*

These lines reveal the essence of therapy as well as uncover a central conflict within the therapeutic journey. Is therapy a structured deductive guide of how to come to terms with life (by comparing yourself to a set of rules or "shoulds") or is therapy an inductive approach, an open-ended exploration of unknown territory as you strive to be all that you can be while still in relationship with others? The latter, the inductive approach, is much richer for me, yet not in keeping with society's cost-containment philosophy and investment in following its own "rules." Therapy can thus sometimes be a place of major conflict with society, a counter-cultural movement.

---

1. Walt Whitman, Leaves Of Grass (Philadelphia: David McKay, [c1900]), ll. 1314–1316.

As a Canadian physician, I am frequently caught in that dilemma. Much of my funding comes from government-supported insurance programs, which require "facts" and labels (called "diagnoses.") Yet I work with people who are at dis-ease: clients who struggle with issues such as abuse, depression and addiction. Sometimes the intensity of my client's pain (and the manner in which it is displayed) means that I can give a medical diagnosis such as "depression" or "panic disorder." Seldom do I believe, however, that the diagnosis helps me in addressing the issues with which the client is struggling. Most of the time I simply help people to become more mature in their approach to life. Then I ask myself: "Is personal growth something that I can legitimately charge to government-supported insurance programs?" I have no easy answer to this question. Generally I choose to regard therapy as preventive medicine, creating a ripple effect of health within a compromised system.

The third theme I will develop in this chapter is that of therapy as change of perception. In my experience, the ability to perceive life differently --- to step out of the view of other people and take a fresh approach --- is the central theme of good therapy, whether it be deductive or inductive. For myself, this theme comes out of my decision to function primarily with an inductive approach. Frequently I am very much outside mainstream cultural belief systems. My challenge is to explore how flexible I can be as therapist (participant-observer), while working in association with how flexible the client can be with the issues at hand. In opening myself to unusual approaches and seemingly impossible ideas, I am amazed and in awe at the power of these approaches to initiate change in myself and in my clients.

This chapter will explore the actual process of therapy (as I offer it.) It will explore the pattern of my therapy work with clients (and the skills that can be brought to the possibility of change for the client.) In particular, I will emphasize the nature of change in therapeutic work. Finally, I will explore some of the traps that prevent the full realization of therapy or, more accurately, of human maturation. I will also expand on this theme of human maturation in the next chapter.

In the development of the Blowing Out! process, I am outside the mainstream. The vast majority of our culture, as I experience it, supports that idea that anger and rage must be controlled to the point of non-expression, and that expression actually increases the risks of violation. As indicated in the previous chapters, I agree that unsafe and ineffectual expression does do this. Yet I suggest that this is a simplification and devaluation of what human beings need so as to reach the transrational. This chapter will also develop the theme of the importance of the subjective and its devaluation by our culture; and it will emphasize the possibility of healing at the individual level. The following chapter will explore the possibility of healing at the societal level.

5.1. Myths And Illusions Of The Therapeutic Journey

When client come to see me, seeking solutions to the difficulties they are experiencing, they usually have a number of myths as to what will happen in the therapeutic process (see Figure 57.) These myths are not only about the process of therapy, but more pervasively, they are about what life offers. None of these myths seem to be true. They relate to our desire to live better lives. The principle myths are:

1. we think we can bypass pain, and

2. we think we can live life on the positive side only.

The first principle myth is that life somehow should be easy. Buddhism named the First Noble Truth: "life is painful." I do not know of any evidence that changes this presupposition. As I encounter people in my life, some have much joy within their pain but I do not know of any who truly has no problems. How this first myth has come about is not at all clear to me. Part of the problem is that our society has made numerous promises, many of which have not been kept.

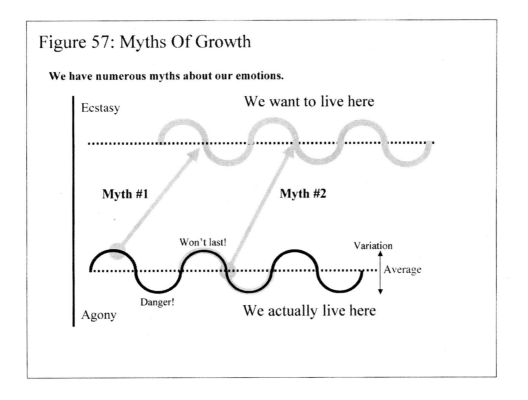

Figure 57: Myths Of Growth

We have numerous myths about our emotions.

Ecstasy

We want to live here

Myth #1

Myth #2

Won't last!

Variation

Average

Agony

Danger!

We actually live here

--- Author's Personal Commentary ---

I will illustrate the impact of this discordance with a personal story. When I was eleven years old in 1954, the leading newspaper in my community had a four-column spread that suggested that the major problem of the 1990s would be too much leisure time, that our technology was such that work would essentially be eliminated as a major component of our daily lives and thus we would struggle with how to fill our time. I routinely ask my client groups how many people struggle with too much leisure time, especially leisure time because there is no work to be done. Needless to say, few people put up their hands in the affirmative.

Telling an eleven year old that life will be leisurely is emotionally equivalent to promising a four year old that you are going to give them an ice cream cone. What happens when you then fail to provide the ice cream cone? "Temper tantrum!" (at least, that's what we adults call it.) The four year old is simply expressing the pain of disappointment in a healthy way, at least until he or she learns the consequences of this manner of expression. Similarly, if you promise an eleven year old that life in thirty years time will be easy, be prepared for pain.

Another contributing factor to this first myth is our profound rule: "Don't hang your laundry out in public." We hide our pain from each other in many different ways, thus making it difficult to correct this first myth as it arises. I do know a small number of people who have had what I would consider idyllic lives: everything was provided for them. They grew up in good family dynamics, with enough money to have some luxuries, and received good educations. They had siblings so as to learn something of conflict and its resolution. They had good health, both individually and within their families. They have gotten good jobs, have married well and have great kids. Yet, these same people often struggle with life being too monotonous --- without passion. Another day, another peaceful time. This lack of passion has been their pain and, for them, it has been significant.

Most of us are not so apparently "fortunate." We live our lives like thermostats, with an average temperature and variation within it. Often the average is quite uncomfortable; sometimes, it is not. If things are good, we know they won't last; if things are difficult, we strive to get away from the pain. We want to live better lives but we are often trapped by the first principle myth, that we can by-pass our pain. The reality to the first myth is that we arrive at joy by going into and through the pain (see Figure 58.) And it is painful --- there is a cost.

Simplistically put, in order to expand into joy, it seems we must expand equally into pain. As we move into the pain and resolve it, however, we bounce back into joy and learn how to manage it as well.

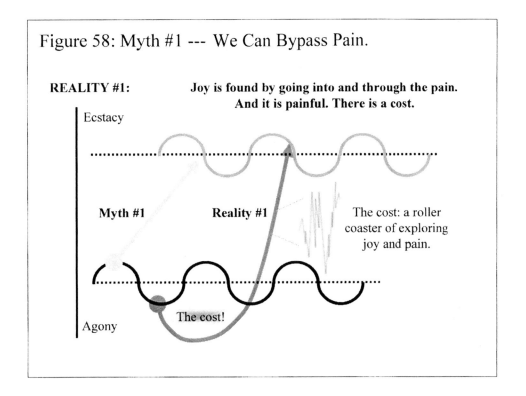

Figure 58: Myth #1 --- We Can Bypass Pain.

REALITY #1:   Joy is found by going into and through the pain.
And it is painful. There is a cost.

Ecstacy

Myth #1   Reality #1   The cost: a roller coaster of exploring joy and pain.

The cost!

Agony

The second principle myth is that we can stay in the joy and consistently live on the positive side of life (see Figure 59.) In my experience of life, it does not seem that this second myth is possible. As we expand our emotional lives, we are called upon to deal with more painful issues. Eventually, the average of our lives may become joyous, but the range of our emotional lives is much broader --- we have both more joy and more pain. There is compensation, though. A third dimension of peacefulness softly pervades the emotional variations of our lives. In some regard, whether our current experience is joyous or painful becomes unimportant --- much of it is peaceful even in the extremes of emotion.

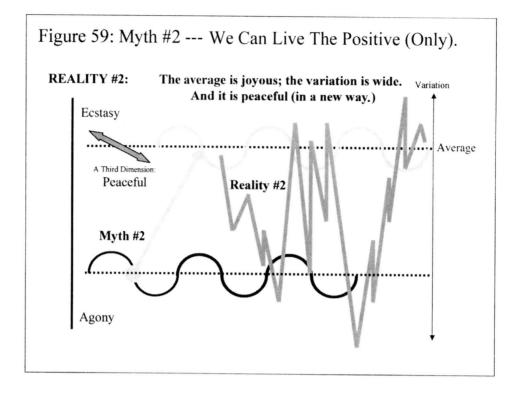

Figure 59: Myth #2 --- We Can Live The Positive (Only).

5.2. THERAPY AS EXPLORATION --- BEING IN ACTION

In this section, I will describe my own style of working with clients. The major tool I bring to my professional work over time is my own integrity. While mine is an unique style, it nonetheless provides a lens into the journey of therapy. In particular, it emphasizes several levels to therapy.

5.2.1. LIFE'S PAIN

In general, the journey of therapy progresses along several predictable stages. A client (or a group of clients such as a family) comes to a therapist because he or she have some form of emotional pain, and wants to get out of it. The pain comes with many names---marriage breakdown, anger and rage, fighting with parents, alcoholism, etc. The pain seems like a huge problem (relative to the size of the person.) As therapist, I do not know how to solve big problems; I can only handle small problems. So, in many cases, the client's pain becomes the basis of the initial exploration that we as therapist and client undertake. This initial exploration is often like a connect-the-dots puzzle; only at the beginning we do not even know what or where they are. Each session we may find a dot or two (small problems); after a few weeks or months, the connections between the dots start to make sense. Patterns emerge and along with this recognition of patterns come new possibilities for change, eventually leading to a deeper appreciation and resolution of the big problem.

Further breaking down the stages of the therapeutic journey, in most problems of my client's life, my client would like the world to change so that he or she does not hurt. Unfortunately this usually will not happen. At the same time, my client does not recognize the ways in which he or she contributes to his or her own problems in life. As a child (usually), he or she has learned ways of being (thinking and feeling) and of behaving (doing) that have kept him or her safe. But now as an "adult," these ways no longer work effectively. The people with whom my client interacts are different; and the situations of his or her life are different. Even so, my client continues to do the old ways. This is the beginning of "growing up." My client is physically an adult human being at an emotionally immature level. Most of us start here.

If you are my client, the essential questions that I explore with you at this point are therefore:

- What is happening in your life that you hurt?

- How do you contribute to or create your own pain?

- What are you gaining or maintaining by your "negative" state?

- How are you willing to be different from your current state so that your pain will shift for the better (and also allow others to be different with you)?

At a deeper level, the therapeutic process is about becoming more aware of who you are and making better choices for yourself, of knowing where you stop and the other person(s) begins. This is the process of developing an Ego, of establishing personal boundaries and personal power, and of building high self-esteem (essentially all the same processes under different names.) At a deeper level still, therapy becomes an exploration as to the nature of life and of being alive, of transcending your Ego, of surrendering to life. Therapy is a transition to spiritual journey, encompassing humility, compassion and respect for all life. Often associated with religion, spirituality is simply a deeper stage of life and need not involve belief systems, especially not religious dogma. As the therapist, I am also on a spiritual journey.

What does it actually mean to be in therapy? What are the issues (the dots) that I can work on in therapy together with my clients? For the most part, therapy is an exploration of how you, the client, live your life, perhaps at many different levels simultaneously.

There are two big groups of issues:

1. Those that you the client initiate. These can be anything with which you are dissatisfied.

2. Those that I as therapist initiate. These can be anything that is part of being human.

So what do you as client do here? One approach could be:

a. First, identify some component of your life with which you have pain or frustration or simply questions as to what is happening to you. The more emotional intensity and anxiety you have around this component of your life, the more likely that the issue is significant to you.

b. Second, identify what you already know about this component of your life --- at this stage your description will be incomplete. If you could describe it completely, likely it would not be a problem. If you think you know what the answer is, likely you do not have the complete answer

(else the issue would be resolved.)

c. Third, identify what you would like to have different in your life around this issue, however impossible it might seem to you at this stage. Your wish may be practical or not.

d. Fourth and most importantly, recognize that you are stuck and be prepared to be stuck further.

5.2.1.1. WHAT HAPPENS IN THERAPY?

Therapy is the process of examining how you the client actually do these steps "a-b-c-d", especially step "d." It is also an emotional process, not an intellectual process. There are several routes we could take to examine what happens to you in steps "a-b-c-d." Increased awareness of your experience is the basis by which you make new emotional choices in your life. Maybe you get stuck and we examine how---what has actually happened to you that you feel confused, angry, sad or whatever. Or maybe we simply identify some human characteristic of yours. Then we explore further to acquire resolution of the issue in some manner, especially to seek greater awareness of what is happening.

All of us would like our difficulties simply to disappear and life to be joyous. They won't. Even if they did, likely we would be unhappy. What would we do without difficulties in life? They energize us; they challenge us; they ask us to be the best people that we can be.

Though not solvable, many of life's difficulties are resolvable: processes can be brought to bear on the difficulties such that you no longer carry any apparent pain about them. Most difficulties recur as time goes on; and different aspects of the difficulties become apparent. If you have dealt with the difficulty successfully a number of different times and the pain has apparently been resolved, sooner or later it does not recur, especially if the difficulty was one that you created yourself.

5.2.1.2. WORKING WITH CLIENTS

I work with clients in group settings, largely because the growth process can be much more active in this context. Within the group, I usually work with one individual at a time but often ask that client to interact with others, both to encourage emotional experiencing and to highlight "stuckness." I encourage action --- simply talking about issues is a relatively slow (sometimes inadequate) process in the resolution of human difficulties. Talking impacts the cognitive brain but is not generally effective in creating change. As an example, witness how successful most people are at keeping "New Year's resolutions." An old adage states: "You can act your way into a new way of thinking; you cannot think your way into a new way of acting." Although changes in acting and thinking are deeply related, my experience is that the emotional brain changes best with an "authentic feel-good" experience. Then the change is more likely to be permanent. The amount of action (physical or imaginative) that can be brought to the therapist-client interactions is especially limited by the risk-taking of the client. It is emotional action that leads to change. As a therapist, I recognize that a group setting is not comfortable for some people. With time, most clients become comfortable in the group context if they will risk being known; many of those initially reluctant often come to prefer the group setting.

Otherwise, I choose not to do individual therapy because, while it can be a place of deep exploration, it is often a place where clients can analyze their issues rather than experience them in action. In this sense, it can be a place of familiarity to "always do what you have always done." Talking generally is low risk and accesses the conscious mind. We as humans are not stuck in our conscious minds --- if we were, it would be a simple matter of making new decisions and sticking to them. We are stuck in our other-than-conscious minds and in our bodies. Talking does release some energy --- it translates story into muscular sound. Much of the time though, we talk to our friends who either encourage us in our anger or criticize us for our actions. In both these cases, the energy tends to increase rather than get discharged. The energy may even become more stuck, depending on the circumstances, especially if we are not allowed completion of our intense emotional story. Individual work also does not offer the "in the moment" validation that comes from working with peers. A major advantage of group work is the experience of witnessing how others struggle with their own dilemmas, a process that encourages the client to explore their own involvement in the same dilemma. Furthermore the feedback that results from interaction with peers is a profound mirror of who they are. One of the principal ways that people learn who they are is by studying their reflection in the eyes of other people.

So, what happens in the therapeutic group setting? Often a client starts into an issue and gets stuck. When we are stuck, many reactions could occur. We may be about to cry, choking on our voices, angry and stuffing our anger, shamed and feeling like a six-year-old again. There are many ways to handle this therapeutically. Often I ask a client to pretend, to fantasize or to act out a fantasy; or I may ask him or her to draw a picture. I will choose some action that seems to highlight the experience that the client describes. As an example, if the client is talking about what a heavy load he or she carries, I may ask him or her to hold a very heavy pile of books in his or her arms, without instructions from me as to what he or she does with the pile. I am waiting to see what they actually do with the pile; what I am really asking is for the client to have a larger experience in some fashion of whatever the issue is for him or her. Responses of clients vary widely. Many people simply tolerate my adding more and more books, while complaining about the weight. I then question them as to how this response is typical of what they do with their real-life situation.

I present this example as illustration that, in my own therapy and in my professional training in general, I find the best way to respond to a client's "stuckness" is through some form of action, perhaps including energy release if appropriate for the client. So in the moment of emotional intensity, I may suggest processes for energy release, always on a voluntary basis. Specifically, as I described earlier in the book, I often encourage release of emotional energy through the Blowing Out! process. To be clear, energy release through the Blowing Out! process is NOT an excuse for a client to hurt him- or herself or others clients in the group setting. Nor is it an excuse to violate anyone, anywhere. Thus I implement the ground rules of "No SAD" and "STOP" (see Sections 3.3.1 to 3.3.1.2 to review details of the ground rules.)

Four aspects of the Blowing Out! process are important for me. First, it is my personal belief and experience that this way of working is incredibly powerful in allowing for growth, far more powerful than simply talking about the problem. Second, I am attempting to find a balance between augmenting the intensity of the emotional issues without overwhelming the client. The group setting and the mandate of every client to say "Stop" are very important in maintaining an atmosphere of trust in this work. Third, we are working at an emotional level. It is my personal belief that to talk about the need for energy release without the actual act of energy release takes away from the benefits of the process. Fourth, there are risks. There is some possibility of physical harm, again similar to that of any vigorous sport. The client has a responsibility in choosing to act on my suggestions or may know him- or herself of a need for physical release. As therapist, I attempt to ensure safety and I can only guess at the risks for the client. I ask that the client be cautious of any problems or risks to self or others at that moment.

Having started work on an issue together, likely I will then examine with the client whatever experience has occurred. I explore how this experience (the feeling or human characteristic) is familiar in the client's life and how he or she has learned to behave and feel in this way. How is it related to who he or she is as a unique human being? How is it related to unfinished business from his or her past? How was it protective of him or her in the past? Because the client still has this experience, this way of being now, I also explore how does it protect him or her now? What does he or she gain from it now? What is its positive intent for him or her? As a therapist, I act from a belief that all human behavior is sustained in the present and has a current benefit, a positive intention for the individual, and

250

a cost, an undesirable component or consequence. The benefit always exceeds (or, in the past, exceeded) the cost, although we usually keep the benefit out of consciousness, especially if we have internal conflict about the behavior.

Having gained some new awareness, the client is now in a better position to make choices. Perhaps he or she wants to keep this way of being --- therapy is not intended to make clients do anything they do not want to do. Therapy is about clients consciously living their choices. If however, the client wants to change this pattern, then we will explore alternate ways of being, i.e. new behaviors. We ask what might be the benefits and costs of these new behaviors and how might they be instituted? Some of the new ways of being might be instituted at a cognitive level; others might involve more direct emotional experiencing; some may seem very strange at first to the client. The basic intent of all this is for the client to reach a state where he or she authentically feels better with his or her life, and where he or she has an "authentic feel-good" experience that is so crucial for change-work.

If we (therapist and client) are unable to work together effectively, I neither make the client nor myself, the therapist, wrong if we are not able to work together. I do not believe that it is possible for myself or any other therapist to work with every person --- therapy is simply too much of an art. I simply want to work in a way that is satisfying both to the client and to myself, the therapist.

5.2.1.3. DETERMINANTS OF GROWTH

What determines success in therapeutic explorations? What determines growth?

First, the exploration is likely very risky on an emotional level; and a key component of the journey is trust. Trust requires risk. To use myself as an example, in my own struggles with important issues (i.e. my own therapy), I have felt a mixture of intense feelings: very vulnerable, afraid of criticism or judgment, afraid that I would break the rules, and afraid that I would be abandoned. In these times, I needed to trust my therapist, which took time to develop. I also needed to trust the atmosphere and space where I was working, whether it was on an individual basis or in a group. In a group process, I needed to trust the other individuals with whom I was working.

Trust is not an all-or-nothing phenomenon; it builds slowly and requires risking being known by others and learning to know others. If my clients had ideal trust at the start of therapy, they probably would not need to be doing therapy. As their therapist, a big part of my work is to allow and assist their trust to develop. Conflict and misunderstanding do arise between therapist and clients. My hope as a therapist is that, at any time, there is enough trust between myself and my clients that we can discuss and negotiate new options for all concerned, so as to allow the work of growth to continue.

A second determinant of growth that, again using myself as an example, I needed to explore was who I am. And I needed feedback, someone to act as a mirror to show me who I am. I also needed to be challenged occasionally; otherwise I started to believe my own truths excessively. Therapy is about learning, learning who I am and what is the nature of being human. There is a cliché that rings true for me emotionally: "The hardest thing to learn is what I don't know because I don't know that I don't know it." And the therapist could not do it for me. At some deep level, I was and am alone; and I must journey alone. The therapist could travel with me but could not do my traveling for me. I needed to identify my own patterns and take note of what I gained from them as well as what they cost me. When I took responsibility for them, I had the choice to continue them or not! When I simply allowed a therapist to identify my patterns for me, I didn't have to choose.

Third, I needed to risk. A big part of therapy was taking on new behaviors as an experiment seeing if they fit. Otherwise, I was simply exploring (in thought or emotion) old pony tracks (for further explanation of pony tracks, Section 5.2.4.3. Patterns Of "Stuckness.") There were a thousand new ways I could be. Being mature meant that I accessed these ways and also meant that I do so with integrity and commitment. At that point, I could fully enter into the process of life's journey. There has also been a price tag to learning from new emotional experience. It was often hard painful work and frequently brought me into conflict with others, conflict that I wanted to avoid because of its pain to me or others. For me, this cost of learning was compensated for by the long-term gains of being more fully alive. I was also more available to be in effective relationships with others.

Fourth and finally, in the complexity of the other determinants of growth, I needed simple tools that could guide me whenever I found myself immersed in an emotional swamp or morass. These tools allowed me to orientate myself and get out of whatever emotional trap in which I found myself. A major aspect of therapy was to provide me with a safe environment in which to learn and practice these tools. Then hopefully, I applied the tools in the environments where I usually had the most difficulty.

5.2.2. VALUES VERSUS BELIEFS

In the previous chapter, the skill development of awareness was emphasized through the assessment of patterns. In conjunction, the development of a value system, through the therapeutic journey, will be highlighted in this chapter.

When clients first come to therapy, they generally do not have a well-defined value system by which they live. The emphasis in our society is on belief systems. The *Webster New World Dictionary*[2] defines "belief" as the "mental acceptance of something as true, whether based on reasoning, prejudice or the authority of the source." It also defines "value" as "to rate highly because of worth" and defines "worth" as "an intrinsic excellence resulting from ... moral, cultural or spiritual qualities." To live by a belief system can be fraught with difficulty, very subject to the society's "crab trap." Belief systems are most useful when reasoning and emotionality are well balanced. To live by a value system has a greater possibility of authenticity. It asks that we examine our own truths and our

---

2. Webster's New World Dictionary: College edition (Toronto: Nelson, Foster, Scott Ltd, 1959).

own truthfulness. To do so with genuineness, we must access both emotionality and reason.

Currently, do we live our lives according to our values? Invariably! We call them important because they contain energy. They are the storage houses of energy. Do we consciously live our lives according to our values? Rarely. The values we verbalize (and keep at conscious awareness) may not be those we live by at the other-than-conscious level. Many of my clients do not know how to identify their values or how to develop a values list. The following exercise develops this skill[3].

****

Skill: Developing And Exploring Your Values

Part A.

Make a list of the activities you like to do and the people with whom you like to do the activities. Then for each item on the list (activity or person), ask yourself: "What is important to me about this item?" Answer the question with one or two words only. Ask the question repeatedly until you have explored all of the possible answers that are important for you. Write down your answers to these questions on a second list. Examine this second list for common words and grouping of words. Generally these will be your values and represent your value system. (This value list is of course not set in stone and can be modified as you repeatedly examine and clarify your values.)

Part B.

For each of the words on your value list, speak the word aloud

---

3. See also Jack Canfield and Mark Victor Hansen, The Aladdin Factor (New York: Berkley, 1995). I often recommend this book as a guide to help people explore what values they want and how to ask for them.

and find out your sensory experience of the word. Notice where in your body you feel the word. (Perhaps you do not keep this value in your body and thus are disassociated from it.) Notice any movement associated with the word. (For example, when I say "honesty," I have the sensory experience of a quiet strength in my back, a visual brightness in front of me and a slight lifting of my chest towards the brightness.) For each word on your value list, explore what meaning you give to the word and when the value is especially important to you (i.e. in what contexts: in all circumstances or only some.) Do the same procedure for each of the words on your value list, allowing enough time between words for the development of your awareness. It is important not to rush this process or intellectualize it.

Part C.

For each value on your list, live it one at a time for a day or so as the highest priority of your day. Experience the word in your daily life, repeatedly coming back to the sensory experience as described in Part B.

Next, live several values together for a day or so as equally high priorities. Observe how the different values come together to support each other or how they conflict with each other. This part of the exercise will allow you to explore how each value actually can be integrated into your life as a living process rather than as an intellectual process.

Continue this process until you have explored your entire value list. Add, modify or discard values as is needed in order to come to a place of knowing what you want in life and how you want to live.

Skill: Detailed Assessment of Anger Patterns
(Using Values As A Basis Of Assessment)

The following is a structured exercise of exploring one episode of anger. The process can be repeated with other episodes as a means of noting your patterns.

It initially asks you to develop a list of your values and explore how you bring your value system to any problem. This invites the development of clarity to the value system that you live and how you live it. It also invites attention to the subtle shifts of awareness that are important in the possibility of creating change.

You need here is to act out the example you have chosen. Much information is stored in your body and not available if you explore from the dissociated position or even if you explore from an associated position without movement.

1. Make a list of the values that are important to you in major relationships, e.g. respect, kindness, being understood, etc. Ten values is an adequate number for the exercise although it can be done with any number of values. Copy each value onto an individual slip of paper. Add two extra blank slips of paper to your pile.

   If you are unclear what are your values, make a list of what you like to do. Step into each action and explore what is important about this action. For example, I like to have a cup of coffee with a friend. What is important to me is to "sharing with others" and the sense of "sensory aliveness" I receive from a good cup of coffee. Thus, sharing and sensory aliveness are the values hidden in my action. (See the above skill Developing And Exploring Your Values for a more detailed description of how to carry out this part of the exercise.)

If you are still unclear what are your values, the following is a partial list of value words from which you can choose.

acceptance	acknowledgment	affection	aliveness
amazement	appreciation	awareness	awe
balance	caring	certainty	challenge
clarity	co-operation	comfort	commitment
common goals	common values	communication	congruency
courage	creativity	dependability	determination
discipline	diversity	eagerness	effectiveness
empathy	financial stability	flexibility	freedom
fun	growth	harmony	honesty
honor	humor	integrity	interaction
joy	justice	leadership	love
loyalty	nurturing	openness	passion
perseverance	playfulness	pleasure	predictability
punctuality	resolution	respect	restfulness
safety	sensuality	sexuality	spirituality
spontaneity	stability	support	teamwork
touch	trust	understanding	vision
warmth	willfulness	willingness	wonder

2. **Remember a time you had a conflict (an argument or a fight) that created stress within yourself. Recreate and act out that scene while holding in your hands the slips of paper with the value words written on them (including the two blank slips.) While you are recreating the scene, consider your values and drop any slip of paper that you did not maintain in the conflict. (Some of the values you have chosen may have no significance to the particular conflict you are re-enacting; put these in your pocket for another exploration.)**

3. **Take up the position of the other person in the conflict. Explore what you did from their perspective. Continue to drop any more values that you find that you did not maintain from their perspective. (Part of living by a value system is being congruent in how you present to others the values you live.)**

4. **Stand on a chair (elevated 3rd position) and look down at yourself in the scene. Continue to drop any more values that you did maintain. Take other perceptual positions as desired.**

5. **Return to your original position and leave the values you dropped on the floor. Explore the impact on yourself of dropping these values.**

6. **Take the two blank pieces of paper and write down the values you held that allowed you to drop any of the other values (safety, a need to be right, etc.)**

7. **Explore what needed to happen for you to start dropping your values. For example, ask yourself: "If I get angry, what needs to happen for me to get angry? What do I see or hear?" Continue to ask until you find the tiniest detail that is the trigger. Test by asking, "If this tiniest detail was different, would I get angry and drop my values?"**

8. **Trace back in your life to other times when you had the same or similar feeling that the "trigger" gives you and find out if it is connected with someone in your childhood or youth.**

9. **Explore for yourself: "What needs to happen for me to maintain my values? What needs to change so as to change my triggers?"**

10. **Re-enact the scene, this time taking whatever steps necessary to hold onto your values. How does the situation change?**

****

A friend of mine, Joe Schaeffer, was a cultural anthropologist in Waterloo Ontario. He spent twenty years working with small groups in community building activities. He probably worked with forty thousand people in that time. In every group he worked with, he asked the people what is important to them in their lives. Essentially every group gives the same list (see Figure 60.) The words listed are my summary words for what people say they want: aliveness, integrity, good relationships and a sense of contribution.

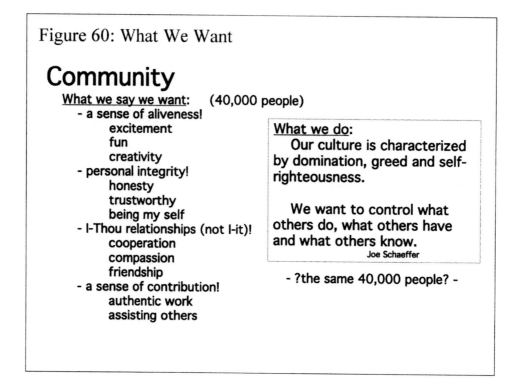

Figure 60: What We Want

Community

What we say we want: (40,000 people)
- a sense of aliveness!
    excitement
    fun
    creativity
- personal integrity!
    honesty
    trustworthy
    being my self
- I-Thou relationships (not I-it)!
    cooperation
    compassion
    friendship
- a sense of contribution!
    authentic work
    assisting others

What we do:
    Our culture is characterized by domination, greed and self-righteousness.

    We want to control what others do, what others have and what others know.
    Joe Schaeffer

- ?the same 40,000 people? -

Joe's statement is: "Our culture is characterized by domination, greed and self-righteousness. We want to control what other people do, what other people have and what other people know." Generally the people who say they want these positive characteristics are the same people who demonstrate at least some component of greed, domination and self-righteousness. What people do versus what they say they want simply represents different Sailors at the helm of the ship at different times (see Section 2.1.2.2 Sailors On A Ship.)

A major need of the therapeutic journey is thus to develop and live by a value system that is authentic for the individual. I believe that this is only possible if we bridge emotionality and cognitive processing to achieve the transrational. As pain avoiders and within the sins of laziness and sloth, the task has many traps.

5.2.2.1. LIMITATIONS OF THERAPEUTIC WORK --- AVOIDANCE

Before discussing the many traps of the therapeutic journey, I will outline here some of its limitations. Some of the major limitations result from a client's avoidance of dealing with his or her emotional issues. Related, a client needs to find a therapist in whom the client trusts when working with his or her emotional issues.

Within our current culture, the active exploration of emotional issues is easily misunderstood. We talk about therapy as "psycho-babble" and accuse people who want depth as being narcissistic or selfish. There is some limited truth in this belief, depending on the participants, but for the most part these comments stem from a "crab trap" mentality.

The term "narcissistic" means "not considering of others." What does this word "selfish" really mean? The suffix "-ish" means "to have the characteristic of." So selfish is "to have the characteristic of a self." How have we as a society come to make this a negative term? Principally, I believe, because "self" also means being not controllable by others; and we want to control "what other people do, what other people have and what other people know." Yet any research I am aware of, especially the works of Abraham Maslow, emphasizes that the development of one's self means that we becomes more aware of and considering of others, not less. The criticism within the term "selfish" is thus to be considered as "you should," another example of the "crab trap" mentality. Because we are also a culture that confuses anger and rage with violation, we criticize emotional expression as not being safe; it is much safer to talk about issues than it is to confront them. It is much safer to dissociate from emotional expression than to engage with it. This is generally true of all emotional expression, even the positive, but especially so with anger and rage.

So what happens when a client comes to a therapist? The client is aware of some problem, the actual events with which the client is upset. The problem is explored and perhaps resolved; yet the deeper issue is not complete. So the client comes back to deal with another problem, perhaps related or perhaps not. This proceeds for a time until the therapist starts to probe deeper and asks the client to explore issues that appear, to the therapist, to underlie the stated problems (see Figure 61.) The client, consciously or not, knows that this new assessment has considerable pain associated with it. Perhaps the client is not

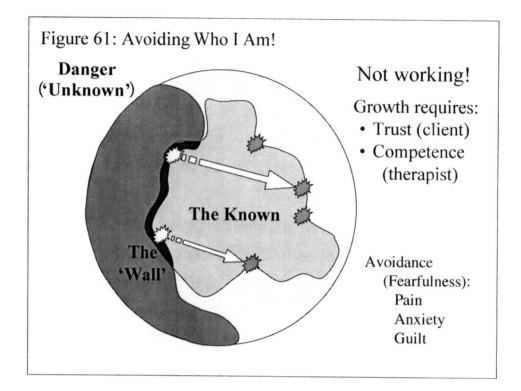

Figure 61: Avoiding Who I Am!

Danger ('Unknown')

Not working!

Growth requires:
• Trust (client)
• Competence (therapist)

The Known

The 'Wall'

Avoidance (Fearfulness):
Pain
Anxiety
Guilt

ready to risk that much with this particular therapist. So the client picks another problem upon which to work. Some resolution is achieved, and time passes. The therapist again comes back to the deeper issues and the client again avoids the work. By the third time the therapist broaches the deeper issue, one of two outcomes is likely to occur. If the client has enough trust, the client explores the deeper issue and the real work of therapy begins, hopefully with a successful outcome. If the client does not have enough trust (consciously or other-than-conscious), the client may leave at this point ("the therapy is not working.") Is there a sufficient match between therapist and client? It could be that the client is not ready; equally it could be that the therapist is not ready. The therapist may not have come to terms with the client's specific issue in his or her own life (that of the therapist) and is only telling the client what he or she "should" do. Trust is the principal limitation of therapy. There is no easy answer to the problems of avoidance. Therapy is an art form, not a science.

5.2.3. Difficulties and Traps: Devaluing The Subjective

One of the major tasks of the therapist's work is to help clients access and trust their subjective experiences. There are many difficulties in this process of growth. And therefore traps to avoid. Watzlawick et al[4] define significant difficulties as "an undesirable but usually quite common life situation for which there exists no known solution and which --- at least for the time being --- must simply be lived with." The mishandling of difficulties creates traps; that is, if a complete solution to a difficulty is sought, either by inaction (such as denial) or inappropriate action (such as explosion when thoughtfulness is required), then the energy is trapped, with all the consequences explored in previous chapters. In our current culture, we have created huge traps for ourselves.

Probably the greatest trap that we have created for ourselves is the denial of the subjective. The difficulty is that each of us has our own experience of the world, our own unique perspective; thus, it is incredibly easy for us to misunderstand each other. From this position, we get caught defending our position (or its variations such as self-righteousness) and, by taking a relatively fixed position relative to our unique experience, it is almost guaranteed that an argument and conflict will ensue.

One way out of this misunderstanding or conflict has been to emphasize the objective in our culture, for example, scientific data, expert opinion, hard cold facts --- all information about which we can agree as being the "real" data. In some respects it has been incredibly valuable to emphasize the objective; it has allowed us to create our technological civilization. But at the same time, the solution is inappropriate because it has locked us into deductive models of how to respond to life, in which we compare life to the model of what it "should" be. We think we know what the problem is; it is just going to take us a little time to fix it.

---

4. Paul Watzlawick, John H. Weakland and Richard Fisch, Change: Principles of Problem Formation and Problem Resolution (New York: W. W. Norton & Company, 1974), p. 38.

For me personally, I see that this denial of the subjective has pervaded medical care in our modern era. In the Western world, allopathic medicine (standardized medical care based on careful scientific investigation) is the dominant model. After thirty years as a physician, first as a specialist anesthetist and then a psychotherapist, I can truthfully say that the medical system is an excellent system, especially for acute disease. However, there are many problems. For example, incredible distortions, intentional and not intentional, have occurred in the pharmacological industry, especially the psychopharmacology industry, and are only now slowly beginning to be teased apart.

I also frequently question the efficacy of allopathic medicine in chronic disease. Because the standard medical thinking repeatedly attempts to bring acute treatment to chronic process, such that if only we find the right pill or the right diagnostic procedure or the magic bullet, then all will be well. This fundamentally denies that the end-point of life is death. There is no other end point known. Repeatedly I have heard derision of alternate systems, such as holistic care and preventive medicine, not from data but from opinion, usually sarcastic opinion. Yet I have benefited tremendously from alternate systems. At a personal level, I have many significant health issues; and I know I would not be alive today if I had not gained much from each system.

Still, neither system gives credence to the fact that I will someday die. This is not a "maybe" but a certainty.

Another problem in emphasizing the objective is that, as a species, we have not yet learned how to agree on a consistent approach to the vast amount of data that is now available. Opinion abounds but not agreement. For example, if I do not have accurate data of my health, I cannot develop an accurate map of how to proceed. In our "age of information," the quest to find the right information has become the major trap. Generally there is too much information for me to digest. Vast numbers of medical studies are published each year, each making claims about our health and sometimes contradicting each other? Seeking the original research to check for its accuracy and completeness is an impossible task.

Furthermore, I have major difficulty accessing the information. Literally, there exist thousands of sources of books, journals, internet articles, chat lines, etc. that I could tap into if I took the time and effort to do so. This overall dilemma of "too much information" is especially true in therapeutic issues. People have their pet theories of what works and what doesn't (as do I, as demonstrated by this book.) The field of Anger, Rage and Violation is rampant with politics as to what services are supported and how.

A third trap in emphasizing the objective is that it has allowed us to dissociate from our problems – to put them "out there" as if we were not major contributors to them. I see this as the central issue of most global dilemmas, including problems of hunger and war, our vast appetite for toys such as the biggest car or fifteen varieties of toppings on our hamburgers, and the dehumanization of our technologies that use euphemisms such as "down-sizing" when jobs and livelihoods suddenly no longer exist.

I have no solution to the traps of overemphasizing the objective other than to attempt to create a ripple effect; any other process traps me in the third limb of the triangle, a position where I create "stuckness" for myself and others. Creating a ripple effect is one of the principal intentions of my Anger workshops --- to impact people in such a way that the over-all health of their emotional system is improved, even if slightly. This may then impact a dozen others and eventually a thousand others. The basic intention of my work is to augment other people's skill in accessing their experience of the subjective, their own truthfulness, so as to bring greater health to all concerned. I ask the same augmentation in my personal life. In creating a ripple effect, I get to explore the value of the subjective.

My truth is that, only in accessing the subjective, do I experience authenticity as a human being and have a sense of personal power and strength, not power over others but power with them as we co-create our lives. When I interact with others in assisting their growth or in augmenting my own growth as I work with them, I gain a tremendous amount. First, I gain a sense of aliveness. Generally it is exciting, creative and fun to help others grow. I challenge myself to be honest with people, and be myself. In that, I am an expert: "someone who is not anxious about what they don't know." I gain a sense of compassion and cooperation with the limitations of what life offers at that precise moment. I gain "friends" --- not people who are nice to me but people who are real with me. I certainly gain a sense of contribution to the lives of others in ways that assist and challenge them (and myself) to grow. I also gain the opportunity to explore my powerlessness at many different levels. I get to explore my own limitations in wanting to influence others. I get to explore how much I want my ideas of human subjectivity to be a force of authentic growth in our society. I get to explore how sad I feel at the dilemmas of human misery: including the homeless of our society, the conditions of hunger and starvation under which much of the world's population suffers, and the rigidity of social systems. I get to contrast my hopelessness at these conditions with the immense trust I have in the spiritual as underlying and supporting these many dilemmas. In essence, when I strive to create a ripple effect, I get to live the way I say I want to live. I do this by valuing my subjective experience in all its complexity.

5.2.3.1. Specific Traps

Within the trap of devaluating of the subjective and over-emphasizing the objective, I suggest there are a number of specific traps to avoid in the therapeutic journey. These include ascribing blame and fault, self-righteousness, fearfulness and laziness, denial, the crab trap of "shoulds" (and focusing on others) and the anxiety we experience of the third limbs of our numerous emotional triangles. I will speak briefly about each of these traps.

Blame and fault do not work. In ascribing blame and fault upon others for our problems, we make them responsible for what is occurring inside ourselves. Blame and fault are generally externalized onto others; and, if given the opportunity, others can invariably explain why they did what they did. In addition, blame and fault are simplistic; they do not take into account the complex interdependence of human emotional systems. Remember the story of the "Belloc Ploy" in Chapter Two in which the executive assistant and her boss were at odds with each other, likely blaming each other without taking into account their own roles in the problem. It probably would have continued until termination (firing or resigning), except that the executive assistant was able to have a new perspective that allowed both she and her boss to change overnight.

Self-righteousness is in some respects a form of blame. It says: "I am right and you are wrong." Yet every human being is always doing the best he or she can and every human being believes what he or she is doing right, or at least, the best choice at the time. The only way this dilemma can be resolved is if we all deeply accept that we are all right, and that we are simply different. The question then becomes: "Can we negotiate the differences?"

With respect to fearfulness and laziness, Julian of Norwich, a fourteenth century mystic, nicely summarizes these two traps for me. At a time when the Catholic Church had hundreds of names of sins, she wrote: "We suffer from two kinds of sickness [sins]. One is … impatience or sloth …; the other is despair and fearfulness[5]." Only two sins. For most clients, these two sins are the major limitation to making significant positive changes in the therapeutic journey. For there is no gain without risk.

Denial is a huge trap in the therapeutic journey. I believe it lies behind all of our addictions and much of our depression as a culture; and it repeatedly shows up in our language. In my therapeutic work, I emphasize this trap of denial by calling its derivatives "swear words" and asking people not to "swear in the office." I do so not to actually stop people from using them but to play with identifying their denial so that they will pause in self-reflection. There are seven principal swear words that I identify:

1. "I can't" instead of "I won't." There are very few things human beings

    cannot do. I cannot for example live on a planet around a star trillions

---

5. Julian of Norwich, Revelations of Divine Love, 1393.

of miles away (if such a planet exists.) We simply do not have the technology for me to get there alive. I can live on the planet Mars; likely it would cost billions of dollars to get me there nor do I know how to access these resources reliably. So I won't live on the planet Mars. But I can. I could devote my life to the possibility even though the likelihood of success is incredibly remote. Similarly, when I ask a client to talk about a painful issue and they say: "I can't," what they really mean to say is: "I won't; it is very painful and I won't go into the pain."

2. "I'll try" instead of "I'll do." Although "trying" can authentically mean that a client will do an action and does not know what the outcome will be, most of the time "I'll try" is an excuse covering up lack of commitment to do it. It does not generate an authentic result; it sets up an excuse.

3. "I don't know" when it is applied to one's internal state. The only person who can know one's internal state is oneself. "I don't know" usually closes the door on looking into oneself. If it is an authentic "I don't know," generally it needs to be followed with the statement "and I will find out," or sometimes with "and I don't really care to know."

4. "Maybe" and its synonyms like "possibly" or "I guess." These words disconnect one from experience. As reader, please say the following statement aloud, completing the statement with some action you are very likely to do (such as having supper tonight): "Maybe I will …"

Feel the impact of saying it, feel how you resonate with it. Now say the identical statement without the "Maybe": "I will ..." The difference between these two statement will likely be immense for you in its felt resonance.

5. "Why" when a client is seeking an explanation of the current undesirable state. People who frequently ask "why" are generally stalled in their lack of internal activity. If there were a good answer to the question "why," likely they would have found it out long ago. And generally, if and when the answer is found, it does not provide a resolution. It simply explains how the person is helpless and powerless. This is not generally a useful stance. As example, someone whose marital partner has had an affair may spend years wanting to know "why" the affair happened. The partner may be unable to give a "satisfactory" answer. The couple argues, repeatedly, re-hashing the same data over and over. The positive intention is frequently somehow to justify or guarantee that the affair won't happen again, but the actual outcome is to spend years bickering without reaching closure and moving on. It is an ineffective pattern. From an outside perspective, the couple's energy would be far better spent on working out their difficulties so as to maximize the love that has existed in the relationship.

6. "But" and its synonyms "however" and "yet." These words are generally in the middle of a compound sentence and imply that the first

part of the sentence is not accurate --- the real explanation will follow.

Seen another way, these words likely represent Sailors in conflict.

7. The same is true for "should." "Should" represents a Crab Trap mentality with all its implications. It also represents Sailors in conflict in that "should" is a statement that indicates someone who both wants to something and doesn't want to do it.

The final trap of the therapeutic journey is anxiety. When a client gets anxious of what others do (and attempts to change the others) or when others get anxious about what a client does (and attempt to change him or her), much suffering is created. Many traps are encountered. Anxiety pulls a client into the third limb of the triangle, with all its implications as discussed in Section 2.3.2. (We Interact --- We Live In Emotional Triangles.)

5.2.4. LIFE IS PAINFUL

In this section and its subsections, I will discuss a fundamental difficulty --- that life is painful. I call the consequences "suffering" when clients attempt to avoid the pain of life. When clients come to see me, it is almost invariable that they are in pain of some kind. (Why else would they come?) Yet they generally have a peculiar kind of pain --- at some deep level, they know that life should not be the way it is at present. They may or may not know how they are contributing to their own pain or even that they are contributing to their own pain. On rare occasions, they are not contributing to their own pain. The bottom line is life is painful. Buddhism covers this stance in the First Noble Truth of the Buddha. A major component of Buddhism is the study of consciousness (the practice of meditation), exploring what makes effective living. The Four Noble Truths are a distillation of this wisdom[6].

****

---

6. Please note that the translation I have given is not strictly in Buddhist language; I do believe the translation is accurate of intent. Apologies to the purists.

The Four Noble Truths Of The Budd3ha

1. **On The Nature Of Pain:**

   Life is difficult.

2. **On The Cause of Suffering:**

   The cause of suffering is that we

   do not want to believe that life is

   difficult. Life should be easy.

3. **On The Cessation of Suffering:**

   Pain is inevitable;

   suffering is optional.

4. **The Way Out (The Eight-Fold Path):**

   The path out of suffering necessitates

   acceptance and discipline.

****

As far as I know, the Four Noble Truths are accurate descriptions of what life offers. Life is sometimes painful and sometimes joyous. Although we generally want the joyous, most of us have not come to terms with the flip side of the coin that life is painful. On those rare occasions when the client is not contributing to his or her own pain, he or she will likely experience sadness, grief, angst, terror, anger and rage. Ultimately though, there is acceptance. Most client's issues are more complex; the client is contributing to his or her own pain in significant ways. Thus, they are "suffering."

5.2.4.1. "It's Not Fair"

Clients name their suffering in relatively specific ways. Often the suffering is expressed by the client by stating what "should" be or by being angry about the fairness of the situation (I have previously defined fairness as the keeping of agreements in Section 4.3.4.3.) It is when I hear these comments that the therapy often begins. The client is in some way saying that life "should" not be this way and that someone else "should" be fixing the problems. The client often says: "It's not fair." When I question the client on this idea of fairness, he or she readily agrees that, truly, life is not fair. For me as therapist, it is a form of denial as described above. I question to myself: "So why then does this person say the first statement that it is not fair." From my perspective, they are basically presenting a "Crab Trap" mentality, such that it "should" be fair. My basic response to the client's statements or questions that contains the "should" word or the idea of fairness is to ask "according to whom?" And then we begin a dance of exploration.

Has the client come with the expectation that I the therapist am going to fix his or her problem? Generally I have enough difficulties in my life without taking on the difficulties of others. Even if I told the client what to do, my solutions are based on my ability to manage my own complexity. I do not live the client's complexity. I can offer examples to the client that have worked in my life or perhaps for someone else I know, but they are examples only. Even if I attempted to do the client's work, it would not help; such behavior on my part contravenes the first law of Emotional Triangles. It will ultimately lead to our being stuck and my getting the pain of the problem. No thank you.

5.2.4.2. RESOLVING PATTERNS

As a therapist, a major component of my work is to identify the patterns underlying the problems presented by the client and to assist in the resolution of the problem. As I indicated above, clients come to see me because they are usually in repetitive patterns that lead to some kind of discomfort for them. When a crisis or trauma in their lives occurs, it may feel like they are walking along and suddenly they find themselves in the middle of a deep hole, characterized by pain, shame, self-pity, etc. (see Figure 62.) They then spend days or weeks getting out of the hole and back to some place of "normality." Normality is a relative term --- a friend of mine once defined "normal" as "a small point on the bell curve of insanity." There is a lot of truth in this statement.

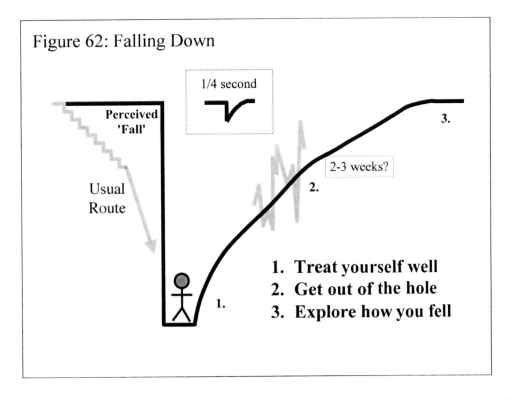

Figure 62: Falling Down

1/4 second

Perceived 'Fall'

Usual Route

2-3 weeks?

2.

3.

1.

1. **Treat yourself well**
2. **Get out of the hole**
3. **Explore how you fell**

Generally a more accurate description of the process that sets in motion a crisis or trauma in a client's life is that the client has a shovel in his or her hands and is slowly digging him- or herself into a hole, deeper and deeper. At some point, the client becomes conscious of the process and feels like he or she has fallen down. The pattern that leads to "falling down" is usually some variation of the traps of the therapeutic journey: denial, avoidance and blaming others for the current problem. Then, suddenly, the client finds him- or herself in a deep hole with a shovel in hand. What is the first thing he or she needs to do? Should the client figure out how he or she got in the hole? Will this help? Should the client get out of the hole? How? I suggest the best option is to put the shovel down. Stop digging and assess what is happening. I tell the client: "Treat yourself well." As indicated in an earlier chapter, it is generally pointless to castigate oneself for longer than ten minutes. A common trap here for the client is to analyze why the client fell down. It is generally a waste of energy because the client likely does not feel safe, cannot think clearly and cannot easily determine the relative contributions of self and others (note that these are all the characteristics of a full pot.) In addition, knowing why a client got in the hole does not usually aid him or her in getting out.

The next step is to get out of the hole. This may takes days or weeks depending on the nature of the problem. It generally entails management of the client's energy (who is, in some fashion, stuffing or releasing it inappropriately) as well as some kind of response to the precipitating events that lead to falling down in the first place: journal writing for clarification, apologizing, etc. Resolution of the immediate problem may or may not occur; ideally it does.

Finally if the client is willing, the last step is to look back at the process of falling down and study the pattern --- is there anything that is predictable or anything that is familiar in the process? How significant is this pattern in the client's life? In effective growth, the client studies the pattern of falling down and notes its characteristics (often by journal writing since it offers review of data over time[7].) As the pattern is studied and solutions explored, the pattern often recurs. More data is gathered. Eventually the pattern becomes clearer. Eventually as well, the pattern changes. It may not be apparent what the change is (perhaps the client is speaking out about his or her truths, perhaps he or she is more relaxed, perhaps he or she have begun to accept the inevitable, etc.) When the client falls down again, whereas before it might have taken two to three weeks to get out of the hole, now it is consistently taking only two or three days to get out. The client continues to study the pattern. Eventually again something is different. Now he or she is only two to three hours in the hole. If the client continues, it is usually possible to shift the issue so that he or she falls down and picks him- or herself up in less than a second. The outside observer does not see the fall; the client knows he or she has fallen but the time span and pain of it are minimal.

---

7. The final exercise of the last chapter illustrates a series of questions that can be asked so as to collect data about the pattern.

In a related fashion, the client learns how to relate to other people in more effective ways. For any given life issue, we are not isolated beings and not all of our difficulties reside within us. We need to learn what part is our internal contribution (our lack of acceptance of our "powerlessness" as discussed in Chapter Three) and what part is contributed by the external relationship (the "conflict.") As outlined in Chapter Three, different skills are needed for the different contributions.

5.2.4.3. Patterns Of "Stuckness" --- Pony Tracks.

I name these recurrent patterns of falling down (as described above) "pony tracks" (see Figure 63.) I imagine that you the reader have been to a circus or amusement center and have seen the kids riding around on the ponies, on a well-worn track. The ponies are dressed in bright spangles, and the kids are generally having fun. But what about the ponies? How are they doing? Generally they look bored, joyless, apathetic, perhaps even pained. Day after day, it's the same old track. Even if the circumstances were to allow the ponies freedom to roam, they might do so briefly but, given that they have been trained into expecting others to feed them, eventually they would wander back to the pony track.

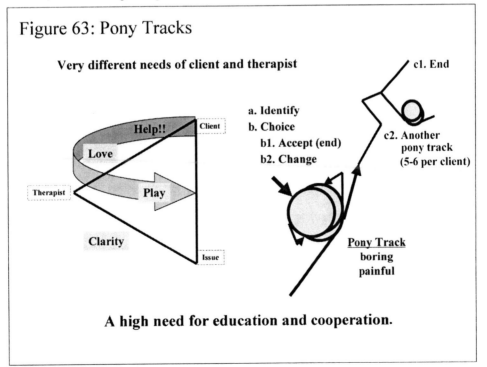

Figure 63: Pony Tracks

It is often this same pattern in the early stages of therapy with clients who have had little experience of what therapy can offer. They look for external solutions or ways to get away from their problems but, if they do get away, they soon wander back onto the same pathway again. My job as the therapist is not to fix the client; it is to identify the pony track and act as guide if the client wants to change it. In my experience, I can work with about ninety percent of clients (ten percent want to work with a woman, or think I am too intellectual or too abrupt.) After I begin to work with a client, it then generally takes three to six sessions together to identify the pony track in enough detail that the client can appreciate the track (sometimes I get lucky --- a client's pony track is identified on one session; sometimes not --- it may take weeks of work as we explore the issue together.)

Once we have identified the pony track to the satisfaction of the client, the client has a choice. Accept the situation and continue to do the same pattern or enter into a process of exploring some different outcome. Of the original ninety percent of my clients, about thirty now choose to do the same and stay on their pony tracks --- but with a significant shift in their focus. They recognize that the pony track is their contribution to a complex issue and that the cost of changing that issue is greater than they are willing to pay (it might mean the ending of their marriage, it might hurt their kids, etc.) In accepting this reality however, the clients are now more at peace with their pony tracks and create much less suffering for themselves. At this point, our work is essentially finished; there is some clean-up to do but the therapy is complete. The clients have gotten what they want out of the process even though it's not what they anticipated.

The remaining sixty percent of my clients are not satisfied with the current status and want something different. They want to change their pony tracks. So we explore, bringing various tools and disciplines to seek resolution of the problem. Eventual resolution occurs and the client comes to a place of personal satisfaction. Usually this exploration to the point of resolution requires three to six months of work in therapy. About half of the individuals (thirty percent of the original) are now complete and terminate the therapy. These clients may or may not return, months or years later, with new pony tracks.

The final thirty percent of individuals are also generally satisfied with the outcome of the therapeutic process, but they recognize that they have another pony track to explore. They could not see this new pony track before because it was obscured by the first pony track. In my experience, most people have five or six pony tracks in their lives, with each pony track requiring three to six months of work until resolution. If people will do the necessary work to achieve resolution, they will dramatically shift their ability to be satisfied with life. Fundamentally these people will learn to be at peace with the pain of life, living the Serenity Prayer rather than just giving it lip service. It generally requires about two to five years of committed searching to learn the skills of effective living. In particular, it does not mean that the lives of these people are problem-free; they simply have the skills to deal with what life offers. Apparently unrelated problems will seem easy to resolve and life will become much more peaceful and joyous overall.

5.3. THERAPY AS EXPANSION

What is it that makes for good therapy? Much research has been devoted to this and I will not reiterate this research here. Much of what follows will be my subjective experience of being involved with therapy for close to twenty-five years. During this time, I have been exposed to many different therapies, many different therapists and in many cases have been at one time or another, either client or therapist. In doing so, I present my own truthfulness, not because it is right but simply to record it as a starting place to challenge some of the current societal models.

Two metaphors are pertinent here. One is the story of the seven blind men each exploring the same elephant --- each will give different emphasis yet the descriptions will be limited principally by their willingness to explore. The second metaphor is that, if two established artists are asked to paint the same external landscape in their usual styles, they will each present a satisfying "thing of beauty" yet the paintings may bear little resemblance to each other.

5.3.1. DETERMINANTS OF THERAPY

Essentially therapy is a relationship dynamic between therapist and client(s), exploring the experiential world of the client and inviting the client into new perspectives, thereby seeking an authentic outcome for the client. The presenting problem is seldom the problem, merely the "weakest link" where the stresses come to the surface. (We say a chain breaks at the "weakest link" essentially because under enough stress, that is where the chain breaks. Each link might be identical --- the chain has to break somewhere.)

The major determinants of skill on the part of the therapist seem to be (in probable order of importance):

1. the personal maturity of the therapist (exploring their own life issues determines the flexibility and rapport building of the therapist in responding to the worldview of the client),

2. the clinical experience of the therapist (exploring the issues both with the clients and with other therapists who have experience in similar issues), and

3. the theoretical foundation of the therapist so as to frame and explain what is happening. Much research has demonstrated that what the therapy is named is a very poor determinant of outcome. The theoretical foundation simply gives the therapist a way of categorizing the exploration of life issues so as to be able to discuss them with others.

The major determinants of outcome on the part of the client are:

1. the willingness to risk new awareness and experience, and

2. the inherent emotional intelligence of the client. All else being equal, some people simply have more skill at emotional issues.

Especially important in all this is the ability to establish rapport between the individuals concerned, client(s) and therapist, as the basic glue that allows trust to develop in the relationship. Often the first few sessions will determine if a successful outcome will be achieved. Therapy thus is an art form and is not transferable from one therapist to another. Often clients do not realize this; they do not search for an appropriate match (for many valid reasons.)

5.3.2. STYLES OF THERAPY

The art form of therapy comprises a multitude of models, all of which attempt to explain the major components of being human, of being conscious. Ideally the intention is to give resolution to the difficulties experienced by the client. Some of these models are:

1. Biologic and/or pharmacological models. These are the major models of current medical practice, with a heavy emphasis on psycho-pharmacology.

2. Rational-emotive models, of which Cognitive Behavioral Therapy (CBT) is the major current model. As discussed below, it is currently heavily aligned to the medical model.

3. Existential models that grapple with the fundamental problems of death, aloneness and loss and how they influence other issues in our lives.

4. Mind-body models that usually have a physical intervention component as the starting place. These would include Gestalt Therapy, Bio-Energetics and other body-related therapies.

5. Relationship and systemic models such as Family Systems which

explore the interactions of people as the primary basis of intervention.

6. Transpersonal models with an emphasis on the inter-relatedness of all life, especially at the spiritual level.

7. Power therapies that are non-cognitive and that work rapidly in creating change. Many work with energy meridians, often with a basis in Eastern Philosophy. I devote Section 5.4.3. in this chapter to some of these therapies.

Each model has its own perspectives. And fundamentally each model is accurate in that it has originated (presumably) from the truthfulness of one or several individuals who have struggled with their own issues within their own limitations. Given the presupposition that each model is accurate, I take the perspective that any truly effective model must somehow include and bridge all of these models. This bridging is what I attempt with the Blowing Out! process. Specifically, I use skills from Cognitive Behavioral, Gestalt, Bioenergetics, Transactional Analysis, Neuro-Linguistic Programming, Life Staging, Family Systems and Transpersonal to name a few. Also, within any model, every therapist is unique in his or her approach to the art form such that the final product is subjective and cannot be interpreted out of context. None of these models are bad models; they simply are all ways of exploring and categorizing the components of humanness.

Therapy seeks new emotional resolution to old emotional issues. It is always a combination of conversation, relationship and task, often with multiple levels of experience simultaneously. It seeks to open out into new possibilities, seeking an authentic experience that resolves the dilemmas of the client. Generally, it is not a process of narrowing into a known solution to a problem (deductive.) Ideally, it must be open-ended and go where the client wants to go (the directedness of therapist generally inhibits options for the client.) Therapy is a dance between the directed and the non-directed, depending principally on the skills and maturity of the therapist and the client.

5.3.3. DEDUCTIVE VERSUS INDUCTIVE PROCESSES

My experience is that there is a major gap between the theory of therapy and the practice of therapy. Therapy as theory presents a model to be analyzed. Therapy as practiced is often systemically inductive, occasionally deductive. A problem is named, usually by the client. A deductive approach uses a known model for exploration, to identify components of the problem, to identify mechanisms of the problem relative to the norm and then attempts to correct the faulty mechanism. Finally the outcome is checked. The major advantage of deductive models is that outcomes can be standardized and comparisons made between what is supposed to work and what actually works. In this sense, CBT, the pharmacological models and perhaps other models offer relatively quick fixes and easy number-crunching of reportable results which thus appeal to the need of governments and insurance companies to contain costs and have a predictable budget.

In an inductive approach, one starts with the assumption that both the model and the mechanism are unknown and are to be explored or evolved. Then, one explores with curiosity. The exploration is not an accumulation process in a logical fashion. Clinical notes of past conduct and past exploration may have little significance at a later stage of exploring. In this sense, every session with the client can be a unique session, supported by but not necessarily consistent with previous sessions. Attempting to follow a consistent pattern, if used as the starting point for so-called "new progress," may actually inhibit the creativity necessary for good therapy. Emergent patterns are compared against other positive models and the system is repeatedly tweaked for possibilities as a test of change. The system is allowed to rearrange and then the outcome is checked. It is possible that the therapist may not have any idea of the final outcome, even when achieved, yet the client may have gotten what they want. If the system is accepted as unknown and people truly are allowed to find their own truths in an inductive fashion, the outcomes are unpredictable. One must operate within the assumption that any healthy shift within a system will ultimately result in the over-all increased health of the system. And one must be open to the possibility of finding that which is truly brilliant and yet not previously conceived.

The presuppositions of an inductive process deeply challenge our human propensity to arrogance and self-righteousness, thinking that we have the answers to highly complex systems. It also challenges our assumptions that we can control emotional systems from a purely rational perspective. Speaking for myself, as an individual who has been exposed to "scientific thinking" over the past forty-five years and as an individual who is somewhat widely read in the politics of "science" in the twentieth and twenty-first centuries, I have great distrust of our cultural arrogance and self-righteousness. My distrust is especially prominent when the "therapist" or psychiatrist becomes the judge of what is best for the client --- a dominant theme in current medical care, especially emotional care, at all levels of our culture.

5.3.4. THE USE OF MEDICATIONS

In keeping the assumption that each model presented above has its own perspectives and that fundamentally each model is attempting to describe a common worldview, discussion of the use of medications is paramount. One of the strongest perspectives of our culture is that, if only we can find the right "magic bullet," our emotional dis-eases and problems will go away. What reality it there to this perspective[8]? Here I will only comment on my own experience. Where do I recommend and/or prescribe medications? My basic answer is: "Infrequently. And always as a trial of medication." I am interested in the client

---

8. Whole books have been written on the use of medications for mental illness. For detailed descriptions of the conundrums of psychopharmacology, I specifically refer the interested reader to Thomas S. Szasz, The Myth Of Mental Illness: Foundations of a Theory of Personal Conduct (rev. ed.) (New York: Harper Paperback, 1974); David Healy, The Antidepressant Era (Cambridge, Massachusetts and London, England: Harvard University Press, 1997); and Grace Jackson, Rethinking Psychiatric Drugs: A Guide for Informed Consent (Bloomington, Indiana: AuthorHouse, 2005).

being convinced that the medication is important, that it is helpful, perhaps short-term, perhaps long-term, depending principally on the client perspective.

First, what medications do I recommend? (As sidebar, when I practiced as a specialist anesthetist, essentially a specialist in drugs that impact consciousness, I was well aware that the most dangerous drugs were the drugs that others considered safe. If a drug seems too safe, it is generally over-used.) Most of the time, if I am going to recommend any drug at all, I will suggest one of the newer anti-depressants such as fluoxetine (Prozac) or venlafaxine (Effexor.) Generally they have good anti-anxiety effects with relatively few side-effects. For appropriate benefit, I suggest to clients that they need to be on these medications for approximately two years, including slow withdrawal in the last six months.

My belief is that most of the time medications are simply a stopgap for the client while other therapeutic tools can be developed. Unfortunately they also diminish the pain, the motivation, of the client that is necessary so as to do the growth work. For some, medications are necessary. As example, I would never deny insulin to a diabetic; I would however strongly suggest that the diabetic become more of an expert in their disease than their own doctor. This expertise would include personal management of dietary and nutritional needs as well as knowledge of blood biochemistry so as to monitor their own health.

I suggest medications in three areas of my practice. Other than the first area, I only suggest medications after extensive exploration of the therapeutic issues.

1. If the client is sufficiently disorientated or disabled by the intensity of their dis-ease such that they are not able to engage meaningfully in the exploration of therapeutic issues. The nature of my work is that these clients seldom stay in my practice.

2. If the client simply has no interest in or grasp of the therapeutic issues. In this scenario, I question myself as much as the client as to what is the limitation. Is the client limited or am I limited in my flexibility of what I

offer? Once again, these clients seldom stay in my practice.

3. If, despite extensive therapeutic work on the part to the client, we still encounter major limitations such as clinically obvious characteristics of Schizophrenia or Attention Deficit Disorder, I will cautiously prescribe medications, attempting to find a balance between the biochemical, the psychological and the spiritual. Always I am dealing with a client in distress, not a diagnostic label.

--- Author's Personal Commentary ---

As indicated previously, my own life has had its ups and downs. My personal truthfulness is that if I had not found good therapy in my forties, I would not be alive today --- I would have committed suicide like my father. The therapeutic journey was very painful but well worth the effort. As a young adult, I could not have conceived of the richness of my life as it is today.

Concerning medications, I have used them and I continue to use them. Currently I take a small dose of fluoxetine (Prozac®) on a daily basis. I am hesitant to discuss this topic of my own use of medications in the expectation that some readers may now choose to totally discount the theses of this book by this simple statement of my using an "anti-depressant." Therefore nothing else I say has validity.

Yet I also need to state my truthfulness on this topic --- it is part of the complexity of evaluating the subjective. My use of medications has much complexity hidden within it. A major difficulty of my life has been this intense self-criticism. I had resolved much of it. I have used fluoxetine occasionally, especially when the environmental stressors have been intense. Currently I do so. Why? In the numerous explorations I have done, I accept that early childhood brain development is a fundamentally critical time for the operating system of emotional development. Much of it likely can be reversed by good therapy (see the shifts possible as illustrated by the remainder of this chapter.) But can it all be reversed? ... I do not know. Has my brain been damaged irreversibly by the coping within my childhood? ... I do not know.

Given the intense emotional shutdown I chose as a young child so as to fit into my family and despite the extensive growth work I have done since my forties, I remain somewhat irritable about interruptions in my daily life. If fatigued, I am grumpier than I would like and if really stressed (by environment or society), I am still prone to moderate despair. I do not wish to live this way and it is simpler to take a pill on a daily basis than it is do the searching within despair for further changes. It is a choice on a spectrum of using my current life for internal searching versus external contribution to the growth of others. But it is not "the answer." It is not a "magic bullet" for me. It is simply another tool available at this time in our culture.

5.4. THERAPY AS CHANGE OF PERCEPTION

A major need of good therapy is to hold the analytic mind in abeyance so as to allow the purposeful but apparently non-rational processes of both therapist and client to evolve (this is part of the "magic" of therapy.) Playful, off the wall therapy often works best. And the best therapy is usually a profound shift in perception, from a previously difficult problem to a suddenly interesting possibility with resultant behavior change that results in dissolution of the problem. This way of working may require extensive preliminary growth work to get to sudden shifts in perception. Psycho-education of the client may take years, hopefully with enough little shifts of patterns that the client remains committed to the process. This may be all that happens but often, with sufficient experience, the shifts become more integrated and at a deeper level.

5.4.1. THE ISSUES OF LIVING

Over all, the issues that the client brings can be considered as falling into several different areas. First are the issues of childhood in that we grow in our families from a stance of powerlessness, hopefully to a place of internal power wherein we are confident and have resources to respond to life's ongoing problems. To the extent that we remain trapped in the limitations of our childhood, others-focused on what we did not receive as our "fair share" in the family, angry at what we have been handed in life, we will be victims. As such, we will feel and act powerless. Much of therapy asks us to step out of this stance and explore what resources we now have as adults and how we can manage our lives different from that which we did as children.

The second group of issues is that of "putting out the garbage." Life has pain --- life offers an ongoing need to respond to problems and clean up the residue; if I want to make a meal, there will be scraps of food left, there will be dirty dishes and pots, there will be work to do to maintain sufficient stability in my life. Especially prominent in "putting out the garbage" is that it is not all my garbage. I live in relationship with others, sometimes cooperatively, sometimes not. Ideally these problems are resolvable but sometimes it seems so complex and convoluted. If I want to be healthy, life requires work or more specifically, discipline.

The third group of issues is the existential problems of life. Life simply has aspects with which we are uncomfortable. We are all going to die. We have no absolute way of knowing truth. We have no absolute way of knowing if life is meaningful or not. Thus each person is required (or not) to come to terms with what life offers, contributing in whatever way is optimal for that individual. If God actually exists, he or she probably could not have designed a better system to encourage growth or flexibility of response. Discipline is again required to manage the dilemmas and pains that life brings.

The *Webster New World Dictionary* definitions of discipline range from "training that develops self-control" to "punishment." Although the first (training) is satisfactory, it does not give enough information to motivate discipline. My most useful definition is "discipline is doing what I want to do even when I don't want to do it." When I was forty-one, I met an eighty-six year old man who was stronger and more flexible that I was --- he had practiced yoga since his age of forty. I wanted to be like this. So for the past twenty-three years, I have practiced yoga myself. As mentioned previously, my commitment is to do two minutes of yoga a day. The perceptual shift of recognizing that I only needed to do two minutes to maintain my discipline was a major shift in recognizing that I can create life the way I want, with relatively little effort --- as long as I am effective in my choices.

5.4.2. SHIFTS OF PERCEPTION

Another major truth for me is that my emotional brain is orientated not to conceptual data but to metaphor and sensory data. By tapping into this manner of processing, the possibilities are awesome. Here I want to underline that shifts in perception are a major component of therapy; they are an area where extensive investigation is needed to clarify the mechanisms and possibilities of "shifts of perception." I believe them to be the single most powerful way in which people change.

Underlying shifts in perception, and part of the "extensive preliminary growth-work" mentioned a few paragraphs earlier, are the skills of awareness, clarity and precision of language mentioned earlier (especially in Chapter Three.) Although simple in concept, these skills are fundamental and may require extensive discipline in their development. They are also very subtle and easily dismissed as "imaginary" or "superficial." As a culture, we do not yet have enough knowledge or clarity as to how the body-mind-heart-soul-spirit, especially the neurological systems, creates the complexity of the mind. Presumably that clarity will come with time.

In the meantime, I can only speculate as to how the mind uses perception, especially at the other-than-conscious level. My own experience is that I always process at the sensory level, even in imagination. I associate into the experience briefly, make a shift in sensation within the experience, re-imagine the experience and notice that other components also shift simultaneously. Then I make a decision as to whether to continue in this process, perhaps utilizing to proceed to the next moment of interaction with the present moment.

--- Author's Personal Commentary ---

As example, yesterday, my wife and I were sitting at a table with friends talking about these concepts of perception. My wife asked me "Think about your favorite vacation possibility. What do you actually do when you do this?"

Although very rapid in development, I was able to identify the following. I heard her words auditorily and presumably gave them conceptual meaning. Very quickly (and more quickly than interpretation of the conceptual meaning), I had a pleasurable body sensation (kinesthetic) in the center of my chest immediately followed by an internal visual picture of a "parrot fish," a fish with which I am familiar from snorkeling in the Caribbean. About this time, I become aware of the conceptual meaning of "vacation" as a subtle internal jarring (kinesthetic) in my head and, again internally, I asked myself "... favorite?" (my internal dialogue, auditory.) Very, very rapidly, I scanned several specific memories visually (skiing, bird-watching, etc.) with equally rapid kinesthetic shifts as I eliminated these memories as less desirable. Then I had a rush of pleasant sensation over the front of my chest that somehow had the impression of "Yes, it is," referring to the snorkeling experience. Visually I then had a much broader visual picture of being underwater seeing many different aspects of a specific memory of snorkeling in the Virgin Islands.

All of this likely took several seconds as I pondered the sequence; the actual sequence probably took less that a second. Then I told my wife what was happening in answer to her question of how I created my response.

I believe that this is the way all human beings process --- as sensory-grounded short-term energy transformers. As one component shifts, so do many others. It was not until about ten years ago (after many years of being a therapist) that I came to appreciate how pervasive and how powerful shifts in perception are in the change process. Intellectually I knew they were powerful very early on; energetically I had no idea as to how powerful.

Perceptual shifts in my life have occurred in many ways. Let me now chronologically describe some of the perceptual shifts, sometimes as illustration of life's complexity and sometimes of what can be done with life's complexity in startlingly simple ways. The shifts I will describe are the dramatic ones; I suggest that many shifts of lesser impact occur frequently on a daily basis for all people.

5.4.2.1. MYSTICAL SHIFTS

As I review my student days, there were numerous times wherein I would be studying something and suddenly I would "get it." Suddenly it all fit into place and the usage of the knowledge was now available. Most of the time, the experience was simply an intellectual illumination. However, one time while studying stands out clearly. During my first years of university in Physics, I was studying the mathematical model of the Bohr atom (the hydrogen atom), baby-sitting my young nephew and nieces who were all asleep. Suddenly I lost my awareness of the room where I was studying and I found myself surrounded by pale light with the sense that I was moving rapidly around a central object --- both literally and figuratively I had the sense of being an electron spinning around a nucleus. I have no idea of how long it lasted, possibly seconds or minutes, but I was in a profound state of peace and bliss as if the universe was fully alive and conscious. Then I became aware of the room again and the state quickly faded, leaving me with a sense of awe and contentment, a state that was uncommon for me given my family background. What happened? To this day I have no explanation of mechanism but am now widely read in mystical experiences. This was one of my first major mystical experiences.

So what are mystical experiences? At the very least, sudden profound shifts in perception such that everything is now seen in a new light. How? Essentially the mechanisms are unknown but, for example, they are now being correlated with neurophysiologic structures in the brain[9]. Speculation abounds --- has this

---

9. For more information, see Andrew Newberg, Eugene D'Aquili and Vince Rause, *Why God Won't Go Away: Brain Science and the Biology of Belief* (New York: Ballantine, 2001).

occurred as a part of evolution to allow us to be satisfied with our existential aloneness or is there truly a God to whom we are capable of connecting. I will speculate on this in the next chapter.

When I was thirty-one, I had an even more intense mystical experience, one that lasted three <u>years</u> in total. On a bright cloudless winter day, crisp and clear, I was walking back to the hospital where I was doing my residency in Anesthesia (at the time attempting to understand the nature of chronic pain and its relationship to consciousness.) Suddenly, totally unexpectedly, someone turned the lights "on." Colors were immediately a hundred-fold brighter and more separate. Sounds were crisper. Immediately I had an immense sense of peace and acceptance. This lasted forty-five minutes or so. I had few friends and no mentors to whom I could talk about what had happened to me. Then, it faded. Two days later, this sensory-emotional state of peace returned, this time twice and lasted longer. It kept recurring. By a month, the state was continuous and characterized fully by a deep acceptance of life as mystery and peace, knowing that "love" is truly a universal principle.

This state remained at a peak for six months and then started to fade. I read voraciously during this time, especially the first six months and at about the five-month period, I can across the book *Cosmic Consciousness*, written by the Canadian physician Maurice Bucke in 1899[10]. Therein, he described his search of his own personal experiences and the experiences of his friend, the American poet Walt Whitman; he also attempted to understand the writings of such individuals as the Buddha, Mohammed, Dante and William Blake. On page 79 of the 1969 edition, Bucke lists eleven characteristics of the state that he called Cosmic Consciousness. When I first read this list, I could immediately say "yes" to almost all of what was listed (exceptions were those dependent on the reports of others --- I had no one to give me feedback on my state.)

Thereafter the state faded over the next three years. I did not know what to do about it. Gradually a subtle sense of despair occurred, a despair that lasted

---

10. Richard Maurice Bucke, Cosmic Consciousness: A Study in the Evolution of the Human Mind (New York: E.P. Dutton, 1969; Innes & Sons, 1901).

about five years and only resolved with my entry into my own therapy. During an intense experiential process at a therapy retreat, I again had a sudden shift of perception, an image of "galaxies dancing" that represented to me the joyousness of the universe. The retreat experience did not restore Cosmic Consciousness --- it did however allow me to integrate the state into my authenticity such that I could now proceed forward in my life. I was able to recognize Cosmic Consciousness as a gift and come to the conclusion that my life was about honing the vessel, me, so as to hold the gift if it ever came again.

So what actually happened; and what does this have to do with a book on therapy, especially anger management? First I want to emphasize that each of these state changes were almost instantaneous in its shifting of perception. Second, each somehow was deeply resonant with my whole being --- what I have come to call an "authentic feel-good" experience. They were not fluffy superficial experiences. Highly subjective, they had an ineffable knowing that resonated within the totality of my being. Each somehow had a preparation state that was consistent with the outcome although totally unexpected, in essence inconceivable during the preparation state.

It is this type of shift that I believe underlies good therapy. Unfortunately it is neither predictable nor deductive. Is it possible to standardize it? I do not know --- I suspect not; like great art, it can be predicted but not guaranteed. Nor is this all there is to good therapy. Much preparatory work in done by clients and this preparatory work itself may give the client the outcome he or she seeks. I do suggest however that the truly transformative work has the impact of the "authentic feel-good" experience.

5.4.2.2. THERAPEUTIC SHIFTS

Let me now explore some therapeutic shifts that I myself have experienced. As stated in the introductory chapter, I will describe my own experiences --- I will be stating my own truthfulness rather than attempting to describe someone else's. Hopefully, this allows a greater depth of clarity of what actually happened.

(I have also been able to lead many clients through similar processes, after which they give me feedback consistent with my own outcomes. These are all skills that can be done with or taught to clients if they so wish. One of my long-term goals with clients is for them to be able to do their own exploring as they continue to create the lives they wish to live.)

My own background is complex and varied, as previously stated. My first university degree was in Physics. From Physics I moved to Biophysics, then Medicine and eventually got a specialty degree in Anesthesiology. I practiced Anesthesia for ten years, being socially successful and emotionally numb. Then during the despair of my major mystical experience, I encountered therapy and my life changed. Truly a mid-life crisis at age forty. After a few years of good experiential therapy (and knowing I wanted to be a therapist), I entered a Master's degree program in Applied Behavioral Sciences (a combination of psychology, sociology and anthropology focusing on how people function in groups.) The program was very eclectic; the emphasis was on Family Systems Therapy. At the same time, I entered a Gestalt Therapy training program and eventually got two diplomas in Gestalt. At heart I am a Gestaltist --- focused on awareness, contact and personal responsibility. It was with Gestalt that my primary skills of awareness were developed. It was also with Gestalt (with some Bioenergetics and Transactional Analysis) that my early ideas of anger and rage were developed (and my awareness of how much rage I then carried within myself.) It was with Bowenian Family Systems (a particular style of Family Systems Therapy, especially as taught by Edwin Friedman) that I learned what to do with what I was feeling. The tools of Gestalt were creative but somehow limited.

So in my searching of various disciplines (both spiritual and psychological), I then encountered Neuro-Linguistic Programming (NLP), a cumbersome title but a profoundly creative and playful therapy. NLP has proved to be the most powerful and fun therapy that I have explored thus far, awesome in its capabilities of perceptual shifts. Most of my profound and rapid perceptual shift experiences have followed my training in NLP. The trainings in Gestalt and Family Systems remain my basic philosophy, both for therapy and for personal life; NLP had given me tools to live my philosophy.

Earlier in the book, I described my shifting of despair ("Search Mode" as described in Section 4.3.2.1. The Positive Intention Of Emotions.) This despair would occur whenever I had more that one emotion present. Once I recognized the positive intention of the despair (my mode of searching within), the despair instantly disappeared and essentially did not recur for a year and a half. In these contexts, when I use the word "immediate" I mean within a second or so --- truly immediate in its perceptual impact. Several years later, a similar despair recurred when I had an internal conflict of values. Working again to recognize the positive intention of the despair, the naming of the process as "Values Conflict" resulted in immediate resolution.

A third example is more complex. Growing up in my family, I was often described as "intense." The term came to have many negative and painful connotations for me until I explored the positive intention of the pain. This occurred during a time when I was doing voice training, previously having had a significantly monotone voice, for which I would also receive much negative commentary. Recalling the previous shifts of "Search Mode" and "Values Conflict," I realized that "intense" was a combination of my need to go inside to process emotional data and at the same time it was a state of shame. As a strong introvert, it may take me hours or a few days to process new intense emotion-laden data; not right or wrong, this is just my internal process. But being "intense" was shameful in my family of origin.

When I named the process described above as "data processing," there was no shame attached and I could then examine the nature of the shame. As I studied the shame, I recognized that my soft palate would go into spasm and that, spontaneously in my imagination, I would exit my body and step into the belief systems of another so as to experience their beliefs. I did not live up to their expectations and would then create the emotional state of shame as a result.

Once I named the state as "shame-frame," I recognized that this was my way of experiencing the "crab trap" at the experiential level and that my entry point into the experience was via spasm of my soft palate. In my voice training, I had recently learned how to relax my soft palate. Taking this a clue, I relaxed my soft palate. The shame immediately vanished. "Shame-frame" thus became an option of experiencing the belief systems and rule bases of others by choice.

I continue to "data process" --- it is very useful to me. Since that time however, I no longer experience shame in my life unless I choose to do so. When I need to test my environment relative to my behavior, I step into this energy space that holds the belief systems of others, so as to explore the expectations of others. Perhaps I experience shame or not. Having tested the experience, I simply step out of the energy space by relaxing my soft palate.

5.4.2.2.1. Rapid Change Of Beliefs

I will now describe another process, one that is quite different. Somewhere around this same time of "shame-frame", I knew a woman who had a child with Attention Deficit Disorder. He was a nice kid but very interruptive, especially verbally. Referring to myself, I grew up in a family with the rule base: "children should be seen and not heard." Obviously not a good combination when dealing with a child with ADD and the expected conflicts arose, including conflicts between the woman and myself.

Remembering that I am a sensory-based energy transformer, I then studied how I created the conflict for myself at the sensory level. As peculiar as it might seem, I recognized that I store my beliefs about children in a small space about two feet in front of my head slightly above eye level. I found that, when I encounter children, I search for the information I need about children (like the central processing device of a computer seeking information from the hard drive), bring the information internally to be processed and then go to the next step in the program of interaction with the child. Choosing to play with this fantasy, I reached up in my imagination to lift the belief from its location (and physically acted out the process.) I noted its size, shape and other features in my "imaginating" of how I stored it. Deciding it was in my best interest to have a new belief, I created "children have their own wisdom," shaped it to fit the old space and put the new belief in the old space (like writing over the memory of the computer storage device.) In less than a minute, I changed a childhood belief and also changed my interactions with this boy. It may sound strange or hokey indeed, but even today (about ten years later) I get slightly confused as I attempt to access the old belief, now without the previous energy it carried. And I no longer interact with children from "children should be seen and not heard."

5.4.2.2.2. Rapid Change Of Emotional States

One final example of this kind of shift is pertinent. About five years ago, I was driving my daughter to the airport for her to return to university. As we drove, we talked about our mutual propensity to compare ourselves to other human beings, usually in a negative fashion. I recognized I did it often, at least a few times a week, and that I used it as a motivator to encourage me to be more skillful (the positive intention) --- it was not a feel good state but it did motivate me. I dropped my daughter off and then, alone on the return trip home, I decided to explore how I actually did this process. The investigation took about three minutes in total --- around this time, I started developing skill at the processes I called truth-testing. Truth-testing offered me a way of checking if my imagined shifts in perception had a reality to them; it was a way of validating the subjective. This validation of the subjective has proved to be invaluable in seeking my own experiential shifts --- it has allowed me to trust the exploration of the subjective long enough to explore the powerful processes contained in the shifting of perceptions.

While driving in the car on my return from the airport, I imagined someone to whom I wanted to compare myself and noted that I spontaneously created a visual shell of that individual somewhat off to the front and right of my body, at about a thirty degree angle and just out of reach (about five to six feet away, quite close to my previous place of shame-frame.) The shell was thin, brittle and had the size and shape of the individual to whom I was comparing myself. In my imagination, I then moved my body (my kinesthetic sense) to attempt to fit into the shell. I didn't fit and the shell shattered. I then brought this information back at the auditory level with a short statement like "Oh sh--," a brief statement with a thousand words attached. From there I spiraled down into shame as a motivator to get me moving. This process worked to get me motivated but it was not a pleasant experience in how it motivated me. Accessing this pattern thus far took about one minute of processing.

The second minute was spent exploring how I compare myself to myself. Over the past twenty years, I have made amazing shifts within myself and am generally delighted in who I have become. It turned out that the process of comparing myself to myself used a structural pattern similar to the above unpleasant pattern but did so in a way that created an "authentic feel-good" experience. For this comparison, I spontaneously created the visual shell of myself behind me to the left, about three feet away and on the same thirty-degree axis as the other comparison. Then I stepped kinesthetically into this shell of myself as I was in the past. From this shell, I compared myself with my current shape in the present and liked the feel. I brought the information back auditorily as an "Hmmmm," with a strong feel good experience. Then I spiraled up into delight. A much better process, more effective and more pleasant. So I decided to explore how I could change the negative comparison process.

I played. I changed the visual location of the original shell of the other person; I changed the space available within this shell; I changed how I moved towards the shell. Some minor shifts occurred but nothing had an "authentic feel-good" experience associated with it. Then, spontaneously the shell shifted such that it stood beside me on my right hand side, about two feet away. I now had a companion rather than a competitor. This immediately felt good. My other-than-conscious had presented me with a resolution. I did nothing further and continued the drive home. The entire process took a total of three minutes while driving the car.

With this shift, I essentially stop comparing myself to others. At about the six-month mark after this occasion, I noted myself comparing myself to my wife, a gifted therapist of whom I had always had some jealousy. It lasted ten minutes until I shifted "her shell" to that of a companion. I simply now recognize her as a gifted therapist. A year ago, having just started writing this book, an author friend was visiting and I found myself briefly comparing myself to him for a moment or so. And then I let it go.

These two occasions have been the only occasions where I have compared myself to another human being in the five-year period since this piece of change work. I now function with companions, not competitors. After three minutes of exploration!

If you had asked me "Is this kind of deep emotional change possible?" prior to this actual event, I probably would have answered "No". Trusting my own experience, trusting my own truths, now allows me to answer a definitive "Yes, with the right tools".

5.4.2.2.3. Integration Of Subpersonalities

As these skills have developed, they have led to other profound skills. In my Gestalt training and other trainings, I had no concept that the Sailors on the ship could be combined and integrated so that processing goes on much more easily at an other-than-conscious level. As an example, an early internal conflict I had was around eating junk food, especially potato chips (described earlier as part of Sailors On A Ship in Chapter One.) One Sailor "potato chip kid" loved potato chips; "critic voice" knew better and shamed me whereas "Doctor Dave" was always planning new ways of solving the conflict. As the expression goes, "the more things changed, the more they remained the same."

One day while working with a client, I chose to use this as an example of integration so that the client had a model to follow. Over a five minute period (total time), I characterized these three Sailors in a number of ways: their beliefs; their energetic locations; the characteristics and locations of their voices; their direction of movement; and such energies as location of past, future, the familiar and the different. They negotiated with each other aloud (for the benefit of the client), agreed to common locations for energetic storage, especially that of voice and direction, familiar and different, and agree to integrate. Since that time, potato chips have not been a problem. Sometimes I choose to eat them, sometimes not (over-all I eat less than ten percent of what I once ate.) Again bizarre, strange, possibly not believable, yet highly effective in creating the kind of life I want to live, one that is authentic of who I am.

5.4.2.2.4. Shifts --- Metaphoric Or Real

Although deeply spiritual (with mystical experiences as described previously), I had never really considered the implications of truly being spiritual, especially the implications beyond the conceptual and philosophical levels, until the events described in this section. To give it a particular frame of reference, I will tell a story of Carl Jung, one of the great twentieth century psychiatrists and researchers of spirituality and religion. Towards the end of his life, he was asked if he believed in God. After some reflection, his answer was something to the effect that "No, I do not believe in God. To believe in God is to consider the possibility of doubt. I do not believe in God --- I know there is God[11]."

So if God is truly Spirit and I am truly Spirit, what else is Spirit? Others have written much about these concepts, sometimes at the experiential level[12]. Here I want to tell my own experience as a basis of challenging the current paradigms of our culture, especially the paradigms of therapy.

If I authentically explore the implications of spirituality, I also must consider that my life energy somehow exists after this earthly manifestation and before this earthly manifestation. Intellectually I believe I could be wrong but my truthfulness and my mystical experiences allow me to say I "know" that life is a spiritual process. If my energy exists both before and after this manifestation, then perhaps other energies also exist. Perhaps previous lives and reincarnation

---

11. C.G. Jung et al., Memories, Dreams, Reflections (New York: Vintage Books Edition, 1989).
12. See Adam Crabtree, Multiple Man: Explorations in Possession and Multiple Personality (Toronto: Collins, 1985).

do exist as more than metaphor. Perhaps other conscious energies exist; these may be what are commonly referred to as ghosts, spirits, entities, etc. Or perhaps these are simply metaphors for some other kind of energy that is yet unexplored.

Metaphors are incredibly powerful means of transformation, of reframing experience so as to have a possibly rapid perceptual shift. Accepting this, I have worked extensively with myself and others on pre-birth experiences. By stepping onto a line on the floor, one that I accept as metaphoric of my life line (so-called time-line work), I have gone back in early childhood experiences of which I have no conscious memory, of birth and intra-uterine experiences and of experiences prior to conception. Working at this level, I have changed aspects of these memories (usually the meaning I give them) with resultant change in my everyday life. I have changed anxiety about past situations and current occurrences. I have also worked extensively with what I will call "entities," metaphoric energies of consciousness and intention other than human.

--- Author's Personal Commentary ---

About fifteen years ago, at a time of major relationship stress, I suddenly started criticizing myself without mercy. As I studied this, my truth was this was a spiritual experience, not a psychological one --- this was an energy outside of myself (although I had not yet articulated the implications of being spiritual as more than metaphor.)

I jokingly said to myself "Get thee behind me, Satan," referencing a well-known biblical passage. My criticism immediately stopped! I was amazed and had no explanation, either for its occurrence or its disappearance. Gradually the criticism recurred and as I studied it, I characterized it as a "Sailor" on the ship, naming this Sailor "Nevill" (evil in the middle.) Slowly Nevill came to be similar to Golem in "Lord

Of The Rings." For several years, I attempted to integrate Nevill as above but without success. Nevill, it seemed, had no positive intention for me and had no intention of integration with me. Nevill "liked" my being anxious, shamed, etc. In my imagination I conceived that I had invited Nevill as a young child to help me deal with the complexity of my early childhood.

Then one day, while talking with a friend about Nevill, she asked me how I knew Nevill was truly part of me. Did Nevill come from outside? My immediate other-than-conscious answer was "Yes, Nevill does come from outside." I have learned over the years to trust and pay attention to this kind of answer. Fortuitously as well, I had recently attended a NLP conference in which the keynote speaker had demonstrated techniques of de-enmeshing psychological energy such as the holding on of anger towards a parent. So I decided to de-enmesh myself from Nevill. I explored how Nevill was connected to me at the sensory level and decided what else would fit in its place (an image of who I truly wanted to be.) I asked if anyone else in the universe wanted Nevill for their protection and growth (both of which Nevill had given me) and received the spontaneous answer "Yes" in my imagination. So metaphorically I cut the umbilical cord, handed Nevill off to the energy that wanted Nevill so as to heal his end of the cord and attached the new symbol of who I wanted to be to my end to allow healing of my end (and no space for Nevill to return.) It worked! Nevill has never returned

--- periodically I playfully wave to him in some distant galaxy and he waves back in my imagination.

Is this for real? I don't know. All I truly know is that it works. I have done it many times with myself and with many clients. If carefully and effectively done (about a hundred times now), it has always lead to profound shifts in the person having the change work, shifts that have an immediate "authentic feel-good" characteristic. I also do not care if it is "real" at the objective level. At this stage, I am concerned with exploring a subjective landscape that is unknown, a landscape that requires an inductive approach. To apply a deductive approach to this kind of exploration would require that I fit the above into current belief systems such as those of psychiatry. I would likely need to label myself as psychotic! This does not appeal to me. My worldview is complex, fascinating and enriched; it is not a place of dis-ease, simply a place of profound compassionate curiosity.

5.4.3. POWER THERAPIES

To close this section, let me now consider some of the so-called power therapies. For the past thirty years or so, there have been a number of therapies developed that are rapid in effect (seconds to minutes), with prompt healing in many cases; these include eye movement desensitization and reprogramming (EMDR), thought field therapy (TFT), emotional freedom technique (EFT), whole-hearted healing (WHH), psycho-energy auro technologies (PEAT processes) and many others, either developed or developing. They remain controversial in allopathic medicine.

At the end of this chapter, I include the process of EFT in that it is available freeware on the internet (http://www.emofree.com) and is also incredibly effective as a simple shotgun approach to many issues.

****

Skill: Emotional Freedom Technique
(see insert at end of chapter)

****

I started using EFT a number of years ago, after my NLP skills were fairly well developed and many shifts had occurred in my life. It thus has not had a great impact on me personally except in minor ways but I have been impressed with how effective it is for most clients, even on their first exposure to therapy, let alone to EFT. Routinely I include it in my Anger, Rage and Violations weekends because it is often so effective in allowing a client to let go of pain with a minimum of skill development.

I recall a client who wanted to murder his wife because of the incredibly horrific ways in which she treated him. After a lifetime of crime, he had been a client for a number of years and had made major shifts in his life. In keeping with family dynamics, his wife became more and more unhappy as he changed; as a criminal, there had been more excitement and much more money. He finished his work with me and hoped for a good life. Eventually she cleaned him out including sending several men to beat him up (they did not succeed.) After all this, he wanted to kill her.

He came back to see me after four months of this and I asked him, on a scale of one to ten, how badly did he want to kill his wife: nine and one-half (if ten, he said he would have already killed her.) But to kill her would have meant he would spend the rest of his life in jail --- not a good option for him. I took him through one round of EFT and he was a zero. A second round was again zero. He left and still today he has no energy invested in his previous marriage. Wow.

EFT has been so profound for me that it is my first approach when it is not clear what other tools would be useful in resolving the issues. In many cases, I am amazed at how effective it is in totally resolving the presenting issue for people. In similar ways, I have also used WHH and the PEAT processes with equal success although they require a little more attention to detail for them to be useful.

Four themes seem to emerge when these power techniques are explored for mechanism as to how they are effective:

- First, emotional energy is stored as energy in a time-less fashion, ready to activate current life experience with the right trigger.

- EFT, TFT and EMDR (speculating on the latter two in my limited exploration) seem to distract the mechanisms whereby the energy is hooked into the current life experience, perhaps allowing the energy to dissipate because it is not recharged. (Like a rechargeable battery, memory seems to require periodic boosting.)

- WHH and the PEAT processes require stepping into the experience fully associated, gradually allowing the energy to dissipate, either actively into the breath or into a bodily letting go of the energy. My guess is that they are ultimately more effective.

- Fourth, the energy is frequently recognized as relating to Eastern philosophy and physiology as meridian lines to provide a means of accessing the negativity.

Whether or not the above is pure speculation or not, I do not know. My subjective truth is these processes are incredibly powerful in quite unexpected ways.

5.5. THE POWER OF THERAPY --- THE POWER OF THE SUBJECTIVE

At this point, I will briefly summarize the power of the subjective.

We are subjective. The only way we get to the objective is through our subjective experience. Our subjectivity is an outcome of our complex biology.

We are emotional and we are metaphoric. It is the manner in which we create and evaluate our reality, our experience of the objective. Our subjectivity is capable of immense wisdom if we will tap into it. We name it with many words such as instinct, creativity, first impressions --- this is only the beginning of the skill; it is only the undeveloped expression of the skill.

We are afraid of it --- it represents the unknown, the possibility of change in an unpredictable fashion. In our fear, we limit ourselves and we attempt to limit others. Some of this fear is appropriate --- we lack skill at using the subjective. And in our fear, we pull away from the subjective so that we do not develop the skills that are possible. A profound Catch-22.

If we will learn to trust ourselves, to trust the predictability within the unpredictability, the skills are awesome. If we are committed to growth, our own growth in conjunction with growth of our emotional systems, many skills are available. With appropriate skill development, the actual change work can be easy; the exploration may be long and sometimes difficult. Authentic use of the subjective leads to wisdom, the ability to interact with others in a manner that will ensure our survival as a culture and as a planet. I know of no other skill that has this capability.

The development of subjective is the therapeutic journey. It begins in pain, there is a long road generally and there is much joy along the way when we learn to live the journey. Eventually it is simply acceptance of life and discipline in doing the work required.

Skill: Emotional Freedom Technique
http://www.emofree.com

Basic assumption: "The cause of all negative emotions is a disruption in the body's energy system."

EFT IN A NUTSHELL

Memorize The Basic Recipe. Aim it at any emotional or physical problem by customizing it with an appropriate Setup affirmation and Reminder Phrase. Be specific where possible and aim EFT at the specific emotional events in one's life that may underlie the problem. Where necessary, be persistent until all aspects of the problem have vanished; fractionate the problem as needed. Try it on everything!

[This process is best done initially with supervision or a guide until such time as the mechanical movements become rote.]

THE BASIC RECIPE

Identify issue in 3-4 words (reminder phrase, RP) and assign a SUDs (subjective units of distress.) E.g. "afraid of sharks" with a SUDs of "9" (10 would be panic mode now.)

1. The Setup...Repeat 3 times this affirmation of RP:

   "Even though I have this .(RP)., I deeply and completely accept myself" while continuously rubbing the Sore Spot (chest) or tapping the Karate Chop point.

2. The Sequence...

   Tap about 7 times on each of the following energy points while repeating the Reminder Phrase at each point.

   ### EB, SE, BE, BN, Ch, CB, BA, BN, Th, IF, MF, BF, KC

EB: Eyebrow	SE: Side eye	BE: Below eye	BN: Below nose	Ch: Chin
CB: Collarbone	BA: Below armpit	BN: Below nipple	Th: Thumb	IF: Index finger
MF: Middle finger	BF: Baby finger	KC: Karate chop area.		

3. The 9 Gamut Procedure...

   Continuously tap on the Gamut Point (back of hand near and between 3rd and 4th knuckles) while performing each of these 9 actions:

(I) Eyes closed	(2) Eyes open	(3) Eyes hard down right
(4) Eyes hard down left	(5) Roll eyes in circle	(6) Roll eyes in other direction
(7) Hum 2 seconds of a song	(8) Count to 5	(9) Hum 2 seconds of a song.

4. The Sequence (again)...

   Tap about 7 times on each of the following energy points while repeating the Reminder Phrase at each point.

   ### EB, SE, DE, DN, Ch, CB, DA,BN, Th, IF, MF, BF, KC

Use the Basic Recipe up to ten (10) times on the issue, until the SUDs comes to zero (∅) on two consecutive occasions.

If two ∅s are not achieved, check your need to hold onto the issue. If appropriate, fractionate the issue into smaller chunks and eliminate chunks until the complete issue is resolved.

Note: In subsequent sessions, the Setup affirmation and the Reminder Phrase can be adjusted to reflect the fact that you are addressing the remaining components of the problem.

306

CHAPTER SIX --- SOCIETAL CONSIDERATIONS: MATURITY

Summary

Earlier chapters have presented many skills; some can be immediately practical and some require extensive development prior to effective application. With each skill, there was a somewhat clearly defined process available to learn the skill. In this chapter, the emphasis is on the application of values to our lives.

I do not pretend to know the mosaic of our culture, especially our gradually evolving global village with its numerous political and social issues. I suggest repeatedly though (especially in this chapter) that major illusions and distortions underlie the emotional issues with which individuals struggle in our culture. Specifically in the issues of anger and rage that beset our current North American society, I suggest that these issues are largely a societal issue presenting itself as difficulty in individuals unable to cope with the system. And if this is so, then identification of the fundamental problems as being at the individual level is likely to perpetuate the problem rather than resolve it. By stating this, I do not in any way intend to exonerate the individual. I am simply stating that the societal issues need to be addressed. How this will happen, I do not know. I believe that the valuing of the subjective and the valuing of the inductive are essential components in this.

Yet we are society, we as individuals. Society will not change until we change. The focus in this book is thus that of change within the individual, such change then perhaps creating a ripple effect within society in the long-term.

The chapter thus focuses on themes that repeatedly arise in my working with clients in their attempts to create change within their lives. These themes relate to values and spirituality, the nature of relationship (especially romance) and child discipline. The chapter close with a brief exploration of laughter as energy release and resource.

CHAPTER SIX --- SOCIETAL CONSIDERATIONS: MATURITY

The focus thus far has been on what the individual can do to manage himself or herself in difficult emotional problems. But we do not exist as isolated human beings; we are part of society. I suggest in this chapter that there are major illusions and distortions occurring in our society. We need to mature both as individuals and as a society so as to come to terms with these problems. We can do this best (from my perspective) by developing and living our values with clarity.

Given the nature of emotional triangles, I strongly believe that the living of healthy values into a societal system will then lead ultimately to healthy change within society. How such change of society will occur is unclear and I do not pretend to know the answers to what "should" be done. Such "should" will trap me in the difficulties of the third-limb. I do believe that personal maturity is devalued in our culture and that it represents a major key to the development of maturity as a society. I also believe that an inductive approach to problem solving is key --- it opens the possibility to unusual shifts in perception, such shifts often leading to profound change (certainly at the individual level where I work with clients.) I repeat the definition from Ken Wilber found in the Opening Considerations: "ecologic wisdom does not consist in how to live in accord with nature; it consists in how to get subjects to agree on how to live in accord with nature." My best definition of maturity is "the living of wisdom;" this would include honesty, authenticity, congruency and the resolution of conflict by cooperative problem solving. This chapter will comment on the complexity of maturity and how it can be achieved. It will also comment on the relationship between the maturity of the individual and the maturity of the society.

A fundamental question to be addressed in this chapter is that of the nature of society relative to the topic of anger and rage. Are anger, rage and violation individual problems or are they systemic, societal issues. After twenty years of exploration, I suggest that the problems of anger and rage are principally a societal problem that presents itself as difficulties in individuals who are unable to cope with the system. If this is so, then the identification of the fundamental problems as being individuals at fault is actually part of the problem rather than part of the solution. This is not to say that the individuals are any less dangerous or any less responsible or any less accountable for their personal dilemmas. Much work needs to be done at the individual level.

However, much work also needs to be done by the individual at the societal level. Society is not likely to change just because I want life to be different. Yet a basic principle of emotional triangles is that if I change, others (including society) must change --- it is just not predictable how they will change or when they will change. Another definition of "maturity" that I use is the "ability and willingness of the individual to change in order to cope with the difficulties of society." This chapter will thus look at a variety of issues related to these systemic factors of maturity. If we do not deal with the systemic issues, the solutions attempted will simply be surface solutions. They may work, especially in the short term, but likely will not be effective in the long term. Fundamentally we will not know where we are and hence we will not get to where we say we want to be.

6.1. THE NATURE OF OUR SOCIETY

So what is the nature of our society?

Our technological competency has been incredible. At age sixty-four, I can still remember when television was introduced in my childhood. Atomic energy was first used (the bomb) after I was born. Space exploration has started in my lifetime. Almost all of the marvels of modern medicine have become routine within my starting of my training as a physician. Wow!

However, we are a society that gives surface (and occasional deep) credence to the worth of the individual. Many examples abound of our wonderful caring. Witness the 2004 Tsunami and the 2005 Hurricane Katrina. Yet how very quickly it is old news. If we truly value the individual, how then do we have such problems with poverty and hunger (amongst many others), both nationally (Canada and the United States) and internationally? At various times, I hear reports that the issues of hunger are resolvable yet I do not see outcomes that are consistent with these statements. I hear reports of how inefficient we are in government matters. When I watch video documentaries such as Fahrenheit 9/11[1] or Bowling At Columbine[2] or The Corporation[3] or when I hear stories such as the Enron story or the Watergate story, I am left with deep distrust of our integrity as a society. I also read of incredible distortions of research studies in the psychopharmacology industry. Even if I take these documentaries and stories with a large grain of salt, I am still incredibly skeptical of the honesty of our culture.

6.1.1. INCONGRUENCIES

How do I cope with the contrast between words and actions in all this? With difficulty! When words and actions do not match, the emotional brain is activated by the possibility of pain in the mismatch. I suggest that this is one of the major problems of our society. Our advertising, our slogans, our media all promise one thing and life presents something quite different, especially for the large portion of North Americans who are being marginalized. And this only represents a small, generally affluent portion of our global village. On a daily basis, via radio and other media, I am inundated with advertising as well as stories of violations, corruptions and societal dangers. Fortunately I have the choice to say "No" to the bombardment, much of which has no direct impact on my life other than to raise my anxiety about fearsome possibilities (crime, tornados, faulty equipment,

1. Michael Moore, 2004
2. Michael Moore, 2002
3. Abbott and Achbar, 2004

corruption, etc.) I do not know how others cope with the invasion of details and noise. I suspect: poorly.

As a result of our technology, we have created a society with too little time. We quite routinely now have two income families (so as to have enough income for the toys we are supposed to have and yet our kids are in daycare or under high stress keeping up with volumes of homework and vast numbers of structured activities.) Or the statement that I frequently heard as a young adult in the 60's, "the difficult we do immediately, the impossible takes a little time" --- cute on face value, dehumanizing and paradoxical if we actually take it seriously (and it was meant to be serious.) We also have a society with too many answers, without agreement as to consistent responses. I repeatedly hear stories of pending ecological and/or global financial disasters yet there is no apparent consensus as to what to do about them.

It is thus no wonder to me that most individuals are highly stressed and have shut down their skills of awareness. The people (men and women) who come to my anger management weekends span the entire spectrum of intelligences and professions. They are not evildoers who intend violation --- although about a third have been sent because of legal difficulties of family violation. They are generally likeable individuals who are stressed by the issues of unrealistic expectations and limited skill development in human affairs. They are people who are lost in having no authentic vision of how to live life well. By living well, I do not mean living life wealthy with lots of toys and vacations; I mean living life satisfied that one is living according to one's values, authentically contributing to a sense of global community and with "enough" to have a few luxuries. Thus I contend that the high stress of our dehumanizing society is one of the major components in the issues of anger and rage. As long as we focus on the individual as the problem, the systemic can be ignored (at high cost.)

6.1.2. DISTORTIONS OF OUR CULTURE --- GENDER ISSUES

One of the central areas where this dehumanization plays out (relative to anger and rage) is in the context of gender politics and domestic violation. In so far as I am able to gather reliable data, my opinion is that the polarization of domestic violation as an issue of male abusers and women victims has been one of the great distortions of our society. To illustrate, I was listening to a radio program the other day in which the staff of a women's shelter were being interviewed. They were celebrating their thirtieth anniversary. Yet the principle message that came across was how little the celebrants perceived they had accomplished in thirty years. At the risk of offending the reader, I suggest that this lack of progress means that women's shelters are somehow part of the problem of domestic violation rather than part of the solution. I say "at the risk of offending the reader" because the issues of anger, rage and violation are highly charged issues in our society. It is not my intention to offend anyone --- it is my intention to invite a broad look at the entire subject.

The major difficulty for me with the topic of domestic violation is gathering good data. Almost all of what I read is opinion and conclusion rather than data. Let me discuss the following three sources. I present them not because they are good scientific studies but because they are conclusions presented to the general public. As such, they have more energetic impact in our culture than scientific studies presented in prestigious journals. The data presented by the three sources below are certainly consistent with what I perceive to be mainstream thinking about domestic violation. Yet there are some distortions that can be identified and which point in interesting directions.

In March 1996, *The Toronto Star* presented fourteen newspaper pages on "Family Violence." It was a detailed presentation of women who are abused by men and the difficulties they face in our society. My initial thoughts when I read it were: "Incredible violations; certainly needing attention as major social issues.

But there are only two sentences (in fourteen full pages without advertising) of reports of women beating men."

On May 29th, 1998, another study reported in *The Toronto Star* began with the following statement: "The first statistical look at family violence in Canada paints a grim picture of one of the most closely guarded secrets in society" (see Figure 64.) From the data, I could guess that there was a ratio of two or three male murderers to one female murderer in Canada. The next paragraph categorized most abusers by type of relationship: men, parents and children. My thoughts ran along the same lines as when I read the first *Toronto Star* article in March 1996: " Again, it does not name women as abusers."

Figure 64: Domestic Violence

from The Toronto Star (Friday, May 29th, 1998)

"The first statistical look at family violence in Canada paints a grim picture of one of the most closely guarded secrets in society."

"No age group escaped the abuse. Husbands assaulted wives, parents murdered children and children attacked their aging parents."

Family Homicides (accused,%,4193),1977-1996---

Husband/CLHusband:....	34	Wife/CLWife:......	12
Ex-husband:..............	3	Ex-wife:.................	0.5
Father/step-father:.....	13	Mother/step-mother:.	9
Son/step-son:............	9	Daughter/step-daughter:	1
Brother/step-brother:...	6	Sister/step-sister:.......	1
Other relatives:..........	13		

Similar information appeared in the publication *Redbook* in October 2000 in an article called "The Secret Violence Of Women." One of the lead statements was the following: "Male batterers are also more deadly, estimated to be responsible for 60 percent of deaths in domestic violence cases." I thought: "This seems compatible to *The Toronto Star* data. Yet if male batterers are responsible for sixty percent, who is responsible for the other forty percent? Cats, horses, …? Women!"

The *Redbook* article gave a slightly different slant on domestic violation as being a male issue, whereas female violation was "but by no means a rarity."

On the topic of domestic violation, the best writings I know of are by Dr. Warren Farrell, a psychologist from San Diego who has written many books over the years on the subject of gender issues. I personally have met the man on several occasions and have been impressed by his intelligence and skill. I understand he was the first man elected to the Board of Directors of the National Organization of Women (NOW) in the 1970s. At the time, NOW was one of the leading feminist organizations in the United States. He was on the Board of Directors for three consecutive terms. I therefore believe he was widely respected in feminist circles at the time[4]. In his books, he routinely lists three hundred to five hundred references from world literature, thus documenting his sources. Of the references I have personally checked, he accurately presents the data he describes. Given all of the above, I trust Farrell's data, certainly much more than I do undocumented conclusions; and I strongly recommend his writings to the reader. I barely touch on the comprehensive studies that he has done --- they present data that has astounded me.

Bearing the work of Farrell in mind, let me now consider the May 1998 *Toronto Star* article reporting on the so-called "first statistical look" at domestic violence in Canada. This claim is grossly inaccurate. It is not the "first statistical look." Farrell indicates in his book *Women Can't Hear What Men Don't Say*[5] that there have been over one hundred prospective research studies done since 1975 (in the United States, Canada, England, New Zealand and Australia.) Moreover, domestic violation is not a closely guarded secret --- we have been talking about it for approximately thirty years. Finally, the *Toronto Star* data concerning family homicides suggests that there are two to three male murderers for every one female murderer in Canada. Farrell indicates that in all of the prospective studies he cites, men and women were demonstrated as being equally violent.

4. For further details, go to http://research.umbc.edu/~korenman/wmst/farrell_who.html and http://www.warrenfarrell.com. The first reference includes much discussion of the controversy surrounding these issues.
5. Warren Farrell, Women Can't Hear What Men Don't Say: Destroying Myths, Creating Love (New York: Tarcher/Penguin, 1999), p. 129..

Exploring further, Farrell[6] presents information for the United States that seems to correspond with the same kinds of study in the (Canadian) *Toronto Star* data and the (United States) *Redbook* data (see Figure 65.) Farrell notes that women are responsible for forty-one percent of spousal murders. This is presumably the missing data from the sixty percent of murders committed by men as reported in the *Redbook* article. Farrell then compares the methods by which men kill and by which women kill. Men kill by gun or knife; women kill by poisoning or by getting someone else to do the killing. Farrell suggests there is a major discrepancy in how these different methods of killing are reported --- the forty-one percent of female domestic homicides do not include the second and third most common methods of how women contribute to the death of their male partners (getting others to do the killing.). Thus, the sixty-forty split is nonsensical; it compares apples and oranges. Given the major beliefs of our society that domestic violation is a gender issue (as demonstrated in *The Toronto Star* and *Redbook*), I do not know how to establish the validity of Farrell's data. I do know that Farrell's data is the best data available to me and that it encourages me to explore more deeply what underlies the issues.

Figure 65: Domestic Violence Revisited

from Women Can't Hear What Men Don't Say, p151 (1999)

On the surface, the Bureau of Justice [USA] reports women are the perpetrators in 41 percent of spousal murders. However, the male method of killing is with a knife or gun, done by himself; it is easily detected and reported. ...

The first mostly-female method is poisoning. The second is the wife hiring a professional killer. The third is the wife persuading a boyfriend to do the killing.

These last two methods, if discovered, are never listed by the FBI as a woman killing a man. They are listed, rather, as "multiple-offender" killings. ... that is, the 41 percent figure does not include either of these female methods of killing [in domestic violence reports].

---

6. Warren Farrell, Women Can't Hear What Men Don't Say: Destroying Myths, Creating Love (New York: Tarcher/Penguin, 1999), p. 151.

Suppose I had unlimited time and resources to do the research on domestic violation myself and the methods of statistical analysis necessary to deal with the vast amount of data that is available. I would need to sort the data carefully from the emotional agendas of individuals who would be impacted by the conclusions drawn from the research. I would then generate another report on "domestic violation." Would this have any more impact than any other report? I doubt it. There would always be flaws that could be identified in my research methods, at the very least in my attempt to sort the information from the emotional impact. For instance, what criteria would I use to do the sorting? As well, the report would be inherently limited in its impact because of the Laws of Emotional Triangles. I would simply be generating further commentary on the third limb of the triangle consisting of myself, the scientific community and the nature of domestic violation.

Considerations such as the above have led me to two conclusions. First, our society's current focus on the objective (that which is measurable and subject to consensual validation by others) as the primary methodology of establishing "truth" has led us into a trap of too much information. It does not seem to lead us either towards authenticity or maturity. The challenge to strive towards authenticity and maturity (for both the individual and for society) must begin with the subjective development of the individual. Am I willing to make my best attempt to know fully the nature of issues such as domestic violation and then trust my own truthfulness in the knowing? Am I willing to work to change myself and act from my truthfulness in a way that challenges the growth of society, a way that encourages agreement on "how to live in accord with nature"?

My second conclusion is that the primary issues of violation are societal. As a society, over the past thirty thousand years perhaps, we have valued external achievement; we have valued the objective results of our technology. It has allowed us massive power over nature and meant that our major ways of interacting with each other are as dominators. Dominators do not seek to agree; they seek to dominate (and thereby violate) --- it permeates our culture. Somehow our need to dominate requires a change in perspective. Learning the skills of the subjective and finding a balance with the objective may offer us this change. The work needs to be at the individual level. Given the nature of emotional triangles, only here does it seem possible to gain authenticity and personal power. But given the nature of our society at the present time, it seems a daunting task. Attending only to the individual issues will not make the societal issues go away. In this context of the systemic nature of anger and rage, the individual issues of the people who go to (or are mandated to attend) anger management programs are only the tip of the iceberg. We all need to learn how to get along.

6.2. Authenticity

It is highly unlikely that society is going to change simply because society is part to the problem. Change must begin with the individual. How? I believe the journey begins with authenticity. Am I willing to live according to my values? What are my values? How do I create and live into effective goals? Here I will suggest how one can live in society with one's value system.

Earlier (Section 5.2.2. Values Versus Beliefs), I suggested how one can study one's own value system and begin to bring personal behaviors into alignment with one's value system. It is of course a lifetime of work to do so. But a journey of a thousand miles begins with the first step and then it is one foot after the other. Part of the difficulty is our great propensity to pretense, of being unwilling "to hang our laundry out in public." This is unfortunate as it denies that we are part of the problem. It perpetuates the myth that the (other) individual is the problem and does not encourage the depth of searching of personal issues that are so important to growth in maturity as human beings. It is principally for this reason that I do not do individual therapy --- for me, the processes of group therapy ask that we come to terms with our common humanity and our common fragilities, not as places of criticism but as places of learning skills of maturity.

6.2.1. LIVING MY VALUES

One of my former professors Robert Crosby talked about core moralities, of how to live with the current dilemmas of our society[7]. He listed the following five core moralities (see Figure 66) to which I have added the sixth, that of celebration.

Figure 66: Core Moralities

1. aging gracefully
2. striving for authenticity
3. being in community
4. being a midwife
5. being my word
6. celebrating life

---

1. aging gracefully --- we have little choice about aging. How will we do so?

2. striving for authenticity --- authenticity is never absolute. You can never fully know me and I can never fully know you.

3. being in community --- living authentically with others.

4. being a midwife --- contributing to the growth of others (Dave's comment: not doing the work for them though.)

---

7. Robert Crosby, Living With Purpose When The Gods Have Gone (Ojai: Times Change Press, 1991).

5. being my word --- doing what I say I will do (or at the very least, negotiating alternatives if necessary), and

6. celebrating life.

I have chosen these to be my core values and I strive to live them for myself. When I do, I am able to live life peacefully. To live well, I need community --- it is the place where I get to show up, being present and honest. I need major relationships --- it is where I experience intimacy and ecstasy. I need a sense of meaning and purpose --- it is how I create integrity for myself, living into my meaning. And I need to defuse the Ghosts of my past --- they trap my energy.

I find community by finding like-minded people who allow me to express who I am without criticism or judgment; these people also challenge me when I seem to step outside living my values. For myself, I belong to a long-standing men's group who meet for two hours every two weeks (occasionally we meet all day.) No agenda is set other than to check in with each other as to what is happening in our lives. This meeting is a place where I feel supported to explore whatever difficulties are showing up in my life at that moment. I find major relationship with my wife and family. These relationships offer me the experience of deep caring, my caring of them and their caring of me. As explained later in this chapter (Section 6.3.2.5.), it is a place where I get to live life as gift. Doing so has been the highlight of my life; it has taken a lot of work in personal change to reach this place.

I gain purpose by contributing to others in a way that is meaningful to me. In my particular case, I contribute by supporting and challenging others to grow emotionally. This sense of purpose will of course vary from person to person. Generally we gain purpose by achievement (creating something in alignment with our values), by relationship (contribution to growth of others) or by inward searching in an authentic manner (historically the journey of the spiritual minded.) The most important component is that the purpose must be in alignment with personal values.

Therapy (or some variation thereof) is the place of defusing Ghosts. Then my energy is available to the present moment.

Within these four parameters, I can then live my life as a series of goals or visions of possibility (see Figure 67.) Goals are not only end-points on a journey; they are the scenery that motivates movement along the path. By such scenery, the process can be exciting or it can create a nemesis by which I drive myself to do the impossible. An authentic goal or vision (one that motivates) has certain characteristics:

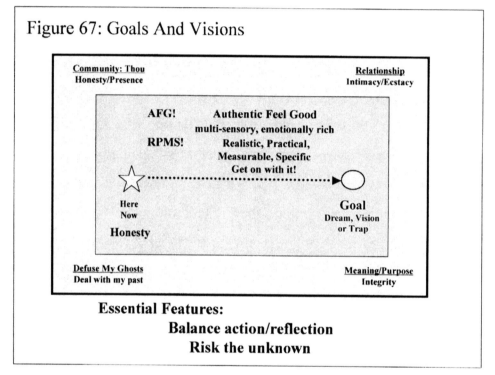

Figure 67: Goals And Visions

a. The vision must excite authentically --- a vision has to have a multi-sensory, emotionally rich, authentic feel-good experience to it. One must be able to step into the vision "as if" one has it and be able to say "Yes!"

b. Second, one must be impeccably honest as to where one is at the present time, at the starting point or anywhere along the path. If I am lazy or careless, I must recognize this and take this into account during the achievement of my vision (otherwise I waste much time in deluding myself.)

c. Third, I need to hold both components, vision and honesty, available to my awareness as I move forward along the path to the goal. I make my decisions relative to these components.

That's it. At some deep level, that is all that is required.

--- Author's Personal Commentary ---

In 1987, I was in a training group and got into a deeply painful place. The facilitator asked me to describe what I was experiencing in metaphor: I felt like I was lying naked in a fetal position, on a bare wooden floor in an empty room without doors or windows. He then asked me to describe what I would rather have: sitting comfortably at a day-retreat center talking with a group of people in a room, with windows looking outwards to trees and water. At the time, I was not able to bridge the two images so the facilitator asked me to explore the initial image, the painful image, each day and add one object of the new image to the painful image, gradually accumulating the objects of the new image into the old. After three months, I was easily able to move from one image to the other.

Several years passed as I continued to work on that vision. After about five years, my life took a new direction and I let go of the possibility of this dream of a day-retreat center. And I moved on. Another five years passed and I was at a dead end, uncertain of what now to do. It was at this time that I bought my present property and set up my current practice, orientated to anger management. Another three years passed and vaguely, on occasion, I had the sense of returning to the dream of 1987.

Then one day, sitting in my office, looking out the window at the trees and the river outside the sliding glass door, I realized that the office room I had created was almost identical to the image I had created in 1987 (and my practice was essentially that of a day-retreat center with my wife.) I had made it happen even thought I had "forgotten" the dream about eight years previously. Such is the power of visioning.

6.2.2. BEING AT PEACE

Within each vision, the path to achieving the goal also has certain characteristics. It is always a balance of what I am able to do and what others are able to do with me. I am not independent (!), ever. When I say "I can do it myself," the "it" is always dependent on something or someone else. "I can do it myself" is often one of the masques of rage.

Suppose I have a simple goal of having lunch with someone so as to get information about a particular subject by questioning that person (see Figure 68.) Before I ask them to have lunch with me, I need to accomplish certain tasks --- check my available money, time, restaurants, etc. This may take a quarter second or three weeks to accomplish. I could ask the other about lunch before these tasks are done; but often it is a waste of energy to ask --- I ask, they make concessions to accommodate me and then I say, "Sorry, I forgot, I'm going to Europe for a few years. Can we have a rain check?" So I do the tasks I need to do. They form what I call my "do-list," the tasks about which I need to be disciplined so as to get on with my life and not have a lot of loose ends hanging (and holding energy.) To do this, I need to be willful of myself --- keep my word, especially to myself.

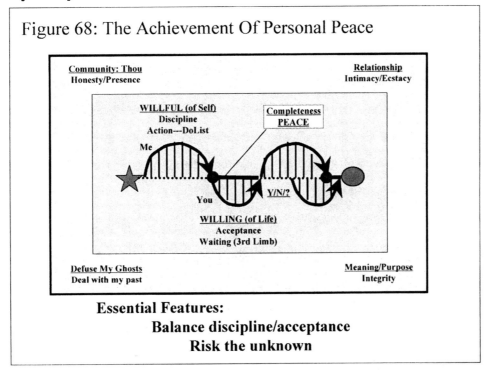

Figure 68: The Achievement Of Personal Peace

Essential Features:
Balance discipline/acceptance
Risk the unknown

Then I ask the other. Now it is their turn. They also have tasks to assess and do --- perhaps it takes them a quarter second or maybe two weeks. The tasks they need to do represent the third limb of my emotional triangle with them. Am I willing to accept the limitations of life, waiting, willing of what life offers (or do I get caught in the third limb, attempting to coerce them to do what I want them to do)? Eventually they answer, "Yes." "No" or "Maybe." "Maybe" doesn't help; at this point I will make two attempts to modify the third limb so as to get my outcome. If unsuccessful, I will assume "No" so as to get on with life. If I have received or assumed "No," then I let go of this goal and evaluate my needs (information and a good meal.) I then find another way to get what I want --- easy if I let go of the third limb. I will have a good meal with someone and perhaps ask someone else of the information I need.

If "Yes," we can move forward to get my goal, Now we both have additional tasks to do (make reservations, get money, drive to restaurant, et cetera), tasks that can now be simultaneous (before the other knew of my invitation, the tasks had to be sequential.) So we both drive to the restaurant, we go in and I get my outcome. My goal has been accomplished.

Certain points on this graph are especially important. If I do my do-list and truly accept my powerlessness as to the third limb, I have completed all of which I am capable in this goal --- I am "complete." And as I await your responses, I am at "peace." Since I keep my do-list small (actively completing tasks) and I only have a small number of goals at any one time, I am thus able to spend a large amount of time at peace. I know of no other practical way to achieve "peace," a state that many people say they seek in their lives.

This is how I achieve it, quite routinely. It requires a balance of action and reflection, risking the unknown, allowing life to be what it is.

6.2.3. STANCES THAT WORK

Part of authenticity is to recognize what stances work. If I am to be in community, be the community a marriage or a business, certain stances are more effective than others. An important truism that connects to maintaining these stances is that "people change and forget to tell each other."

There are three stances that work in my life (see Figure 69.)

- Our issue!

    If a problem is important to one of us, it is important to all of us. We do not exist in isolation and we do influence each other. This is the basis of relationship. We co-exist --- will we support each other in our difficulties? Sometimes this may mean that we require each other to do the hard work associated with our individual issues. This stance is the primary stance. It keep me aware that we are inter-connected and inter-dependent.

Figure 69: Stances That Work

I. Our issue.
        If it is important to one of us,
        it is important to all of us.

II. Not my issue.
        I care; I may be powerless to initiate.
        I am not powerless to respond and care.
        It may be your responsibility to initiate.

III. Authentic powerlessness.
        --- emotional triangles ---

- Not my issue!

   Although I care about your struggles, I have my own struggles. I do not live your struggles, and I do not authentically know what you need. I may be powerless to initiate action because I truly do not know what will be effective for you. In my powerlessness, it may be necessary for you to initiate, to ask me for assistance in specific ways. Mind-reading and assumption become prominent difficulties at this point as we dance with each other, potentially misunderstanding each other. We need to tell each other how we are changing.

- Authentic powerlessness.

   Authentic powerlessness is an underlying strength of emotional triangles (as is authentic power.) Only when I recognize the distinction between "power with" and "power over" will I be able to be authentic in relationship. I can then extend myself in love, clarity and play.

6.3. Complex Issues --- Living My Values

As clients struggle with issues of anger and rage, they often ask about common topics in their attempt to grasp how they create difficulties for themselves. These topics include values and spirituality; romance and marriage; child discipline; and laughter and playfulness. Each topic illustrates the complex relationships between emotional issues and societal factors. In this section, I will comment on the four areas I have mentioned. I realize that whole books could be written on each subject and my comments are not meant be exhaustive. I discuss them in order to point out certain essential ideas or concepts that permeate our collective consciousness and often lead to gross difficulties with our maps. These difficulties have to do with misunderstanding of the dynamics of energy, especially at the level of cultural expectations that fuel the dynamics of energy. I hope to provide guidelines for how to overcome these misunderstandings and lead successful lives.

Before proceeding in depth, I will first provide a brief summary of the four areas to be discussed.

1. Values and Spirituality. What is the nature of spirituality and how is it different from religion? What makes belief systems more important for most people than value systems? How are values and spirituality connected? For me, successful living requires living my values in a way that generates meaning for me.

2. Romance and Marriage. What is romance? What makes for an effective long-term relationship, especially a marriage? What has happened that our divorce rate is so high? Similar to values and spirituality, successful

living for me requires living my values in a way that generates authentic relationship with my partner.

3. Child Discipline. What is effective Child Discipline? How has it become a major problem for most parents? Again, successful living for me requires living my values in a way that allows happy, compassionate and productive future generations.

4. Laughter and Playfulness. We probably have as many societal rules about laughter as we do about anger and rage. How did we get to be so serious as a culture? Successful living here requires living my values in a way that generates joy for me.

In this section, I will often ask the question "How?" and "What?" instead of "Why?" Please note that "How?" and "What?" seek to understand the processes that have generated the outcomes (and perhaps the underlying mechanisms.) "Why?" asks for an explanation. All three words often overlap in their content somewhat but there is a very different focus to each. For example, "How did I go to the store this morning?" "I got in my car, made sure it had enough gas, started the ignition, put the car in reverse, backed out of the driveway, then put it in forward, ..." This answer is different from "Why did I go to the store?" "To get a loaf of bread." and "What method did I use to choose that loaf of bread?" "I smelled it for freshness and squeezed it gently to assess its softness."

Generally the questions "How?" and "What?" give the opportunity to explore what could have been done differently in an action so as to get the same outcome. "Why?" usually gives an explanation of what the purpose was for the action, but comes with two deficits.

The first deficit of "Why?" is that the basic end-point is not an intellectual end-point --- it is when you are satisfied emotionally with the answer and stop asking the question. In other words, when does the answer feel good and hence satisfy you? To illustrate, at what point are you satisfied with the answer "To get a loaf of bread." You could continue asking "Why?" indefinitely. "Why did you need a loaf of bread?" "Because we had no bread in the house." "Why did you have no bread in the house?" "Because …" Like a two-year-old, you can get into an endless series of questions if desired. The second deficit of "Why?" is that the answer usually does not contain information about what can be changed in a current action so as to achieve the desired outcome in other ways. For many people, "Why?" can become either an excuse when the desired outcome is not obtained ("I didn't succeed because …") or an avoidance of one's powerlessness ("Why did that happen? It's not fair!")

6.3.1. VALUE SYSTEMS AND SPIRITUALITY

Many of my clients struggle with finding a sense of meaning or purpose in life. For some, it is a profound dilemma. Traditionally, religion has attempted to provide answers to this dilemma. There are many religions in the world. They range from a belief in God (theistic religions) to the belief that no God exists (atheism.) For the most part, theistic religions have originated from the works of one individual (Christ, Mohammed, Buddha, etc.) These were individuals who had profound mystical experiences and were in turn able to influence other people to follow truths adapted from their mystical experiences. Over time, these truths became codified as "faith traditions" and were called religions. In essence, religions are belief systems that give meaning to life. Generally, they include a sense of ethics. The ethics are often very appropriate. but are usually tied to and lost within the proscribed beliefs. This is because religious concepts are often vaguely defined and represent sloppy language. They are thus potentially troublesome.

For a significant portion of the population, the power of religion has waned in the past hundred years or so. If I ask the vast majority of my clients if they are religious, they answer: "No"; if I ask them if they are spiritual, the answer is usually: "Yes." Yet seldom are they able to give me a statement of clarity as to what spirituality means to them. They talk vaguely about believing in a higher power and attempt to define an underlying experience of life, not just a belief system. But they do not attribute specific characteristics to this higher power. In other circumstances, religious concepts have become rigidly dogmatic in recent years, as in the case of the Religious Right in the United States that has developed immense power in today's society. It is power that is based heavily on the imposition of belief systems and value systems on others and is therefore a third-limb problem. Such rigid thinking is again very much a source of potential conflict due to sloppy language.

What has been the mechanism by which religious and spiritual belief systems have propagated? My best guess is that we do not like "not knowing" --- it is a form of powerlessness. When the "not knowing" is about the nature of the universe, the meaning of life and the ultimate questions (such as "What is death?"), this sense of powerlessness is very strong. Because we want certainty, which we do not have, even when we claim we do, we take on belief systems to stabilize our energy. In Chapter One, I explored beliefs as the underlying mechanisms that provide energy to our emotionality. Here, I suggest that beliefs also provide equilibrium in the uncertainty of life, especially when those beliefs come from highly charismatic individuals. The belief systems of religions seem to guarantee passage through this life in a meaningful and predictable manner. Even science has not offered a meaningful way of coming to terms with the inequities and pain of life. The conflict between science and religion has largely been about the "irrationality of belief." For the most part, twentieth-century science has offered "meaninglessness" as belief. This is not nearly as satisfying as "faith."

Is there a way out of this discordance between the struggle for meaning and the imposition of belief systems? I believe there is --- if we truly recognize how we function as human beings. I suggest that the development of the skills of the subjective underlie the nature of spirituality. These skills clarify three dimensions of the nature of spirituality: experience of mystery, belief systems and value systems (see Figure 70.) Earlier portions of this book have dealt with the first two of these: my own profound mystical experiences (see Chapter Five for details) and the subtleties of belief systems and how they influence our lives. The work of John Fowler[8] suggests the third dimension. He proposes that human beings have a hierarchical staging of faith development that is expressed by an evolving "locus of authority" and a "value system." "Locus of authority" answers the question "To what do I ascribe authority? Do I go outwards to the experiences of others or do I go inward to my own truthfulness?" Fowler's exploration of faith development suggests that as human beings become more mature, have greater wisdom and greater personal power ("power with", not "power over"), their locus of authority moves inwards and they become both more centered in their own personal value systems and more authentically compassionate towards others in their struggles. In other words, they move towards greater subjectivity. Persons such as Gandhi and Martin Luther King Jr. are obvious examples of such individuals; many others are less obvious.

Because of the multi-dimensional nature of spirituality, someone can be intensely religious and yet utterly caught in its belief system. Or someone can have a profound mystical experience without the framework of a belief system. However, certain correlations appear to be reliable. Typically, the more profound the mystical experience, the greater the development of a complex value system and the more the locus of authority moves inward. In extreme cases, other people in relationship with these mystics may become impressed with their leader's subjective wisdom --- hence religious movements are born. With or without profound mystical experiences, as people mature in their value systems, they

---

8. Fowler, John. Stages of Faith: The Psychology of Human Development and The Quest For Meaning. New York: HarperCollins, 1981.

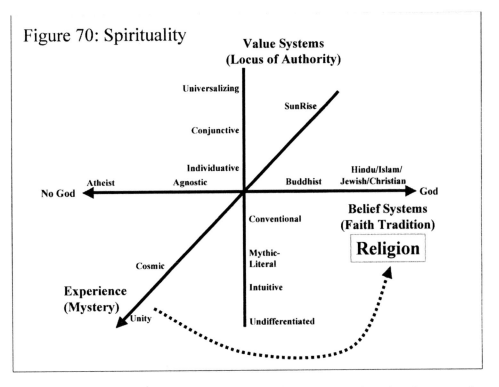

Figure 70: Spirituality

are generally more likely to develop an internal locus of authority, moving away from external belief systems and towards self-authority. As they further develop, they often become more compassionate and more accepting of difference in other people. They become more ecumenical and more religious in the sense that they recognize the complexity and mystery of the universe; their belief systems evolve to include the paradoxes of mystery. Mature individuals are able to live their own truths without the need to impose "truth" on others. They come to value subjectivity as the way to live more fully and freely.

6.3.1.1. WHAT IS FREEDOM?

In *Webster's New World Dictionary*[9], the definitions of the words "freedom" and "free" take up almost half a page of very fine print. The essence of their meaning seems to be "the absence of hindrance." In general, I do not like definitions that function by exclusion --- they do not open up possibility and wonder. So, what are the possibilities here for the words "freedom" and "free?" In my experience, they both have to do with choice. To explain further, let me

---

9. Webster's New World Dictionary, College edition. Toronto: Nelson, Foster, Scott Ltd, 1959

start with a basic assumption. Quite aside from religious belief systems, either there is a God or there isn't. If there isn't a God or a central intelligence to the universe, then somehow the universe is meaningless. In other words, the ultimate outcome of my actions has no meaning and everything that happens is at some level ultimately explainable, or, for lack of a better term, rational (even if it is beyond our intelligence.) In this case, I still have choice. I can choose to give meaning to my life, knowing that it is meaningless. I can function in a way that is authentic for who I want to be. Alternatively if there is a God or the universe has a central intelligence, it presumably has a purpose. The question then becomes "Is this purpose friendly to me or not?" If it is not friendly, then I am "fodder" in some fashion to this unfriendly God. Yet even here I still have choice. I can still function in a way that is authentic for who I want to be.

The interesting option for choice is when we consider the universe to be friendly and that ultimately "all manner of things shall be well" (even if it is beyond our intelligence to see how.) If the universe is friendly, what then is the purpose of this entire struggle of human existence and the pain of living? For lack of a better explanation, I see that the purpose of living is to grow a soul. This appears to me as the journey of coming to terms with what life offers in its authenticity. To use a metaphor, if you want to grow beautiful roses, first you plant them in manure, prune them over a few weeks time and then you wait until you get beautiful roses. Nobody ever said that the roses had to like it. In our case, life does not always or even often offer what we want; within the presupposition that the universe is "friendly," it offers what we need. From my readings, it appears that truly mature individuals of the world all accept the proposition that the universe is friendly. They don't believe it. They know it.

So does this presumably friendly universe offer us choice or are our lives predetermined? To what extent are we free? This has been a perennial and unanswerable question for centuries. I suggest that both the question and the answer are immaterial. "Freedom" as "the absence of hindrance" is never the case. There are always hindrances. Instead, I suggest that "freedom" is "the ability to influence myself." It is the ability to shift my attitude concerning any hindrances that I face. In other words, while I still have little choice as to what life offers, I can however choose how I respond. With the development of my personal skills and maturity as a human being, I can increase that ability to choose. It is optional.

Regardless of whether or not God exists, life appears to operate on four fundamental principles that guide our ability to choose[10] (see Figure 71.) I call these principles the "moral imperatives" of the universe.

Figure 71: Moral Imperatives

Community: everything is in relationship with everything else.

Diversity: everything is different.

Subjectivity: internality increases.

Change: everything changes.

- Community: everything exists in relationship to everything else (no one thing is of greatest value in the universe; it is always relative);

- Diversity: everything is different from everything else;

- Subjectivity: the more differentiated the manifestation of an organism (atom, molecule, rock, bacteria, tree, dog, child, human…), the more internal a sense of subjectivity and the greater a sense of possible internal locus of authority; and

- Change: everything is always in the process of flux.

---

10. I have adapted these ideas from the general writings of Thomas Berry and Brian Swimme. I suggest the book The Universe Story by Brian Swimme (Harper, 1992) as a starting point for further reading.

My contention is that if, in choosing amongst options, one or more of these principles is breached, a violation has occurred. For example, when I intentionally restrict your freedom without permission, I am going against all of these principles. Say I lock you in your house without your permission, I restrict your community (you cannot go out), I restrict your diversity (you are limited in your activities), I restrict your locus of authority (I am the authority unless you fight me) and I restrict your ability to change (you have to deal with me in some fashion before other options in life become available to you.)

On the other hand, any process or choice in keeping with all of these four principles is within the "moral imperative" of the universe. If I live within these moral imperatives, I am able to create a vision of who I want to be, not as an end-point ("When I grow up, I want to be a ...") but as a presently-lived value system of how I want to be at any one time. When I frame my life this way, I come back to my core moralities of:

1. aging gracefully,

2. striving for authenticity,

3. being a midwife,

4. being in community,

5. being my word, and

6. celebrating life.

Can we live in a world without violation? If we manage our energy and manage our subjectivity, I believe that we can. There would still be conflict, but it would be managed cooperatively.

6.3.2. ROMANCE AND MARRIAGE

The definition of conflict is "difference in a closed space." The major areas of conflict for most people are in their closest relationships; and the most important closed spaces are immediate family, extended family and work relationships. How are these the areas of life where we have the most conflict? What contributes to them as places of conflict other than simple proximity? This section will explore romance and marriage and use it as an example of what underlies conflict in many cases of people's closest relationships.

I invite the reader to consider his or her own major sexual relationships in life. What was so attractive about the other person in the beginning? More specifically, did you "fall in love" with your partner as the basis of the relationship? Falling in love, or romance, is the foundation of marriage in most of the Western world today. Does that relationship still exist? If so, what happened to it over time? Likely the relationship changed drastically if you are typical of our culture. How did this change occur? What evolution did the relationship undergo? How? What are the mechanisms whereby the relationship changed? Asiatic countries still have the concept of arranged marriage as the principal mechanism of family perpetuation. It is the cultural norm. Two years ago, I was in India for three weeks. While I was there, I talked to three Indian men, each about thirty years old, who had just returned from Canada to get married. The date was set for two months from the current day. They did not know who they were going to marry --- their families were arranging it. But even in India, the tradition of arranged marriages is waning with the developing global village. It too is changing to romance as the basis of marriage.

6.3.2.1. THE NATURE OF ROMANCE

What is romance exactly? And for how long has it been the model of marriage in our Western culture? My best definition of romance is "lust with potential.". We marry to meet our deepest needs, yet we do not know how to identify them. Romance honors the rights of individuals to have choice; and, in this sense, it is an important principle in our culture. Romance as the basis of marriage has been the model for approximately two hundred years --- this makes sense to me in that the rise of the cult of individualism has only been around for four hundred years.

So what actually is the mechanism of "lust with potential"? My best understanding here comes from Harville Hendix[11] (see Figure 72.) Basically, it starts in utero. Before birth, the fetus essentially exists in a state of perfection --- everything is provided (ideally) and its brain is undifferentiated from the source of provision. Then the baby is born into a family. It is an energy transformer and is designed to copy its family members. This forms the basis of the metaphor of Sailors On A Ship discussed earlier in the book (see Sections 2.1.2.1. and 2.1.2.2.) To the newborn brain, whether the energy it copies is positive or negative does not matter --- this is an adult distinction. From that positive or negative energy, the newborn will develop an image of perfection deep within its emotional brain, an "imago" of how life should be at the energetic level. This imago will be important in later life.

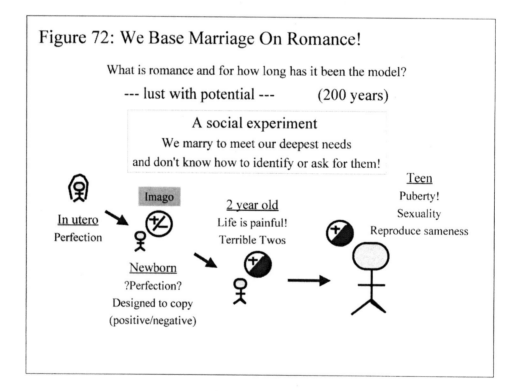

Figure 72: We Base Marriage On Romance!

Around the age of two, when the baby is a toddler who is entering the "terrible twos," he or she starts to distinguish self from other and positive from negative.

He or she is learning that some aspects of life are good and others are painful. He or she may also learn that some of the energy hurts, such as being beaten for disobedience. But that toddler has little power to change his or her world; he or she does however have the power to repress his or her experience. Figuratively, the toddler puts on "horse blinders" and emotionally hides from the pain. When the toddler becomes a child, he or she copies the behaviors of others and also learns his or her own patterns of coping with the difficulties of life. He or she may take on the role of the "good student," the "great hockey player," the "pretty ballerina" or the "street bully," whatever works in his or her family.

Around puberty, the child's imago of perfection that it has been carrying with it since birth (with its developing distortions as the child has grown up) becomes hooked into sexuality. Biologically, the function of sexuality is to reproduce the sameness of the species (with minor variation.) Human sexuality is designed to reproduce the same emotional field of the early childhood experience, both its positives and negatives, especially the powerful energy of the imago that imprinted itself on the newborn's developing brain. (For reasons that I hope will become obvious, I will now switch to using male gender language in my description of the mechanism of "lust with potential[12].") When the child becomes a teenager (or even later as an adult), he may walk around the mall, talking to his friends, looking at the stores, when suddenly out of the corner of his eye, he sees "Perfection!" There could be many beautiful women in the mall that day but he will focus on one woman only, based on his imago of perfection. It may come across as how she tilts her head, her voice tone, the shape of her hip or many other subtle features whereby he says to himself "Wow!" Then, his energy aroused, he may wander over (like a penguin) to where the woman is standing and somehow manage to say "Helloooo." She may reply, "Take a hike, turkey!" His energy rapidly deflated, he sneaks back into his shell. Later, someone else gets his attention, with perhaps the same scenario ensuing. Eventually, the man finds someone with whom he also matches her imago of perfection and who says (perhaps to herself), "Ooooh, interesting." They begin to spin an energy together.

If all goes well, if the energies of the two teenagers or adults match, the energy intensifies and they "fall in love." They say (at least silently to themselves), "Wow. Look at all those positives. I have found my soul mate!" They continue to spin the energy. They may have a few fights along the way, but deep down they still feel that "nobody else understands me in the same way." They are "in love." The couple decides to marry and plans to spend the rest of their lives together (sometimes even in the face of negative comments from parents or friends.) Happily ever after should follow from there.

6.3.2.2. THE TRAP OF ROMANCE

As we all know, "Happily ever after" doesn't really exist. How does it happen that we inevitably get into significant difficulties and conflicts with the person who is supposed to be our "soul mate"? What is the nature of romance that we now have a divorce rate that hovers around fifty to sixty percent and has done so for the past thirty-something years? The difficulties of romance are actually quite predictable (see Figure 73.) They are built into the nature of the imago. We are attracted to our partners not only by their positives but also because of their negatives. Consciously we do not see their negatives; they do however remind us of the emotional fields of our childhoods, especially the painful parts that we were unable to deal with as children. Like moths to a flame, we are attracted. (And you know what happens to moths. They get burned!)

So we marry and for a few years, we experience a honeymoon period. Then the differences between us start to emerge, especially the differences that remind us of the pain we want to avoid: "Yes, I know she is a wonderful woman but there are a few negatives too." Presumably, she is saying the same thing to herself about him. After about five to seven years, we realize we are fighting a lot. We are into what is called the Power Struggle. The Power Struggle occurs as we find

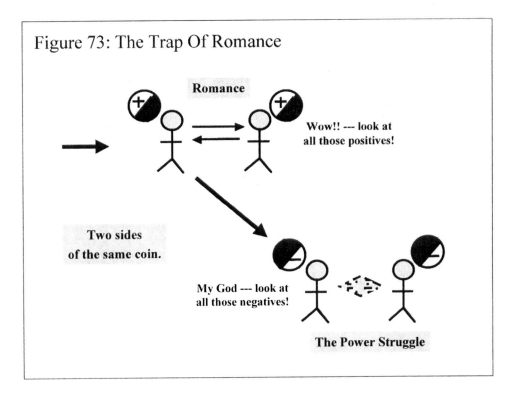

Figure 73: The Trap Of Romance

Romance

Wow!! --- look at all those positives!

Two sides of the same coin.

My God --- look at all those negatives!

The Power Struggle

it more and more difficult to avoid being aware of each other's negatives: "I'm right. You're wrong." It is easier to see the negatives outside of ourselves than to be aware of the pain inside of ourselves. The Romance and the Power Struggle are two sides of the same coin. The intensity of the Romance may well be an indicator of the intensity of the Power Struggle.

If we are unable to negotiate our differences, the relationship degenerates: "D--n it, who is this b---- I married?" She likely has her own expressive description of him. At this point, one of us may have an affair or breach some other major commitment of the relationship. We separate and eventually divorce: "It's hard on the kids but what else can you do? The relationship isn't working anymore." Then we move on into another relationship, believing that the pain we feel inside won't occur with a new partner: "It won't happen again." It does. If perhaps we don't divorce (and stay together because of the kids, for instance), then the relationship may be dead and we fight a lot. In either case, in trying to solve our difficulties inappropriately, romance becomes a trap.

6.3.2.3. THE INVITATION OF ROMANCE

There is a positive and meaningful side to the trap of romance. It is an opportunity for us to really learn about ourselves; it is an invitation to growth. If we really want to know about ourselves, we need to pay attention to two sources of information in our closest relationships. First, because it is easier to see the negatives (of our imagos) in our partners than it is in ourselves, when we are about to criticize our partner, we need to remind ourselves of the Pointing Finger and the fingers pointing back to us. For what is it that makes the imperfections of our partners so painful and frustrating to us and not to others who also experience them? Our Ghosts, of course. Certainly there are aspects of our partners that are immature, aggressive, etc. The same is true of all human beings. But usually these aren't so bad that we can't work around them. What we really find hard to live with is being in closed relationships with our partners where we generally cannot hide from our Ghosts. The second source of information that shows us who we really are comes from any faults that our partners complain about in us from their perspective. Although they have their own imagos and are responding from their own pain, it likely identifies the parts of us from which we both want to hide. In other words, their "Pointing Fingers" still point at us. Corresponding sources of information are available to our partners as well.

As I said above, in spite of the pain engendered by the mechanism of romance, it is also an invitation (see Figure 74.) We may marry at twenty or thirty years old and live to be eighty or ninety. To my knowledge, our emotional brains were not designed for such long-term relationships. So how do we live them? Our invitation is exactly this, i.e. to explore how in our modern-day society. First, because we have choice, we may choose not to grow in emotional maturity. In this case, we will create the same positives and negatives we have always created in each and every one of our close relationships. For some, serial monogamy is the route they take to avoid growth. For others, it is bitterness.

---

11. Hendrix, Harville. Getting The Love You Want. New York: Holt, 1988

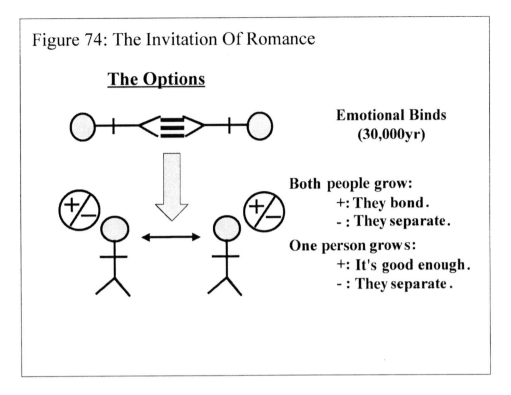

Figure 74: The Invitation Of Romance

The Options

Emotional Binds
(30,000yr)

Both people grow:
  +: They bond.
  - : They separate.
One person grows:
  +: It's good enough.
  - : They separate.

Alternatively, if both partners choose to grow, perhaps they can reach a place where they are able to say to each other: "Wow. You are a neat person. You're not perfect; nor am I." They recognize that they are different from each other and that, yes, they do have their conflicts. But the conflicts are not the relationship, and they now have or will learn the skills of dealing with the conflicts more effectively: "So let's hang out together and have a good life. Let's support each other." The flip side is that one of the partners might end the relationship in a mature fashion: "You know, it's sad. I got attracted to your negatives, not your positives. You're a neat person but now that I have some awareness, there is no passion left in our relationship. I don't want to spend my life just tolerating you. It is time to move on." Potentially, the former partners could be friends or, if children are involved in the break-up, at least both invested in the growth of their kids rather than in constantly fighting with each other. My guess is that of these two growth scenarios, the first one is more likely --- we are all a mixed bag of positives and negatives. And, for the most part, the positives outweigh the negatives when the issues aren't clouded by our Ghosts.

There are third and fourth options that arise when exploring how to live in long-term relationships. These occur when only one of the partners chooses to mature and do the necessary growth work. In the third option, the person who grows may reach a point of saying: "The marriage is good enough. Sure, my partner is crazy (as am I), and I've learned how to respond so that I am no longer trapped. It would cost too much to leave the relationship, and it would hurt the kids too much. Anyway, I was mainly attracted to her positives and they are still there." In the fourth scenario, the partner who grows may decide to leave the relationship: "No, I don't want to waste my life this way. Sure I can tolerate my partner but this is not how I want to live my life. Its time to leave." (It may also happen that the other partner chooses to leave because the partner who grows has changed so much.) My guess is that the fourth scenario would be the more common of the above two. Likely the break-up will have much bitterness and conflict. In the next relationship though, having done some growth work, the partner who chooses to mature is more likely to become involved with someone who is also invested in growing.

6.3.2.4. THE RULES HAVE CHANGED --- SLIGHTLY

In addition to the above difficulties of romance, the traditional rules of how to be in marriage have changed --- slightly! (see Figure 75.) Up until the 1940s or so, the traditional rules stated that we married to create a family. The family was important; the individual less so. The men raised the money, and the women raised the children. Women were property and expected to risk their lives in childbirth and later to protect the children; men were expected to die if necessary to protect their property of women and children, especially in war. There was little or no divorce in these days (ideally.) Love was less conditional then. If the man wanted sex, he would go and find a mistress. Women were not supposed to be overtly sexual.

---

12. As a side-comment, please note that I am heterosexual and so I will use cross-gender language when discussing human sexual relationships --- it is not however my intention to offend any other type of gender relationship.

Figure 75: The Rules Have Changed

STAGE 1 (1940s)	STAGE 2 (1990s)
Survival	**Fulfillment**
Role mates: whole	Soul mates --- synergy
Division of roles	**Commonality of roles**
Women---children	
Men---money	
Risks	**Risks?**
Women---childbirth	no danger!
Men---war	no war!
No Divorce	**Leave if unhappy**
Women---property	
Men---die (less than property)	
"Love"	**"Love"**
Dependence	Fulfillment
Less conditional	More conditional

Modified from Farrell, The Myth of Male Power

Now in the twenty-first century, the traditional rules of marriage have changed. We now want and expect personal fulfillment for both genders. The roles of man and woman are less defined. The risks are supposed to be less. And if one of us is unhappy, we may leave the relationship and start again (usually at a high cost.) The aim of these changes was to bring an improvement to our marital relationships. The problem is that the rules have changed only slightly. The old model of the 1940s was based on the premise that men need to be successful (in order to get the beautiful woman) and women need to be beautiful (in order to get the successful man.) The new model espouses not beauty and success but maturity in relationship skills and the management of energy as key to successful relationships. Yet the old model persists. Go to your local grocery store and examine the magazines at the checkout counter. They show that the dominant model for women in our culture is still beauty. Go to your local video store and watch the action movies. They show that the dominant model for men is still to take out the enemy. These are not models of maturity. They are models of energy: generate sexual attractiveness to get a mate, either by beauty or by success. In many respects the energy of beauty and success is exciting, but it is not a recipe for successful relationships in the twenty-first century.

6.3.2.5. THE NATURE OF EFFECTIVE RELATIONSHIP

Given the trap of romance and only the slight changes to the traditional rules of marriage in our culture, how then exactly are we to be in effective relationship in the twenty-first century? Marriage for me is a special type of relationship. In our culture, it is one that begins with romance and later (hopefully) changes to one in which I have the long-term opportunity to learn about myself. It encourages my ability to give love as a gift to extend myself for my partner's growth and to receive love as a gift. Much work is required in the marital relationship (and occasional delightful fun occurs!) My strong conviction (my truthfulness) after several long-term relationships is that two major commitments are necessary for me to sustain a long-term committed marital relationship.

The first commitment for me to be in effective relationship is to develop and live a value system that is congruent with who I am. The skills of living a value system have been explored earlier. I first need a Captain and then I need a value system. My value system needs to be simple enough that I am committed to it. if it is too complex, requiring constant effort, then I become confused and ineffective. In addition, to be in a successful marital relationship, both myself and my partner need to achieve clarity as to what we want and do the work (and fun) to achieve our goals. It also necessitates that both myself and my partner communicate our values to each other. I cannot know what the other person wants! It is the responsibility of my partner to define and then let me know what are her values. My component is to stay present, authentically, while the other person clarifies what she wants and lets me know how I can be a resource. I can however know what I want. And it is my responsibility to define and communicate them to my partner.

For myself, I have six values that I know need to be met in order for me to remain fully engaged in my marital relationship.

- Honesty. I will not remain in relationship with someone who is dishonest and wants to avoid the truths of living.

- Common vision. My partner and I need to have a vision that engages both of us, a vision that allows each of us our uniqueness but which draws us both forward in relationship.

- Conflict resolution by problem solving. I am not interested in psychological games or repetitive patterns without resolution. (Resolution means to be at peace with a difficulty; solution means the problem has gone away.)

- Satisfying sexuality. I am a sexual being. At some deep level, it is both a sensual and a spiritual experience.

- Sensuality. Richness of sensory experience is very important to me.

- Health. I want good food and enough activity (exercise) in my life for me to remain physically fit.

I do not require my partner to accomplish these values for me; I do require that we co-create them. Because wants vary from individual to individual, and some wants are more important than others, meeting my wants in my marital relationship is my responsibility, not the responsibility of partner. However, it is a relationship and many wants require a dynamic interaction between the players. If I do not get my important wants met (in the long term), there is a very real risk that I will not stay in the relationship, leaving either emotionally or physically. In this regard, I especially need specificity in my value system so as to be committed to remaining in relationship with my partner. I need to know when I am living my values, and when I am not. If my values are being met in the long-term, I am committed to being in the relationship regardless of any current difficulties. I am thus committed to living my values with my partner; I am not committed to my partner.

6.3.2.5.1. Gift-Giving Versus Transactions For Payment

The first commitment for me to be in effective long-term relationship is to live my life as much as possible as "Gift" (see Figure 76.) The alternative to gift-giving is to live my life as a transaction for payment. Both stances are necessary in life but can be kept quite separate. For me, a gift requires no payment, not even a thank you, whereas transactions for payment set up an exchange between myself and someone else. Transactions are a part of life. I work and I get paid. And I need resources to sustain myself in what I do. If I do not get paid, I risk resentment. For the most part, I try to avoid resentment in my life by ensuring that the systems with which I set up transactions for payment are healthy and open systems.

Figure 76: Gift Giving

Gifts vs Transactions For Payment

I can only do two things with others:

a. I can do something for which I expect reciprocity
(a transaction for payment.)
I resent when I don't get paid!

b. I can give them a gift of my time or my energy.
A gift has no price tag, absolutely none,
not even a thank you!
Yet I gain merit (personal value) from gift-giving
(part of the paradox of life!)

Keeping these two actions separate
is absolutely essential.

In my marital relationship, however, I live from the stance of gift-giving: "Your needs are more important than mine in the short-term; in the long-term, my needs are more important." This means that I will bend over backwards to support my partner (assuming that what my partner needs adds to her growth.) Sometimes I do this even when I know my actions will simply add to her comfort (and not challenge her growth.) Because I am not in relationship to make my partner grow --- I am in relationship to challenge my own growth; I do many things that support my partner and the relationship even though they are inconvenient to me. I do these things without expectation, simply because I "want" to. Therefore I do them as "Gift." The beauty of gift-giving is that the other person usually then wants to return a gift. (It is possible for my partner to perceive this return action as a payment but for me I simply accept the action as a gift.) It then becomes possible for both of us to live our relationship as "Gift." Paradoxically, I get my long-term needs met by living my life in this way. It takes effort yet it is highly rewarding.

6.3.3. CHILD DISCIPLINE

Living with children also takes much effort and is potentially highly rewarding. Children are our resources, both for the future and for many of the skills we have lost. They often have incredible wisdom to offer (if we will listen to them.) Yet when I talk with parents (especially parents of teenagers), the problems of disciplining children are major.

With our modern-day valuing of the individual's self-worth, we have (ideally) given up such practices as child labor and violent disciplinary actions when children are disobedient. Yet how have we created so much turmoil in raising our children in our current society, especially in our difficulties with teenagers? Some of the problems are not new. One of my mentors Edwin Friedman used to talk about a Sumerian tablet from 4000 BCE that started with the phrase "I do not know what the current generation of young people will come to ...." However, the writings of authors such as Ron Taffel[13] reveal a tremendously different teen and childhood culture than in previous generations. Quite aside from the horrendous violations that still occur to children such as sexual abuse and pornography, the use of drugs is rampant; early sexual experience is commonplace; and teens often engage in highly violent activities without adult supervision.

---

13. Ron Taffel, The Second Family: Dealing with Peer Power, Pop Culture, the Wall of Silence -- and Other Challenges of Raising Today's Teens (New York: St. Martin's Press, 2001).

How have these changes come about? For one, our younger generations are the first ever to be constantly exposed to new technologies such as television and the internet. Our children are made aware of an incredible diversity of values, both at school and via the media. In some respects they are much more sophisticated than their corresponding adult caregivers; yet younger generations lack experience in sexuality, drugs and violence which they see on television (and which, according to Taffel, they soon seek out.) Our younger generations are also the first ever to be stratified by age and peer group. In previous generations, children were brought up mainly by their extended family. Now, two-year-olds spend a major part of their day playing with other two-year-olds at day care, while four-year-olds across the country watch the same programs on television.

6.3.3.1. CHILD DISCIPLINE --- ADULT CONSISTENCY

Certain principles of living with children are mandatory. Adults have more life experience (and more disillusionment); children have more flexibility (and more hope and playfulness.) Children have a right to be heard; adults have a responsibility to have clarity and generally be consistent. Families are not democracies; there is a power difference between adults and children. Just as Sailors on a Ship require a Captain for direction and guidance, children require adults to provide appropriate safety, energy and choice.

What then is child discipline? It used to be telling the child how to behave and expecting the child to do so: "Children should be seen and not heard." Discipline if necessary often meant slapping the child or punishing him or her by isolation. It was an acceptable form of practice (then) and a model consistent with the 1940s. Society usually turned a blind eye to the minor and not so minor violations, both from parents and children. Now, in the twenty-first century, corporeal punishment is no longer acceptable. We have the problem of how to control the behaviors of a child in a way that others will perceive as a reasonable manner. This is inherently a third-limb problem in many ways, both to "control" a child and accommodate to the expectations of others. In combination with other stressors such as two-income families and the false promises of television and other advertising, the likelihood of being able to control children is next to impossible if we remain others-oriented in our discipline.

In addition, conflicts between parents and teens are now often major power struggles. Many teenagers (and younger children) are willing to phone "911" to report their parents to the police if the "discipline" is too intense. Sometimes a true violation has occurred. Sometimes it hasn't. Like all power struggles, those that go on between parents and teens are energy struggles and subject to the Laws of Energy as well as the Laws of Emotional Triangles. If the parent's or child's attempt to control the other is beyond the boundaries of "public safety," it is truly likely that a violation was both intended and initiated.

The secret of child discipline is hidden in these Laws of Energy and Laws of Emotional Triangles. Parents are not responsible for their children (they do not have the power to make them respond); rather, they are accountable for their children's safety and the consequences of their actions on others. Thus, child discipline is NOT disciplining the child; it is disciplining the adult to provide safety, emotional consistency and age-appropriate choices for the child (see Figure 77.) The best writings I know of in this subject area are those of Dr. Thomas Phelan[14] and Barbara Colorosa[15]. (I recommend them highly.) For the purposes of this discussion, I want to focus in their writings on the topics of the emotional dynamics of safety, energy and choice. These three things provide the major keys in the skill of being disciplined in managing your children.

First and foremost, children need safety. Safety does not mean restricting the choices of a child completely or telling him or her exactly what to do all of the time. Safety refers to creating a boundary where the child can be safe. As a parent, you therefore give the child something to do rather than something not to do: "You can play or explore within these parameters but outside of this area it

14. See Thomas W. Phelan, 1-2-3 Magic: Effective Discipline for Children 2-12 (Glen Ellyn, Illinois: Child Management, 1996) and Surviving Your Adolescents: How to Manage and Let Go of Your 13-18 Year Olds (2nd ed.) (Glen Ellyn, Illinois: Child Management, 1998).

15. See Barbara Colorosa, Kids Are Worth It: Giving Your Child the Gift of Inner Discipline (rev. ed.) (New York: HarperCollins, 2002).

Figure 77: Some Presuppositions Of Child Discipline

1. **You and your child/teen do not inhabit the same world.**

2. **You (the adult/parent) and your child/teen both operate with fundamental needs (in order of priority):**
   1. **Safety**
   2. **Energy**
   3. **Choice**

3. **Child Discipline is discipline of the adult/parent to provide safety, energy (consistency) and appropriate choice for the child/teen.**

---

is not safe." In this sense, the parent's restriction of the child's freedom without his or his permission is not a violation because it is in the interest of the child's safety. Once safety is established, the parent's next job is to establish consistent boundaries of safety. Difficulty ensues when the parent is inconsistent in the issue of safety or when he or she willfully restricts the child's freedom simply as punishment. Problems also occur when parents constantly tell their children what to do (in the name of safety) and do not allow them to experiment with energy and choice.

Second, children want energy. This concept is the basis of a book by Dr. Thomas Phelan called *1-2-3 Magic*. In this situation, the parent needs consistency in his or her management of energy so that the child knows what to expect and when. To illustrate, if you want a child to start something positive (for example, to help around the house), you give lots of positives as early in the life of the child as possible. These are not rewards per se but are meant to satisfy the needs of relationship: praise, respect, caring, authentic teaching, etc. The child will then repeat the behaviors because they generate desirable positive energy. Starting to give a teenager positives when he or she is fourteen where previously there was lots of criticism is not likely to make much difference. If you want the child to stop behaviors, restrict the energy given to them. This is done by time-outs and minimal explanations. It also means speaking to the child in a quiet respectful voice whenever giving an explanation of his or her desired behavior. Over-explaining or yelling simply gives the child a negative energy reward to continue the behavior --- it is a double message. The verbal message says "Stop"; the non-verbal says energy is available if you continue. (And remember that negative energy is better than no energy at all.)

The third need of children is choice. This concept is the basis of the work of Barbara Colorosa. She provides examples of consistent age-appropriate choices that parents can give their children, so that the energy exchange between parent and child stays at a level of natural and expected consequences consistent with the behavior of the child (further explanation below.) For example, if the child wants to play in the rain without a raincoat, he or she is allowed to do so. However, the child soon learns that "wet" has some discomfort associated with it. If the child is asked to put out the garbage before supper, he or she has the choice of whether or not to do so. However, the child realizes that supper is not on the table until the garbage is put out.

6.3.3.2. THE PURPOSE OF CONSEQUENCES

Consequences have a purpose. Children (and adults) learn from them (see Figure 78.) Consequences come in three different forms:

a. natural consequences (if you walk without protection in the rain, you will get wet --- it is predictable);

b. expected consequences (if you steal my wallet, it is predictable that I will get angry so don't be surprised when I do); or

c. punishment (consequences in excess of the expected.)

Figure 78: Consequences (i)

Natural consequences
absolutely predictable
- natural laws -

Expected consequences
very likely to happen
- predictable human responses -

Punishment
3rd limb of the triangle
- I'll make you do it! -

**Consequences determine what I do --- they are energy rewards.
The human brain learns from information (emotional information!)
Choice can be shifted by emotional information.**

**The emotional brain learns from consequences.
Energy can be shifted with consequences.**

Ideally, consequences teach children experientially what can be expected from a given behavior. Punishment, on the other hand, teaches fear --- the child learns that he or she is "bad" or needs to be sneaky about the behavior rather than that the behavior is inappropriate. As part of the parent's discipline, when teaching consequences to the child, these need to be livable for the parent too (see Figure 79.) For example, if your child wants to use the car and never returns it with a full tank of gas, do not ground him or her for a month --- how would you feel being at home with him or her for all that time? Instead, ask your child for money as a down payment which will be returned if the car comes back with a full tank of gas. No money; no car. This way, you are in charge of your own energy and your own choices. Fundamentally, effective child discipline comes down to the parent's management of his or her personal energy.

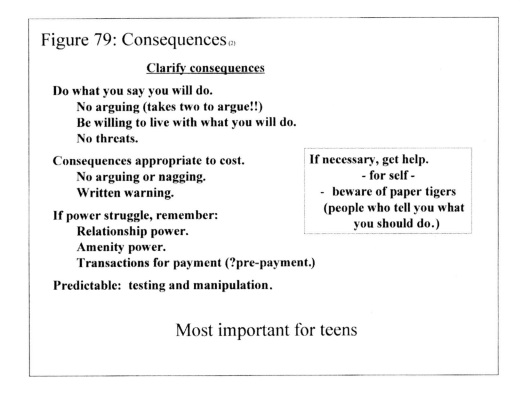

Figure 79: Consequences (2)

Clarify consequences

Do what you say you will do.
  No arguing (takes two to argue!!)
  Be willing to live with what you will do.
  No threats.

Consequences appropriate to cost.
  No arguing or nagging.
  Written warning.

If power struggle, remember:
  Relationship power.
  Amenity power.
  Transactions for payment (?pre-payment.)

Predictable: testing and manipulation.

If necessary, get help.
  - for self -
  - beware of paper tigers
  (people who tell you what
  you should do.)

Most important for teens

6.3.4. LAUGHTER AND PLAYFULNESS

The final area of discussion that many clients raise in the therapeutic process is how to bring more laughter, joy and playfulness into their lives. For myself, the idea of incorporating laughter into my anger work came about because my wife wanted more positive energy around the house. She wanted to shift the energy dynamics of our life. Regardless of how effective my therapeutic program was in helping people change (in workshops or group therapy), dealing with angry people every week was taxing. The energy was generally serious. So we explored how to change the energy.

At about this time we heard a radio program about laughter clubs --- social clubs where people gathered daily or weekly simply to laugh. We were intrigued. So we trained as laughter leaders of the Laughter Clubs International and shortly after became friends with its founder, Dr. Madan Kataria. The idea for a laughter club came in 1996 when Madan, a cardiologist in Mumbai, India, was concerned with how stressed both he and his patients were becoming. While writing an article on "Laughter is the best medicine," he asked himself, "Why am I writing this; why am I not laughing?" So he went out to the local gardens early one morning and invited people to share jokes. Most people would not do so (according to Madan, Indians are very serious), but he managed to get four people to join him. By the end of the week he had close to sixty people. But the jokes were getting sour.

As Madan thought about a solution, he decided to experiment in laughing without humor --- in other words, just laughing for the sake of laughing. The concept succeeded. Now there are at least five thousand laughter clubs around the world where people gather simply to enjoy the power of laughter. But how do you laugh without humor? It's simple: "Fake it 'til you make it." Take a risk in being silly --- you can at least laugh at yourself. It is surprisingly easy to be silly if you are willing to step out of society's rules of not laughing.

6.3.4.1. THERE IS NO EVIDENCE THAT LIFE IS SERIOUS

What is the nature of joy and laughter? Fundamentally there is a lot of evidence that life is painful. But there is no evidence that life is serious. So how did we get to be so serious? Madan Kataria repeatedly states that young children laugh hundreds of times per day (this is consistent with my observation of them) and that adults customarily laugh about eight to fifteen times per day. What happens between childhood and adulthood? I can only speculate that we accommodate to the rules of the Crab Trap. Society has almost as many rules about laughter as there are about anger and rage. Other people mind-read our behavior and give their own meaning to what we are doing. Then they may say: "There is nothing funny about this" or "Get that smile off your face" or "This is not the time for fun."

As the reader, pause for a moment and step into your most serious stance. Choose an event when you were very serious. Where is your energy focused? Most likely on the other person or the situation and not on yourself, the place of power. If you adopt a stance of true wonder towards that person or situation about which you were serious, what happens? How do you step into that wonder? One way is to simply start laughing about the serious moment. You do not need to make the other person or situation explicitly humorous or belittling --- simply laugh to the best of your ability while you think about the moment. What happens? You may find that your emotional focus shifts (as mine does) and that you are reflecting now from a place of curiosity, perhaps even wondering how your seriousness came about in the first place.

This ability to shift our focus occurs because we have the ability to take any situation and play with its energy. To play with the energy does not mean to make fun of the situation, to belittle it or to be sarcastic. It means to adopt an attitude of wonder (see Figure 80.) I can even play while in an argument with another person. To Illustrate, one of the introductory exercises of most laughter clubs is called "gibberish talk" where you have a conversation with another person using nonsense words. Perhaps you have done so with your children on occasion. Usually it is hilarious. What would happen if you were angry with someone and, in their presence, launched into a continuous stream of gibberish words as the means of expressing your anger? What might they do? First they might think that you are crazy. (Not your problem.) Then they might start to laugh, either at you or with you. What would that do to the conflict? What would happen to your energy while you are expressing gibberish? Likely, it would diminish considerably since you could put a lot of your energy into your voice tone and facial movements without being threatening to the other person. What impact would that have on you?

It appears to me that the most successful people in the world are those who play and have the most fun. In my personal experience, I do not make comparisons when I am having fun. I simply have fun. Everything is included and integrated; there are no divisions. Moreover, laughter is unique amongst the expressions of energy. It is contagious. It results in a "feel-good" experience

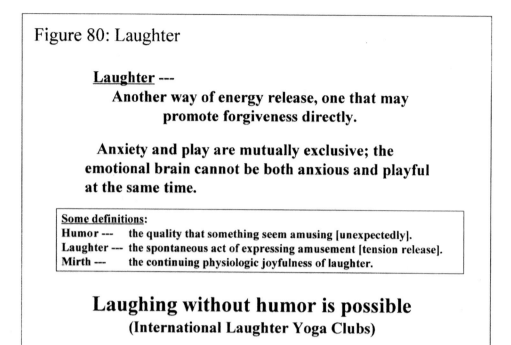

Figure 80: Laughter

Laughter ---
Another way of energy release, one that may promote forgiveness directly.

Anxiety and play are mutually exclusive; the emotional brain cannot be both anxious and playful at the same time.

Some definitions:
Humor --- the quality that something seem amusing [unexpectedly].
Laughter --- the spontaneous act of expressing amusement [tension release].
Mirth --- the continuing physiologic joyfulness of laughter.

Laughing without humor is possible
(International Laughter Yoga Clubs)

called mirth, generally for all who partake of the experience. And it is possible to move into that experience without external humor. It is possible to move energy, any energy, into laughter. Given that anxiety and play are incompatible to the emotional brain, shifting anxiety (or anger) into laughter releases the energy and likely moves us towards forgiveness.

6.4. MATURITY

In my personal life, the major struggles that I have encountered as an individual are those that require me to sort out the nature of life problems and how to respond to them. These struggles can be very painful when they occur. Many times the problem exists because of a deficit in my understanding of what life offers. My resolution has been to update myself and my skills so as to have better ways of dealing with the stress. The skills offered in this book in "Part B --- The Practical" allow for much self-correction and acceptance of life's difficulties at an individual level. Much work is necessary to acquire these skills;

and much of the work requires acceptance and discipline, as discussed earlier. These two words --- acceptance and discipline --- are the essence of the Fourth Noble Truth of the Buddha.

What happens when life's difficulties involve an illusion or misrepresentation at the level of society? Here, updating myself and my skills is still important, yet it does not generally lead to an adequate resolution of the stress. Rather, we need to find ways to get along with each other. The discussion offered in this book in "Part C --- The Philosophical" questions our society's long-term philosophic bases that underlie the problems of emotional issues. For me, this is the place where the Fourth Noble Truth becomes even more applicable, especially acceptance. There are limits to what I can accomplish and what others will allow me to accomplish. Much of the time these limits are appropriate --- we call them "law." They are the ethical agreements of our society as to what behaviors serve us as a human culture. But in our "post-modern" age with its inherent risk that everything is relative, most processes of our society have become extremely complex. Are the limits to what I can accomplish appropriate? As a physician and therapist, I am exposed to this conundrum most obviously in the medical and legal professions. Many distortions come to the surface, yet I have no good mechanisms for "how to get subjects to agree on how to live in accord with nature."

As I have suggested in this chapter, there are major illusions and distortions occurring in our society. We need to mature both as individuals and as a society in order to come to terms with these problems. So what are you waiting for? How willing are you to manage your energy and create the kind of life you say you want?

Part D.
The Challenge

PART D. THE CHALLENGE --- AND THE APPENDICES

Summary

This book has been a detailed study of the nature and mechanisms of emotional issues, especially those of anger and rage (but applicable to all emotional struggles.) Have you been impacted by this book? Has the impact been more than intellectual curiosity? Will the impact be positive in the long-term?

The challenge has been to engage in authentic growth. It is my belief that we need this as individuals and as a culture so as to survive. Perhaps you are already doing your individual growth and contributing well to society. If not, or if your growth has been insufficient to bring you to peace with what life offers, what further do you need to do? What further do you need to do to contribute to society in a way that keeps your focus on yourself, on having power with society?

I suggest that the integration of the subjective and the objective is essential in this growth. I further suggest that the power of the subjective has been fundamentally and deeply discounted in our emphasis on technology and the objective.

The mechanisms and skills offered in this book are one way to grow, individually and as a society. It is not the only way. It seems to be an effective way for those who have recognized its possibilities.

Chapter Seven — The Need For Healthier Systems — presents and overview and conclusions from the previous chapters. It explores what seems to be successful about the weekend workshop on Anger, Rage and Violation. It suggests what the individual can next do in their journey of growth. It suggests how the individual can bridge the gap to impact society: by living one's own values with clarity. Living one's values slowly impacts the emotional systems around you and creates a long-term ripple effect of health in the system. You may be surprised by the changes that occur.

Chapter Eight — The World's Best Kept Secret — alludes to the next step.

The Appendices present information that applies to the remainder of the book. Appendix A gives my definitions of words I use throughout the book — clarity and precision of language is essential for growth and subtle shifts in meaning are important. Appendix B lists a number of books that I have found helpful, some of which have been referenced in the main body of the book and some not. Appendix C illustrates how to create a Truth List, an ongoing statement of what the individual finds true, and one that can guide them on their journey of clarity.

As conclusion, Appendix D discusses recidivism (resistance to change in the "more hardened characters") as a systemic problem. It also presents the stories of individuals who have been impacted by the Anger, Rage and Violation weekend in profoundly positive ways. These have all been "more hardened characters."

Growth is possible. If you change, others must change. So must society.

CHAPTER SEVEN --- THE NEED FOR HEALTHIER SYSTEMS

CHAPTER SEVEN --- THE NEED FOR HEALTHIER SYSTEMS

So, just what are you waiting for? What is it going to take for you, the reader, to engage in authentic growth? Perhaps you already do so. Perhaps you disagree with the premises of this book. Perhaps you are simply scared of what would happen. This is for you to decide.

7.1. THE NEED FOR A MORE INTEGRATED APPROACH

The philosophy offered by this book asks all of us to change at the societal level by deep change at the individual level. It also challenges the lack of authenticity and the devaluing of subjectivity that so characterizes our society at the present time. I believe that the concepts and the tools offered in this book represent the starting point for your own personal integration. From that integration, there exists the possibility of the integration of our society.

Do you resonate with what has been written? If so, what are you going to do differently with your life? In this book I have offered a banquet table of ideas and tools. You do not have to adopt all the tools --- you can come back as necessary. You cannot however learn the skill of a tool simply by reading about it; you must pick it up and use it, making mistakes and learning from the mistakes. If you decide to make a significant change in your world, it will not be easy. First, many of the ideas presented here are far from mainstream, especially those of high energy release. The crab box will react powerfully --- so be careful; especially be safe (no SAD and STOP.) Second, you probably need a guide, at least in the early stages. Find someone who has done his or her own growth --- that may be very difficult to do. Much of what is called therapy is one person telling another what they should be doing; it is likely that the person "should-ing" is not someone who has done his or her own personal growth. And third, risk safely. Risk small steps frequently and know what you will do if you fall down in the process.

I received an unsolicited email a while ago that prompted me to write this book at this time. The email was about anger management programs based on Cognitive Behavioral Therapy. Within the body of the email, there was this statement:

> "The bad part, he adds, is that what little data he has suggests that the methods that work for people who sincerely want to deal with their anger are useless on more hardened characters. They blame the world, their boss or their spouse for their troubles and just want to do their court- or spouse-ordered time and escape. Many people who have been to traffic school can empathize. "What we need to do is design interventions that look at the issue of readiness, then try to see if we can move people to where anger management programs are helpful," says ....

I am not interested per se in attacking CBT --- it is a good therapy when used well within the limits that it offers. But as the email says, "the methods that work for people who sincerely want to deal with their anger are useless on more hardened characters." The intention of this book on the Blowing Out! process was to offer a methodology and philosophy that does get at "more hardened characters" because it has the possibility of getting at all people if they will recognize their need to be authentic. The "more hardened characters" I have met do want to be authentic --- they lack resources.

In the sense that these people are the tip of the iceberg of our societal problems with anger and rage, I say thank you to the more hardened characters for their integrity in holding onto their anger and rage until they have found the tools that work for them to achieve a genuine life that satisfies them. Many of these people have been gifts to me.

7.1.1. Feedback From Clients

As part of writing this book, I also wanted to be able to document the overall effectiveness of the Anger, Rage and Violation weekend in some fashion. The following is anecdotal and therefore subjective, not objective or rigorous. It does however allow a framework in which to place the more specific feedback of Appendix D (comments by the "more hardened characters.")

I ask all clients who attend my weekend workshops for feedback of their experience. Of the last four hundred twenty-nine clients who started the weekend, four hundred two completed the weekend and three hundred ninety-one handed in feedback sheets (ninety-one percent of all attendees.) Eighty one percent of the feedback was uniformly positive and affirmative (three hundred seventeen feedback sheets), with occasional minor comments as to sitting too long and too much information to absorb in one sitting. Most of the remainder had minor comments about too little time or of being overwhelmed by too much theory. Five percent of comments talked about the process being too intense and/or were significantly negative to the point that I would say they did not get what I intended for them for the weekend (eighteen feedback sheets) --- my intention was that they get good tools and they did not.

Approximately thirty percent of the attendees were mandated by some legal process, approximately thirty percent were instructed to be present by their families and the rest were strictly voluntary. These figures are less accurate in that I did not ask for details as to how clients chose to come. (In attempting to record details, I have not yet come up with good questions that give answers that I consider reliable. I would consider them reliable if the answers to the questions accurately reflected the off-hand comments of participants over the weekend.) My guess is that approximately forty percent of the attendees did not really want to attend. Yet eighty percent described the weekend as a uniformly positive experience, getting good tools.

Thus at least eighty-seven percent of attendees (no complaints or minor complaints only) who stayed for the full process got enough to say that the weekend was successful for them --- they got useful tools. Unfortunately the nature of our culture is such that effective tools are not easy to find. In stating that effective tools are difficult to find, I do not mean to say that my methodology is the only way for this to happen; my approach is simply one of a number of processes of which I know that seem to be effective (they all step out of the crab trap in many ways.)

What does succeed with the "more hardened characters?" In Appendix D Recidivism (referring to "habitual or chronic relapse"), I list comments by a number of "more hardened characters" as well as commentary by another therapists or a probation officer who have sent me clients over the years. Although "anecdotal" (and necessarily so --- the subjective is anecdotal by our present research methods), the comments suggest that the Blowing Out! process offers something unique or at least not easily found in our society.

7.2. An Overview Of The Practical

In this book, I have attempted to present a comprehensive view of the nature of human emotional process, synthesizing information ranging from basic biology to psychology to spirituality. It needs to have this span to be thorough. Otherwise, it would not challenge people to seek authenticity. We are biological and in so being, we are short-term energy transformers prior to our being rational computers. We move energy from the environment back into the environment; and in the middle is a marvelous processor that works well when allowed the opportunity. The processor works well at many levels but is best designed for integration of the emotional and the cognitive, creating a bridge to achieve the transrational.

Many factors come together to limit this integration of humanness. The factors are such that when mashed together, they become too complex for most (?all) human beings to manage and thus major distortions take place that limit effectiveness, that limit us from getting what we truly want in ways that are authentic of who we really are. These factors I have summarized as conflict (differences in closed spaces), powerlessness (real and fantasized limitations because of our childhood development and our basic biology), the mobilization of energy (from meaning and intention) and the stoppage of energy (lack of safety) because we have not come to terms with our powerlessness.

It is my experience that the separation of these factors allows more effective management of life issues, management that can resolve many difficulties without the need to impose upon or defy others. However the manner in which this needs to be done deeply critiques the "rules" by which we have learned to limit ourselves --- it steps outside the crab trap of society in many ways. Many of these factors (safety, energy and powerlessness) can be entirely managed by myself (perhaps with additional resources being needed but the work is totally limited by my own determination for growth.) I do not however exist in isolation --- I am always in relationship with others. I am always involved in emotional systems, be they in my family, my work or my society. My system also needs to change for optimal health, both individually and systemically.

I have suggested that fundamental laws apply to emotional systems: the laws of energy and the laws of emotional triangles. These are not laws that have been arbitrarily set by those in authority; they appear to be natural laws of biology. They can be tested, they can perhaps be broken temporarily but to do so generally has significant long-term cost. And limits the human potential. Within this process, it is always possible to empty the pot --- it takes about ten minutes. Dealing with the conflict takes time and effort (which is possible if the pot is empty.) From this place of emptiness, I can both support and request others to be genuine. And from there, I can create a ripple effect whereby I begin to change society around me.

I truly believe that every human being who comes to my anger workshops is doing their absolute best to live life authentically, limited principally by the lack of awareness of mechanisms and tools for effective living. Most are also limited by the human dynamics of laziness and fearfulness. These limitations are changeable. What are needed are experiences that have the characteristic of "authentic feel-good." When this occurs, change is almost automatic --- our basic biology is geared to the good.

7.2.1. WHAT IS EFFECTIVE IN THE WEEKEND WORKSHOP PROCESS?

What then do I believe is effective in the Blowing Out! process as applied to a weekend workshop? What is it about the workshop and its follow-through that lead to effective change.

First and foremost, there are no "shoulds." Part of the weekend is the negotiation of ground rules that limit our behavior; these are ground rules of choice, not coercion. If we do not agree to them as stated initially, we change them so that everyone is aware of what are the ground rules. Most important within the ground rules is safety --- absolute ground rules are "No SAD" and "STOP."

Second, the weekend offers endorsement of human experience. People are given opportunity to talk about their lives in simple fashion without the usual complaining typical of such gatherings. If complaining, they are invited to dump their "anger" in some other way, using the tools of the weekend. (Complaining is simply our common way of scattering our energy.) As part of this validation, I tell my truths about my own life. I do not do this from the intention of dumping "my sad story" on others; I tell it factually that in some major respects I too have had a difficult life and I have changed it effectively to a place of deep personal satisfaction. I challenge others that they can do so also --- all they have to do is pay the price of the tools.

Third, I offer ideas and metaphors that are simple enough to grasp and accurate enough to be useful. As one person described it, I offer "user-friendly information." It is a lot of information because there is a lot of misinformation available from other sources.

And fourth, most importantly, I challenge people (usually gently, not always) to be in action with their own lives. "If you always do what you've always done, you'll always get what you've always gotten." My basic belief is that the vast majority of human beings want to be authentic. It is achievable.

The difficulty is that the price tag is high. It is not impossibly high but it is high. It is especially high when one attempts to do the growth work alone. As stated in an earlier chapter, we need authentic community, we need authentic relationships and we need authentic purpose in our lives so as to defuse the Ghosts of our past and live the lives we truly want to live. It is possible to do this growth work alone just as it is possible to build a house without tools. It is however generally simpler and more satisfactory to use good tools. For those who wish to continue the growth process, I offer ongoing weekly therapy groups focused on skill development (of any emotional life issues.)

There is a societal agreement that we are entitled to living well: the possibility of growth "should" also be fair. One of the more important comments I have read was that of a native elder talking to a white judge, the elder saying, "we know you have a legal system; we're just not certain it is a justice system[1]." By this, I believe the elder meant that the values of the society of the "white judge" (this current society) were rigid and perhaps not in keeping with a humanistic approach to life. But until we examine the beliefs of the societal system by our own growth, change in these societal values is not likely to happen.

7.2.2. SOME SUGGESTIONS FOR GROWTH

The insert summarizes the skills of anger and rage (see Figure 81.) For those who want more in life, I suggest that the way to proceed further is to make a commitment to growth, for new options in your life, and keep the commitment.

Start learning your triggers. People won't like it; don't violate them.

Manage your energy. People won't like it; do it safely.

Learn the messages of your energy. Deal with your past Ghosts, in therapy processes if necessary.

---

1. Rupert Ross, Dancing With A Ghost: Exploring Indian Reality (Markham, Ontario: Reed Books, 1992).

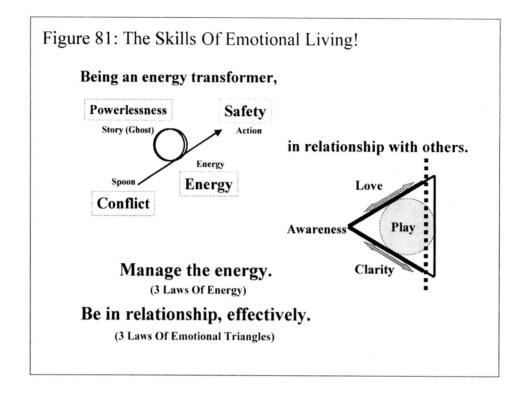

Figure 81: The Skills Of Emotional Living!

Being an energy transformer,

Powerlessness   Safety

Story (Ghost)   Action

Energy

Spoon   **Energy**

Conflict

in relationship with others.

Love

Awareness   Play

Clarity

Manage the energy.
(3 Laws Of Energy)

Be in relationship, effectively.
(3 Laws Of Emotional Triangles)

Prevent violations by others.

Deal with the conflict. The only person who can change is yourself. This requires more than lip service. Learn the skills of creative communication, cooperation and challenge.

Discipline, discipline, discipline. Do your DoList.

Considering the skills offered in this book, my suggestion is to plan an hour a day and start with Emotional Freedom Technique. Practice it twenty minutes a day for three months and defuse many of the simpler issues in your life (at this stage, do not expect it to resolve the big issues but it will clarify the big issues.) Then do three months of "Now I Am Aware Of ...," again twenty minutes a day, perhaps continuing the EFT at the same time. Add "Truth-Testing" and then Journal Writing, over-all an hour a day. Depending on how full the pot is, add energy release processes as soon as you are willing to risk them safely.

As necessary, dive deeper (and re-surface.) Do your own emotional change work as necessary, with or without a facilitator (preferably with, at least in the beginning.) Going beyond your level of comfort is required.

Using the suggestions of this book and working with a facilitator likely will require two to five years of active growth, with some plateaus. Do not expect a quick fix.

Preferably do your work openly, in small supportive groups, so that others may grow from your experience and you can grow from their experiences. This way we support each other in our genuineness.

Do your work with a facilitator who has done their own growth work and has the skill to lead participants through experiential growth processes rather than just talk about issues that are troublesome. Talking usually activated the cognitive brain, not the emotional brain.

Explore to what extent you are capable of impacting the social dynamics around you. Do so --- speak and act your truths.

7.3. An Overview Of The Philosophic

Although I strongly believe that change must take place at the individual level, we must never forget the problems that exist at the systemic. Most of our problems (hunger, the environment, our emphasis on money) are systemic; they permeate the entire system of our culture. Yet in our lack of integration, it seems easier to focus on changing others, not self, and to simplify the system by the process of "blame." When we do so, we say that the problem is "men's violence" or "the government" or "Cognitive Behavioral Therapy." We identify only a limited process and focus on a limited methodology rather than attempting a more long-term and more comprehensive approach.

I have suggested that the most important way for this to occur is through the processes we call therapy. As mentioned earlier, I do not like the terminology. The words carry too many connotations of the individual being sick and needing to be fixed by the healthy therapist. And how incorrect this is. Any good therapist is working on their own life issues as part of their own growth. From my perspective, the healthiest people I know are my own long-term clients in that they are willing to admit that they have life difficulties and are seeking authentic resolution of them. They may look to me as a mentor, a guide, but I hope (and encourage) that they do not look to me for answers as to how to live their own lives. I am a mirror for them, challenging them in many ways to look at their own lives and the choices they bring to their lives. I also have a skill set that, if they wish, they can access so as to create change in their own lives more effectively than the passive and/or aggressive "I can do it myself" stance that permeates our culture and whereby we hide from each other.

Until ten years ago in my own exploration of the subjective, I never had any concept of the incredible power of inductive processes and the shifts of perception that can occur within these processes. The tools I now commonly use (and use effectively) often require that I step far outside the common belief systems of my culture, yet they seem to provide rapid and unexpected shifts in myself and my clients. I have no idea of the objective reality of the work I do --- I am much more interested in people coming away from my work with a sense of empowerment and growth that ripples throughout their lives. Certainly some traps exist and the ultra-powerful tools are only useful for those who have the imaginative risk-taking to take on the possibilities offered. Many do, and mostly with astounding success.

My basic conclusion in this book is that in our focus on others, in our focus on the so-called objective, we have created a society with loss of meaning wherein everything is relative and subjective authenticity is discounted. We do not look to ourselves for the incredible power and strength of which we are capable; we do not value the incredible power and strength of which we are capable. And when this occurs, it is difficult to find one's way out of the swamp.

As part of this, we have created major incongruencies, especially in the gender distortions that we identify. Without question, there have been extensive violations by many of our culture but I suggest the major underlying mechanisms are that we all have been victimized by a dehumanizing focus on the objective and the technological. In attempting to live up to this focus, and in the ways that we insist that others live up to this focus, we have all suffered major losses and we are all at risk of being violators.

My deep assertion therefore is that the way out is to encourage the development of individual authenticity, the valuing of awareness and clarity of subjective experience, trusting that we are capable of growth. This must include a valuing of the biologic, the psychological and the spiritual. But this must be a valuing of experience and personal reflection rather than a valuing of whose belief system is a better system. I suggest that the valuing must be done from a perspective such as the importance of community, diversity, subjectivity and change. It must also include such stances as illustrated by the core moralities of aging well, striving for authenticity, being a midwife, being my word, being in community and celebrating life. The skills of effective marital relationship, the commitment to child discipline as discipline of the adult to provide consistency and the primary intention to live life joyously must also be part of this searching. From these stances, there needs to be a valuing of ecologically sound environmental systems and the development of tools for agreeing on what needs to be done and then doing it.

Paradoxically this developmental searching needs to be done in the presence of others who also seek authenticity --- only there can we learn the skills and tools of testing our own experiences, using others as guides and mirrors. The paradox is to be self-focused while in true relationship with others who are also self-focused (thus the value of small group interaction.) For best impact, a skilled facilitator is needed until adequate personal skill has developed. This then reiterates the need for good therapists as well as good clients and, ultimately, there is no difference between the two.

In closing, let me emphasize a statement of the internationally known anthropologist Margaret Mead[2]: "Never doubt that a small group of thoughtful,

2. http://www.quotedb.com/quotes/1821

375

committed people can change the world. Indeed, it is the only thing that ever has."

If you change, others must change! So must society!

CHAPTER EIGHT --- THE WORLD'S BEST KEPT SECRET

This has been a book about how to manage life energy, especially the difficult times. The emphasis has been on anger and rage; I have repeatedly suggested that the skills offered are applicable to any emotional issues.

The book has also presented a challenge: the need to manage energy and be in relationship effectively. It is my strong belief that this allows the individual to respond well to any emotional difficulty, and thus to manage emotional negativity. This is the world's second best kept secret.

The world's best kept secret is how to develop and manage positive energy. It will only occur when we have mastered the unpleasant energies.

The basis of this is to create a partnership between the objective and the subjective.

APPENDICES

Appendix A --- Some Definitions As Used In This Book

Appendix B --- Some Other Books To Consider

Appendix C --- ?Truths?

Appendix D --- The Nature Of Recidivism

(APPENDIX A)
SOME DEFINITIONS AS USED IN THIS BOOK

The "words in simple quotation marks" are words that I have created so as to get at the concepts that I believe are important in the context of energy management. The remaining words give slightly different emphasis from the standard dictionary definitions. The words are listed alphabetically with reference to corresponding words by the use of "cf".

Anger	the energy of conflict wherein the participant has a sense of power.
Associate	to enter fully (in body) into an experience "as if" the experience is present at the moment. cf. dissociate and contact.
Awareness	attention to one's ongoing spontaneous perceptions.
Authenticity	the genuine integrated living of the complexity of being human.
"Body-mind-heart-soul-spirit"	the totality of being human, that which includes all possibility in being human.
Clarity	the ability to think at the emotional level.
Contact	associating into the immediate present.
Conflict	difference in a closed space or time; any difference to which energy is attached and wherein change is wanted.
"Craziness"	the purposeful (usually at the other-than-conscious level) intention to avoid pain in such a manner that further pain (suffering) is created.
Dissociate	to separate from an experience, perhaps witnessing the experience out-of-body or perhaps associating into another experience without awareness of the shift. cf. contact.

Emotion	a biologically adaptive action tendency, the purposeful beginning of action; a body experience associated with energy and named in meaning. e.g. "I feel angry" (in my jaw; I want to clamp down on the issue at hand.)
Energy	aliveness, the ability to initiate movement. cf. emotion.
"Feeling"	the energy I bring to relationship, a more complex emotional experience that refers to my interpretation of what is happening in relationship. e.g. "I feel betrayed (by …)" Here the speaker is talking about the relationship.
Feeling Judgment	my thoughts about my energetic experience. e.g. "I feel that this is appropriate" or "I feel you betrayed me when you did that." Here the speaker is talking about the story.
Freedom	the ability to influence self in a productive manner.
"Imaginating"	to imagine fully associated. The terms "to visualize" or "to imagine" often limit to visual and dissociated experience rather than entering into the full power of imagination.
Maturity	the living of wisdom.
Objective	that which is measurable and available to consensual validation by others.
"Overstanding"	the analysis of an object, living or otherwise, such that one can explain how its parts function and come together. Overstanding ignores the profound mystery that underlies all creation.
Power	the ability to influence another or something in the environment.
Pain	the conscious awareness of an unpleasant experience that denotes the possibility of harm, at any level of "body-mind-heart-soul-spirit." Many generic terms exist: pain, angst, anxiety, etc.; each of these words have both specific and generic meaning. In general, pain as used in this book refers

to the overall definition.

Play   an activity whose sole aim is diversion or amusement; in
                        the context of this book, play allows one to be present to
                        emotional distress while maintaining a sense of wonder.

Rage   the energy of conflict wherein the participant has a sense of
                        powerlessness.

Safety   the absence of that which poses long-term negative
                        consequences, especially at the physical level. Believing
                        myself to have choice in the present of danger generally
                        means I am safe; I may not feel secure until the danger is
                        past.

Secure   the feeling associated with believing myself to be safe.
                        When an innocuous event reminds me of past danger, I may
                        not feel secure; I am safe.

Sensory-grounded Descriptions   description of processes in which the
                        visual, auditory and other sensory features are predominant
                        and separated from assumptions about their meaning.

Story   the meaning I give to external and internal experience based
                        on the interplay between sensory data and VBMEs; such
                        meaning is always partially fictional (it is my interpretation
                        of the external data modified by VBMEs.)

Strength   the ability to resist another or something in the environment.

"Stuckness"   the limitation of movement, physical and emotional, that
                        results from "craziness."

Subjective   that which arises from the internal processing of external
                        and internal data by the mind.

Suffering   pain that arises or is augmented by the attempt to eliminate
                        that which is inherently painful. For example, breaking
                        a leg is painful; complaining about the pain in excess of
                        appropriate treatment is suffering.

Transrational   the integration of emotion and cognition so as to come to a place of congruent choice, a place of clarity and effective action.

Understanding   the appreciation of the mystery that exists in the "overstanding." Overstanding is important; understanding is essential.

Values, Beliefs, Memories, Expectations (VBMEs)   processes within myself that carry my life energy and contribute to my recognition of my current emotional experience.

Violation   any behavior (other than agreed behavior for public safety) which intentionally restricts the freedom of another without their permission. Unintended violations occur and can be resolved. Intended violations are abusive.

Wisdom   flexibility with "craziness;" the ability to deal with life's pain in such a manner that appropriate judgment, often playful judgment, can be brought to what life offers.

(APPENDIX B)
SOME OTHER BOOKS TO CONSIDER

There have been of course many influences on my life and my writings as presented in this book. The following books are those I recommend to others as pertinent for a deeper understanding to the issues involved in the emotional dynamics of our species.

The books are listed alphabetically with brief commentary. A few are quoted in the main body of the text.

The Practical

Bishop, Jacqui and Mary Grunt, *How To Forgive When You Don't Know How* (Barrytown, New York: Station Hill Press, 1993)

A simple and excellent book on the nature of forgiveness.

Bloomfield, Harold with Leonard Felder, *Making Peace With Your Parents* (New York: Ballantine, 1983)

Since one of the early needs in therapy is coming to terms with what life has offered, this book also offers many interesting comments and exercises.

Canfield, Jack and Mark Hansen, *The Aladdin Factor* (New York: Berkley, 1995)

A useful and practical book that explores the limitations we create in seeking what we truly want (and hence often we do not get what we want.)

Colgrove, Melba, Harold H. Bloomfield and Peter McWilliams, *How To*

Survive The Loss Of A Love (New York: Bantam, 1977)

> An excellent book for grieving, especially in that it is simple and
> describes a 100-day journey as an example of the process.

Colorosa, Barbara, *Winning At Parenting...Without Beating Your Kids*
(Littleton, Colorado: Pannonia International Film, 1989)

> I've only seen the videotape, which I find excellent. Barbara
> Colorosa is very dynamic and an excellent storyteller. Her basic
> principle is that of discipline of the adult to provide natural and
> expected consequences for the child.

Craig, Gary, *http://www.emofree.com/downloadeftmanual.asp*

> A free downloadable manual on Emotional Freedom Technique.

Farrell, Warren, *The Myth Of Male Power* (New York: Simon &
Schuster, 1993)

> I was astonished by this book when I first read it. And overwhelmed
> by the style. More that any other author I have encountered in
> gender issues, Farrell presents data and citations to his sources
> (usually 300-500 per book); thus his presentations are highly valued
> by me.

Farrell, Warren, *Women Can't Hear What Men Don't Say: Destroying
Myths, Creating Love* (New York: Tarcher/Putnam, 1999)

> The most recent book of Farrell's (that I have read) continues the
> tradition of presenting data and citation, generally separating data
> from story.

Gendlin, Eugene, *Focusing* (New York: Bantam, 1981)

One of first introductions to the possibilities of awareness testing; still a very useful process as described by Gendlin.

Gordon, Lori, *Passage To Intimacy: The PAIRS Program* (New York: Simon & Schuster, 1993)

A practical book on couple relationship development with many useful tools.

Gottman, John and Nan Silver, *The Seven Principles For Making Marriage Work* (New York: Three Rivers Press, 1999)

What I especially like about John Gottman's work is the extensive research he has done on what works in relationships, not what "should" work.

Hendrix, Harville, *Getting The Love You Want: A Guide for Couples* (New York: Henry Holt and Company, 1988)

Excellent in its presentation of the nature of the imago and how the emotional brain dictates our choices for partners. From my perspective, the exercises are good, likely mandatory, but rather dry.

Jackson, Grace, *Rethinking Psychiatric Drugs: A Guide for Informed Consent* (Bloomington, Indiana: AuthorHouse, 2005)

An anecdotal investigation into the complexities of "evidence based medicine" and the choices made about psychopharmacological medications.

Kataria, Madan, *Laugh For No Reason* (Mumbai, India: Madhuri

International, 1999)

> Madan is the originator of International Laughter Clubs. I fully
> expect him to win a Nobel Peace Prize in the next ten years.

Lee, John with Bill Stott, *Facing The Fire: Experiencing and
Expressing Anger Appropriately* (New York: Bantam, 1993)

> Until the writing of my book, *Facing The Fire* has been the book
> I have most often recommended to others. Although I have never
> met John Lee, his philosophy of energy management is very similar
> to mine, presumably arising parallel to mine. The concepts of
> Emotional Triangles, to my knowledge, are not part of John Lee's
> work.

Phelan, Thomas W., *1-2-3 Magic: Effective Discipline for Children 2-12*
(Videotape and Booklet) (Glen Ellyn, Illinois: Child Management, 1996)

> The originator of *1-2-3 Magic*, who himself has children with ADD.
> The videotape is excellent and is my preference over the book
> because it is more dynamic. *1-2-3 Magic* highlights the need for
> energy management as well as discipline of the adult.

Phelan, Thomas W., *Surviving Your Adolescents: How to Manage and
Let Go of Your 13-18 Year Olds (2nd ed.)* (Glen Ellyn, Illinois: Child
Management, 1998)

> Skills for managing beyond the early childhood years. Excellent --- I
> prefer the first edition as it has more specific suggestions to offer.

Slavinski, Zivorad, *http://www.spiritual-technology.com*

PEAT technologies, a range of examples of power therapies.

Taffel, Ron, *The Second Family: Dealing with Peer Power, Pop Culture, the Wall of Silence -- and Other Challenges of Raising Today's Teens* (New York: St. Martin's Press, 2001)

An exploration of the richness and pain of current teen culture.

Watzlawick, Paul, John H. Weakland and Richard Fisch, *Change: Principles of Problem Formation and Problem Resolution* (New York: W. W. Norton & Company, 1974)

One of the early books on the principles of playfulness. "The Belloc Ploy" comes from this book.

Weisinger, Hendrie, *Dr. Weisinger's Anger Work-Out Book* (New York: Quill, 1985)

For those more inclined to Cognitive Behavioral Concepts, I usually suggest this book for the many exercises and simplicity of concepts. The exercises need to be done though!

The Philosophical

Bucke, Richard Maurice, *Cosmic Consciousness: A Study in the Evolution of the Human Mind* (New York: E.P. Dutton, 1969; Innes & Sons, 1901)

A classic in the investigation of mystical experience --- the book that allowed me to identify my own experience at my age of 32.

Carse, James, *Finite And Infinite Games* (New York: Ballantine, 1986)

A simple book which develops a profound exploration of theology.

Crabtree, Adam, *Multiple Man: Explorations in Possession and Multiple Personality* (Toronto: Collins, 1985)

An intriguing investigation into the processes of "Sailors on a Ship," extending the ideas beyond the usual psychological descriptions into the realm of mystery.

Crosby, Robert, *Living With Purpose When The Gods Have Gone* (Ojai: Times Change Press, 1991)

One of the major struggles of our society is to come to terms with our secularization, especially manifest in the loss of general value systems. This book is the first that I encountered that clearly invited living in such a manner.

Damasio, Antonio, *Descartes' Error: Emotion, Reason And The Human Brain* (New York: Quill, 1994)

Damasio brilliantly presents the neuro-anatomic basis of emotion as it is currently being understood. Amazingly, from my perspective, he presents almost nothing about the subjective.

Damasio, Antonio, *The Feeling Of What Happens: Body and Emotion In The Making of Consciousness* (Orlando: Harcourt, 1999)

Again brilliant and again little on the subjective.

Fowler, John, *Stages of Faith: The Psychology of Human Development and The Quest For Meaning* (New York: HarperCollins, 1981).

A detailed and comprehensive investigation into the nature of faith and its development as part of human maturity.

Friedman, Edwin, *Generation To Generation: Family Process In Church And Synagogue* (USA: Guilford Press, 1985)

Ed Friedman has been one of my major mentors although the actual time spent with him has been relatively brief. He was an early student of Murray Bowen, one of the pioneers of Family Systems Therapy. Much of my understanding of emotional triangles has evolved from my contact with Ed.

Gladwell, Malcolm, *Blink: The Power of Thinking Without Thinking* (New York: Little, Brown and Company, 2005)

An interesting compilation of stories of those who trust their own awareness.

Healy, David, *The Antidepressant Era* (Cambridge, Massachusetts and London, England: Harvard University Press, 1997)

A history of the psychopharmacological developments of the last fifty years.

Lewis, T., F. Amini and R. Lannon, *A General Theory of Love* (Toronto: Random House, 2000)

Similar to my book, *A General Theory of Love* attempts to base our human experience on our basic biology and then go beyond the biological.

Newberg, Andrew, Eugene D'Aquili and Vince Rause, *Why God Won't Go Away: Brain Science and the Biology of Belief* (New York: Ballantine, 2001)

A study of the neurology of mystical experiences, incorporating much modern investigation with sophisticated brain scanning devices, and subsequently speculating on the evolutionary development and purpose of mystical experience.

Peck, F. Scott, *The Road Less Traveled* (New York: Simon & Schuster, 1978)

In my opinion, another of the most important books of the twentieth century. I recommend all of Scott Peck's writings; I dislike that he does not usually say where he has gotten his data.

Rogers, Carl R., *On Becoming A Person* (Boston: Houghton Mifflin, 1961)

An exploration of the process of being human by one of the classic leaders of therapy.

Ross, Rupert, *Dancing With A Ghost: Exploring Indian Reality* (Markham, Ontario: Reed Books, 1992)

A truly profound book that questions the wisdom of our traditional technological society by developing an understanding of a different perspective, that of the Native people of North America.

Swimme, Brian and Thomas Berry, *The Universe Story: From the Primordial Flaring Forth to the Ecozoic Era--A Celebration of the Unfolding of the Cosmos* (New York: HarperCollins, 1992)

A fascinating book which bridges theology and modern physics, suggesting the underlying principles that I call the moral imperative.

Szasz, Thomas S., *The Myth Of Mental Illness: Foundations of a Theory of Personal Conduct (rev. ed.)* (New York: Harper Paperback, 1974)

A fascinating study of the pathologizing of human experience, eventually leading to the diagnostic difficulties of modern psychiatry.

Wilber, Ken, *A Brief History Of Everything* (Boston: Shambala, 1996)

For me, this is one of the most important books of the twentieth century, a broad synthesis of the subjective and the objective, with many useful concepts.

(Appendix C)
?Truths?

The following are truths for me. I speak them only as my experience, my beliefs, my values, and yet I think they are universal, independent of culture for the most part. I also live them as much as possible; they are always in revision and are not absolute.

I encourage you to examine them closely, not to adopt them but to examine them and come to your own truth list. Personally, the creation and ongoing revision of this "?Truth?" list has been one of the most powerful tools I have in defining my self and my value system.

My original list contains over three hundred items and is listed on my website http://www.aplacetwobe.com/ for those who are interested. I have drawn extensively on this detailed list for the writing of this book.

For the most part, the ideas contained in this Appendix list are those of being in relationship. The list is intended to provide you with a simplified example of a truth list; it also supplements and expands the body of the text.

1. I forget these truths, frequently and repeatedly. Frequently it is not safe for me to learn these truths---there is a price tag to truth.

2. Actions speak louder than words; they are also more truthful.

3. I can never know absolute truth. Depending on circumstances, everything is true and everything is bull. What I gain on the journey is wisdom, the knowing of my own truth. I cannot teach wisdom to anyone else.

4. There are two major measures of truths, including these truths. How inclusive is the truth? (Who is excluded?) How persuasive is the truth.

(How do I resonate with it?)

5. I am currently doing the best that I can. Even when I believe I should be doing something else, I am still doing the best I can right now with the resources that are available to me. I can however do something different (especially if I do not like what I am currently doing) --- I have choice! There is a price tag to choice.

6. For me, the best definition for happiness is "wanting what I get" --- note the differences from "getting what I want."

7. Please do not trap me in the limitations of your map. It is extremely painful to get caught in your interpretation of me when that interpretation does not reflect my reality and you do not have a way to step back from your reality. At a personal level (Dave's), it is the most painful experience of my life (I care about you and your experience.) At a societal level, I think it is probably the most common problem we have in relationships.

8. I am here now. This is very simple yet very fundamental. This is the only time in which I am able to make a difference in life. What, if any, difference do I want to make at this time? Now? Here?

9. The word "present" has multiple meanings; it is called a triple entendre. It means to be "here," it refers to "now," and it is also "a gift to be opened." Are you present? Am I present?

10. My time is my time. No one, absolutely no one, gets my time without my permission. I can give my time freely or resentfully --- either way,

with my permission.

11. I will go as far as I can see; then I will be able to see further.

12. There are no guarantees!

13. Other people have done this journey before me --- they can guide me. I can learn from them and I have to do my own journey. My guides come in many forms --- most important for me is whether or not the guide has done his or her own journeying. If they have, they offer me an example of integration; if they haven't, they offer me beliefs (and shoulds.) At some point(s), I need a guide --- they can help me know what I do not know. They have been here before.

14. Much of every-day life requires discipline in the form of delayed gratification, cleaning up mess (mine and yours) so as to have greater satisfaction. Discipline allows one to do the clean-up with contentment rather than resentment.

15. To live is to have pain (sometimes); to live well is to find meaning in the pain. Life ultimately asks that I take response-ability to find the answers to its problems and fulfill the tasks it repeatedly sets for me, and for each and every individual. These tasks differ from individual to individual and from moment to moment for the same individual.

16. I am often in internal conflict with myself, frequently experiencing this as external conflict in relationship. The more I am willing to sort and integrate my internal conflicts, finishing what is unfinished, the more I open myself to love and play in relationship.

17. Life necessitates struggle, sometimes saying good-bye. To say good-bye is to abandon by choice --- it is characterized by sadness, pain and the expectation that the other will not change.

18. When stuck between a rock and a hard place, I prefer to choose how I am crushed. I have more power and freedom when I choose the consequences with which I wish to live.

19. Violation of self or of others is ethically unacceptable to me (unless in the interests of authentic public safety); otherwise it is a form of evil. Authentic public safety is subject to much interpretation.

20. My relationships with others are based on my being authentic (showing the other who I am), and on my keeping my commitments (doing what I say I will do.) Living in this manner takes much time and effort.

21. Given the complexity of communication, why bother telling others how I feel? The most important reason is to be honest with myself and to define my self. When I do this, I like myself better. And I develop my inner strength!

22. Why do I really care what other people think? In general, when I take a stand on an issue, any stand, 25% of people will like it, 25% will dislike it and 50% won't care. In each group, there will be those who will tell me who I should be and those who will tell me of their own experience. I would rather have people tell me who they are, even if they disagree with me, than for them to tell me who I should be.

23. Telling others how I feel however does not lead to change, especially

it does not lead to change in others. It is not meant to. The only time it really worked this way was as a newborn infant.

24. Honesty without compassion is often disguised hostility. When you make no attempt to truly understand my worldview, no attempt to include my responses in your honesty, likely you are attacking me.

25. I live in an environment, an environment of other people, all of who are also attempting to live in ways that keep them safe, if not joyous. Other people are mirrors for me; it is from others that I learn to see myself. I need to know the authentic experience of others so as to see myself more clearly. To do this effectively, I need ways of sorting the information I get from others. What is authentic experience? Whom/what do I trust?

26. I am dependent on others for many of my needs. This is neither good nor bad, simply part of being human --- I am designed for interaction.

27. I live in a community, an environment of other people. When we are authentic and complete with each other, I am most at peace.

28. You and I are different. Most, if not all, of the differences occur either from intrinsic capabilities (such as intelligence or beauty) and/or from wounds (such as scars and shoulds.)

29. The basic issue is not whether we are different --- we are different. Some of these differences can be modified.

30. The basic issue is whether we violate one another, intentionally choosing to devalue the other, treating the other as an object, sometimes in a harmful fashion.

31. It is in the working through of these differences that I learn trust, trust of you that you will not abandon me and trust of myself that I will not abandon you.

32. Authentic interpersonal relationship necessitates shared honesty and the coming to terms with these differences that exist between us. Conflict occurs when we confront these differences---anger or a precursor of anger is the emotional impact of this conflict.

33. To trust is to have confidence in the reliability, the predictability, of an occurrence in the future. It is usually, but not necessarily, a positive hopefulness. If you are repeatedly dishonest, I can trust you to be dishonest in the future. Not usually the basis of relationship though.

34. Interpersonal relationship with another person has most to do with trust, only partially to do with liking and loving --- I trust you when you keep your commitments and/or when your actions are consistent with my expectations.

35. I have considerable difficulty with language in my relationship with others.

    - To like (what we often call love) someone is to be excited by his or her presence --- this has more to do with me that it has to do with you.

    - To love someone is to "will to extend oneself for their spiritual growth", to "call them to their own unique power" --- this has more to do with my own growth as a human being, my relationship with the universe, than with you.

36. Sexuality both enriches and confuses relationship. Sexuality is a biologic drive consistent with

- a deep sensual experience (sensory awareness with pleasure/ pleasuring), and

- a form of worship (spiritual connection, but only in the presence of intimacy and vulnerability, trust and commitment.)

37. For me, authentic relationship ranges from informal friendship (what society calls "liking") to the legal state of marriage (what society calls "loving") with many variations on this scale.

38. You and I are similar. I feel comfortable with what is familiar. I relax and have fun. I "like" you. We are "acquaintances". Then the differences start to emerge.

39. In friendship, the sexual issues are minimal. I choose to show you who I am, my similarities and my differences, and to work through these differences when they impact us. I have a commitment to work through the differences that keep us apart. Often my commitment is limited---by time, by geography, by interest.

40. I am a sexual being. I get "turned on" by certain experiences, many of which I am not consciously aware. When I am "turned on," my sensations are wonderful; my emotions are powerful; my thinking is very unclear, very foggy. You and I are similar. You do things that remind me of my sexuality. Thus, "romantic love"---a sexual fog! Then the differences

start to emerge.

41. In marriage, the sexual issues are prominent. Theoretically, my commitment is unlimited. I will work through the differences---I will find ways to remain authentic and present, even with volatile emotions.

42. An old adage is that "you cannot make a silk purse out of a sow's ear." The adage does not say however that one is better than the other; maybe I want a leather purse. Relationships require both basic ingredients and transformation. Not all ingredients lead to effective transformation in the direction that I want. Romance is only one of the ingredients. It may be that I want a silk purse and one or both of us are sow's ears --- we need to come to terms with this, perhaps staying together or perhaps separating. Thinking skills, feeling skills and effective actions are all necessary for successful relationships in the complex world that we inhabit.

43. The primary role of the family is nurture and re-creation. I need to love my children for who they are, not who I think they should be. I am accountable to them to provide an adequate model, a mirror for them to seek their own growth.

44. I learn the most about myself, about who I am and what it means for me to trust, from friendships and marriage.

45. In partnership, can we be effective with each other? I believe so. It requires much work for us to be authentically ourselves and still validate the other fully.

46. You are the ultimate Mystery to me. I cannot possibly understand you --- I am not you. What I can do is make meaning of who you are (my story) and authentically share my meaning with you --- I am a distorted mirror for us to experience each other and learn from what we are experiencing.

47. I only am able to hear you when I am moving towards you. "Moving towards" means being interested, excited, physically moving towards, anything such that my interest in focused on you. I want to hear and be heard---what do I need to do?

48. The distinction between "needs" and "wants" is frequently important in relationship. Needs reflect that which would affect my survival, my outcomes as a living being. I need oxygen. I need water. I need food. I need shelter. Wants reflect that about which I have some choice; I can survive without my wants being met, perhaps with sadness or pain. I want successful relationships in my life. I want a comfortable home.

49. If I say to someone, "I need you", I really am saying that I want you in my life. I want the feelings that I experience in your presence. I can survive without this and it might be painful to me.

50. Depending on my maturity, many of my needs and wants overlap or are fuzzy.

51. One of the ways I meet my needs and wants is by commitment. Commitments are statements that define what actions I am willing to do so as to keep agreements, either with myself or with others.

52. Commitments require a vision, a purpose to which I am committed. Big purposes require more commitment and are also more validating of my being, my sense of belonging and valuing of myself and the universe.

53. I can only keep commitments when I know the terms by which I may break my commitment. Often my commitments have time limits or some other way for negotiation of conflicts.

54. I am very committed to you getting your desired outcome in life. I am not at all committed to my getting your desired outcome for you. I am very committed to working with you, to exploring with you. I am not responsible for you.

55. In relationship struggles, I can only:

   - find ways so as to resolve my pain, and

   - be available to you so that you find ways to resolve your pain.

56. In seeking to get my wants and needs met from others, I can either:

   - make hints and expect that they will guess my needs (wherein I am often disappointed and angry---my outcome), or

   - ask for assistance. Telling how I feel and expecting change is not a form of asking. "Asking" means that the answer "no" is acceptable.

57. I can also only really ask two things from you:

   - for some form of behavior change (to which you can answer "yes" or "no"), or

   - for information (to which you usually cannot answer "yes" or "no."

58. Indirect communication is characterized by confusion to these two. For example, "Do you have the time?" is usually a request for "What time is it?" Also I may not like "no" --- the other is free to respond and I am free to ask another.

59. One of my truths is summarized in the poem called the Gestalt Prayer. This is not an easy poem to embrace yet there is much truth in it.

"I do my thing and you do your thing.

I am not in this world to live up to your expectations

And you are not in this world to live up to mine.

You are You and I am I,

And if by chance we find each other, it's beautiful;

If not, it can't be helped."

For me, the final line of this poem does not mean that I passively suffer; acceptance is an active process and I am capable of much change (as are others also capable of change.)

60. All this relationship stuff is hard work, and occasionally delightful fun. The best argument for being alone is its simplicity. Yet it provides only limited possibility for growth. Relationship provides much more.

61. I am not God---only God is perfect, whatever that word means. The rest of us in some way struggle with imperfection --- we are wounded, either from natural abilities or previous relationships.

62. When there is difference, when I am angry with another, I can

- move away from (abandon),

- move against (attack or criticize), or

- move towards (cooperate and problem-solve.)

Only the latter leads to long-term healing and growth of relationship.

63. When I move away from or move against, I am coming from woundedness.

64. As a culture and individually, we deny our individual and collective woundedness. When we do, we are likely to violate self or others.

65. Authentic relationship means that we deal with the anger between us. This requires time and energy, often much time and energy.

66. Problem-solving: what are my needs, your needs, our needs? What alternatives do we have? What flexibility to persist until resolution, perhaps with several attempts?

   What stops me? Usually my story that you are inflexible. Wow!

67. Only when I recognize my wounding, am I able to problem-solve or otherwise move on in some fashion. Only when the other validates my wounding, is healing of relationship possible.

   Perhaps; I am not sure about the "only" part. It is certainly an optimal component and yet it may also create more victimhood.

68. A moral/ethical stance does not suppress choice but educates and allows liberty, encourages growth and fosters relationship.

69. The ultimate human journey is to live in joy and glory, free from

alienation, in selfless service to life. Paradoxically, I believe that I achieve this most effectively by ensuring my own growth, my own truths, my own pleasure and play.

70. A life of sanctity is one in which I give thanks. To truly give thanks is to be in the presence of mystery and awe.

71. What is the bottom line? The bottom line is that I live in such a way that:

    - I act in a way that is consistent with what I say I want,

    - leads to my wanting what I get,

    - allows me integrity in my core moralities, and

    - allows me to have compassion, humility and respect with others.

72. A growing edge for me is to be public in an appropriate fashion, to challenge the stance of others, the judgments of others, in a way that speaks my truth. Fritz Perls said that "The only authentic statement is a demand." For me, this is partly true; another authentic statement is "I stand here."

73. Human beings are magical. The above truths are not and do not need to be consistent --- living is paradoxical. To live fully, I need on occasion to step outside the bounds of rationality.

(Appendix D)
Recidivism

The *Webster New World Dictionary* (College edition, 1959) defines "recidivism" as "habitual or chronic relapse, or tendency to relapse, into crime or antisocial behavior patterns." Previously I talked about the difficulties of the "more hardened characters" and indicated that the Blowing Out! process appears to offer tools for these individuals to change deeply if they so wish. And that my experience is that many do so wish --- they simply have not found the tools.

At this point I wish to comment on the terminology "more hardened characters." At some level of meaning, the term is an affront. It is typical of the objective world to name the problem as "out there" and if only they would change, everything would be fine.

I suggest the problem is systemic. What stops us from recognizing that we are currently ineffective in meeting their needs and that we are likely just as much the "more hardened characters" as they are?

We do such subtle disrespect in many different ways in our society. In medical circles (the area with which I am most familiar), the naming of patients as "non-compliant" is a similar affront. It simply means the patient does not genuinely trust the system. Is the system truly trust-worthy? In my experience we also do it with our psychiatric labels especially that of depression. I suggest that depression is a concept, that depression as a "biochemical illness" is simply a particular belief system as compared to the belief system of it being a "sociological dysfunction in a biochemical processor."

And when I challenge like this I do not mean to insult --- I simply want to find the best map that I can have so that I can get to where I say I want to be. In my sixty-four years, I have not found the socially accepted maps to be very accurate.

In this Appendix, I have asked various clients, especially those whom others have almost certainly considered as "more hardened characters" to comment on what has made the difference for them in being exposed to the Blowing Out! process. I have also asked individuals of various referral sources to comment on the changes they have noted after a one-weekend program, changes that they have often described as life defining.

I have of course picked dramatic examples to emphasize the thesis of this book. For the most part though, the clients who come do change. Unfortunately some then slip back into old habits. Most likely this occurs either because the familiar is easier and/or the ongoing support necessary to stabilize the change is not available. Both of these explanations are perhaps part of the systemic nature of the problems; it is likely that neither the home environments nor the legal-social systems support growth that validates the complexity of the problems of that individual.

The words speak for themselves. I have added nothing other than correcting minor grammatical items.

Clients:

SC, DD, DF, CH, MK, MP, DP

Referral Sources:

FR, JS

Clients

SC, a 48-year-old woman with a long history of drug abuse and violent crimes.

"September 19th, 2005

The first time that I remember violating another person was when I was four. I continued to do so in many different ways throughout my life. Suicide attempts, homicidal thoughts, assaults both physical and verbal.

In fact the energy of the rage I had was so intense, there were days I was fully capable and willing to kill. Either myself or whoever I was angry with. That is how I spent most of my days in recent years; either suicidal or homicidal.

This behavior resulted in psychiatric hospital stays, certified and on medication. I was 18 years old the first time that happened. So over the years I have gone to anger management programs, psychiatrists and psychologists to talk about my problem.

Honestly, none of this helped. Most of the time I heard what I was, was told to talk about how I felt, to think about my rage and what I was angry about, and in some cases, told that if I didn't do what I was told I was going to end up dead or in the penitentiary. When I was spoken to in the "do this, or else" fashion, I took that as a threat. I know that when angered, the last thing I could do was talk or think about what I was doing. The only thing I thought about was getting rid of the rage and acting out violently. It worked.

So one day, I was given a phone number for Dave's workshop. I called him and went. Wow!

I now understand my energy when angered, and what I can do to release it safely. I no longer carry it until I explode in the ways that I did. That is exactly what was missing in other help that I sought. No one told me how I could release the energy of rage.

At Dave's Anger, Rage and Violation workshop, I saw exactly how to release. In fact, it was a beautiful moment when I saw him hit a punching bag with a baseball bat. A way to be violent; which is what I did when angry, without harming anyone. Incredible. That's how I could release my rage. Perfect.

For almost two years now, I have been working with Dave, and in this time I have been able to deal with emotional issues I hadn't ever in the past; molestation, family violence, etc. The most important, of course, has been the suicidal and homicidal behavior patterns. I no longer think about not living, or harming others. Sure I still get angry, I am human. I know exactly what to do with the energy when it isn't appropriate. I release it, and then I can deal with the issue.

This is the greatest gift I have ever received. EVER! I truly enjoy living, and am committed to working on my own personal growth.

I am peaceful with myself most of the time and I wholeheartedly appreciate what Dave has shown me.

Thanks for the love, Davey.

SC"

Statement by DD, a 51-year-old man, with an extensive criminal record (who incidentally wanted to be able to enter the United States for a variety of peaceful purposes.)

"October 26th, 2005

My name is (DD) and I live in (…)

My life seemed to be always on hold, struggling in relationships everywhere it seems.

I've tried Anger Management in (…) and 3 attempts at that and it seemed a lot of talking and swearing, blaming and I was more angry after I left.

In Aug. '04, my world came tumbling down again and I heard of this place in Orangeville called A Place Two Be and Dave MacQuarrie. So I knew I needed help and called him.

That weekend was the most incredible thing I've ever done besides getting sober and finally I realized my problem was me. I learned about pressure and rage and that I knew nothing about releasing this energy. My energy was used in all the wrong places.

I have been going now over one year [to A Place Two Be] and learning to deal with whom I became and undo these emotions so I can live and deal with life problems.. Sitting in group, role-playing and watching others is very helpful to me and knowing that I'm not crazy is great. I have my own anger room at home and it does the trick in moving my energy.

I'm not as angry and I was able to practice that in Buffalo when an immigration officer treated [me in a way] what I believe was unfair and I kept cool and practiced what I'm learning and the judge has allowed me over the border now to visit. I don't always get results but when I stay focused it really works.

Thank God for Dave and his hard work and dedication to his gift that I can enjoy life today a little better.

DD."

Statement by DF, a 51-year-old well-educated man, chronically raging to the point of disability.

"November 21st, 2005

My partner directed me to Dave Macquarie. She had wanted me to have counseling for anger management for a long time and gave me an ultimatum. If I did not go to a weekend anger management course with him, then she would end our relationship.

Needless to say, I did not want to go. I had been in counseling on and off since my last year of high school, and I did not feel that counseling was doing me any good. It was simply a case of one screwball trying to straighten out another screwball. It didn't work and offered me no hope. However, in order to save my relationship, I would commit to the Anger, Rage and Violation weekend workshop. I also decided to sabotage it as much as possible. I e-mailed Dave a series of demands, telling him that I did not want to sit around having a feel-good session with a bunch of testosterone-laden angry men, nor did I want another nut-bar therapist pushing happy pills at me. I had been on antidepressants for years, and they were not helping. To my surprise, Dave agreed to all my demands, challenging me to come. All it would cost me was my time. I cancelled at the last minute so I could sabotage some more.

When I finally did go to a workshop, and met Dave, I was very disappointed.

Here was an unshaven man of advancing years whose clothes were covered in what appeared to be dog hair, wearing mismatched socks. I was right. Here was another screwball that was going to tell a room full of angry screwballs how to fix their lives. It was clearly a lost cause and a waste of my time.

What I didn't realize at the time is that Dave would agree with me. He agreed that he was a screwball (my words, not his) and that he had his own craziness that he had to deal with. I really don't know how or when the change occurred that weekend, I just know that it did. He talked about obscure things that I knew, like how lobsters and crabs get trapped, and used them as a metaphor for life experiences that I understood. What really stood out was that he did one other thing that no other therapist had ever done: he told me that there was hope. He told me that with the right tools, change was remarkably easy to achieve. My previous therapy had not worked because I was never offered the right tools. He didn't lie. He told me that he did not know as yet which tools were the right ones for me. But if I would work with him for a year, we would find out together and use them to bring about change. I left the workshop a changed person.

I have been working with Dave for six months now. He promised me that there would be pain and tears. Sometimes the work would be hard, sometimes easier. He also said that he was not there to change me, but to tweak the strings and see what happened. No hollow promises, no platitudes, just results. So far he has been right. When I first started group sessions, I was terrified, sitting in the back and covering my face so that I couldn't see what was going on. Now I participate as fully as I can at any one session. The results I want are coming. Some come very easily, others are harder. I learn not only from work that I do, but also from what others in the group work on.

I am getting results because of the work I do, not because of anything that Dave does. He merely offers me the tools, steering me towards the right tool for the job. Unfortunately, going to Dave did not save my relationship. It did save me.

DF"

Statement by CH, a 40-year-old man who attended both the Blowing Out! weekend and another anger management program.

"November 4th, 2005

In response to life difficulties, I sought to attend an anger management program. Exploring options via the internet, I encountered and enrolled in Dave MacQuarrie's program Anger, Rage and Violation. This program was a fascinating explanation of anger and how it can lead to abuse. Additionally, it offered a concrete, learnable plan of bodily action with which to actually manage anger.

This additional kinesthetic approach is a highly effective method for "emptying the pot". And "emptying the pot" is the only true foundation for managing one's anger. That is why Anger, Rage and Violation is so vitally important.

I subsequently attended another anger management program which missed the mark by offering only a cognitive approach to managing anger. Much of it consisted of being told what to do by the facilitator while the participants sat in doubt about what they were hearing.

Anger, Rage and Violation has enhanced my life and for me is the pinnacle of anger management programs. I believe it should be the standard for all anger management programs.

CH"

Statement by MK, a 53 year old lawyer in "burn-out."

"December 8th, 2005

mon histoire

My expectations in coming to the ARV weekend? None, really. I knew that something was wrong, but I never considered myself to be an angry person, or having "anger management" issues. I prided myself in my self-control. I attended more to placate my partner than out of conviction that I needed it. I learned that my calmness was part of the problem, and that once I allowed myself to let loose, then the negative emotions that I so carefully denied-out-of-existence could come to the surface where I could finally deal with them. The weekend was not a cure, but it was an awakening to a process of emotional renewal. Here's the kick: I very much dislike the process of introspection and "work" on my "shit". It's not fun. It's painful. It's unsettling and disconcerting. Still, I would not go back even if I could.

It's like being at 10,000 feet on a mountain with blistered feet and aching lungs, marveling at [the] view.

Whenever I was asked how I liked practicing law, my standard answer has been "I hate it". It's not that it never has its moments of reward, but dealing with the constant conflict of my clients and the professional obligation to both promote their cause and resolve it has been extremely corrosive to my emotional health. I often thought that it would be better if I just didn't give a shit: "be a hired gun; as long as you get paid, it's their life, so what?!" Some lawyers do that. Not me. I wanted to make a difference, to actually help, to "see the big picture" and make the world a better place. It almost sounds corny, but I was brought up to care for the weak and less fortunate.

Unfortunately, I was crossing over to the third limb of the relationship triangle without being aware of it, and I was burned out. In retrospect, it was no wonder. Attempting to "help" where I was doomed to be ineffective is a recipe for disaster. With Dave's help (nobody calls him "Dr. MacQuarrie" any more) I was able to come to clarity about this long-standing and personally debilitating misunderstanding. It wasn't that I didn't *know* that the problems of my clients were not *my* problems, it was that I couldn't *feel* the force of that. A few whacks of the baseball bat on the punching bag, and Voila! I was healed. Well, not quite that simple, but it's amazing how effective physical exhaustion in a loving and therapeutic environment can, with Dave's guidance and group support can be. I used to think I pretty much had it together. I see that I was just holding it together as best I could, and now I don't have to. I can still care, but without bearing burdens that don't belong to me I can actually be more effective.

Thanks, Dave. Although I consider myself forever in your debt, I'll pay it forward as you wish.

MK"

Statement by MP, a 47 year old truck driver, deeply caught in frequent raging.

"September 8th, 2005

My Anger Free Life

On August 26, 2005, I had the opportunity to set myself free from my anger outbursts. It all started about 6 months ago when the pressures of life started to get in the way of my marriage. No matter how small the issue was, I would lose my temper and almost lost my family. I would get angry if a dish was on the counter, if the rain blew from the west, or if the television was too loud. It didn't matter that I was not even home if the television was on. I had to seek help.

I called my family doctor and was referred to David MacQuarrie. Could David help? I doubted it; no one has been able to outwit me; I know it all. I'm not angry; the rest of the world just won't co-operate with me.

I went to see David for an Anger Management Weekend. I went from Friday night, 6:30 P.M. to 10:30 P.M. and Saturday and Sunday from 9:30 A.M. to 5:30 P.M. Was I angry? You bet I was. David brought it to my attention through his soft-spoken voice and knowledge that I never believed existed.

I had seen therapists before, numerous times. Have they helped? No, I walked out feeling more confused than when I walked in. No therapist has ever gotten into my head and to the root of my anger like David has. David opened up my eyes, my mind and changed my way of thinking. Many issues have been analyzed and solutions have been thought through.

My wife and I both attend David's therapy sessions now, every Wednesday evening. My wife does not have an anger issue; she's there mostly for moral support which encourages me that people really do care. To be honest, if it were not for David, I would not have my life back. I can negotiate problems and have a much calmer approach to the solutions. It seems that David can change my way of thinking and I don't even realize it.

I am more relaxed in my space, and now my family enjoys being near me, rather than running from me. My wife likes to sit and cuddle with me on the couch, rather than hide in her needlework. My girls come to me for help with homework, rather than hide in their bedrooms, hoping I'll go out or go to sleep. Could I blame them for acting they way they did before I seen David? Absolutely not, I was a monster, my family didn't know me. Now, I can sit and talk, rather than yell, I can sit next to my wife, rather than beg her to be in the same room with me, and my girls can smile again. My wife has the man she married, and my girls have a new friend in the house. I will continue to see David as often as I can, he's my "Higher-Power".

Thank you David, you've given me my family back, and the man that my wife married. In my home, there truly is….NO S.A.D. Thank you.

Sincerely,

MP"

Referral Sources

Statement by FR, a therapist in private practice with extensive training in Psychodrama and addictions.

This highly readable book walks the reader through the concepts, images, metaphors and action exercises which Dave has been developing in his Anger, Rage and Violation workshops. Having heard positive feedback from some of my clients who had attended the week-end, I attended one myself to witness and learn and have since been encouraging current clients to attend to add the tools he offers to their recovery toolbox. In the book he describes in clear simple language these user friendly tools to aid participants to climb out of the repetitive patterns of conflict which show up in many relationships. There is careful focussed attention on language throughout his writing, as in the workshops, which challenge the reader to question his/her assumptions, to risk thinking "outside the box" and to explore how anger operates in our lives.

As a therapist working in the addictions field I can attest to the myriad connections which anger has to other powerful human emotions so I valued his emphasis here on the applicability of these tools to the management of all the emotions. There is a simplicity of language he uses to look at a highly complex subject --- no less a subject than human consciousness and the unconscious as they play out in emotional life. He renders it understandable through using images, metaphor and proverb, a time honored vehicle, employed by many of our great teachers, for making the complex understandable.

As an action oriented psychodramatist I appreciated over the week-end the opportunity which Dave offered, and describes in this book, to explore in action warming up to the groupwork, grounding the intellectual learning deeper through experiential exercises and the group sharing in pairs and in the whole group. The design provided for an integration of the cognitive with the emotional. He speaks with some personal authority in that his teaching is grounded in his own journey towards health and healing.

The metaphors are easy to grasp, not coached in mystifying psychological terminology and are readily usable. One client of mine who attended described coming away with tools which he has been using "on a daily basis to good effect ever since".

Statement by JS, a probation officer of more than 25 years experience.

"November 12th, 2005

DEALING WITH NEGATIVE EMOTIONS
IN 'DIFFICULT TO SERVE' CLIENTS

This subject has been a matter of great interest to me, both as a 'Difficult To Serve' client in my own right, and as a Probation Officer with nearly thirty years experience dealing with 'Difficult To Serve' clients.

I intend to be purposely anecdotal here, and personal. I will leave arguments about theory and method to others. But what I have seen and experienced of the suffering and brokenness of human experience is that, contrary to appearances, nobody wants to live that way. So why do so many of us live in suffering and brokenness for years and years? Why don't we 'do something' about it? What makes a client 'Difficult To Serve'?

In my experience, it is rarely something blameworthy; it is more, I think, a matter of being subject to the human condition. I have met few human beings who would not benefit from some serious investigation into their emotional wellbeing, but many who have no inclination to do so. In my experience, it is often the sheer difficulty of the project that discourages such investigation. It is something like running outside your house and looking in through the window to try to see yourself.

In addition, I see a cruel dilemma: we can't do an effective self-examination alone, and there is a forbidding stigma attached to seeking help for emotional troubles. Moreover, when the individual finally takes that brave leap, and seeks such therapy, they so frequently encounter an unskillful therapist, and I think the increased resistance that results is directly proportionate to the square of the un-skillfulness of the therapist they encounter.

Ok, I exaggerate. My point is that an unskilled therapist can do immense harm. At the same time, it is not my purpose to attempt a general critique of the therapeutic community, only to take a look at, from one perspective, what makes Dr. MacQuarrie an effective therapist.

As a former[1] client, and as a Probation Officer who has referred numerous clients to Dr. MacQuarrie over the past fifteen years, my focus is on results. The initial results I observe in clients (and this is true of my own experience as well) are --- surprisingly --- something intangible. There is just something different. Self-perception and relations with others are, simply stated, better. I can readily identify with these clients (mainly men) who come back from Dr. MacQuarrie's weekend 'Anger Management' program with a sense of excitement, a feeling that something important has happened in their lives, a sense that something weighty and wearisome has been lifted from their shoulders. This is not to say that they cannot identify specific insights they got hold of and strategies they learned, but it is their over-all sense of epiphany that is most striking and familiar to me[2].

A couple of years ago, I had lunch with Dr. MacQuarrie, and while we were talking, it occurred to me that I could not remember one probation client who attended his 'Anger Management' weekend who had re-offended. Since then, I have been unofficially keeping tabs. One (out of more than twenty) of these men has committed a further spousal assault, and one has been convicted of impaired driving.

---

1. I wonder if anyone is ever a 'former' patient/client of Dr. MacQuarrie. It has been nearly fifteen years since I participated in one of his groups, and I continue to be guided by what I learned there. When I have one of those tricky decisions to make, where self-delusion is a temptation, I can picture the group, and see the expectant, knowing smiles of the participants, and my capacity for self-awareness still gets a gently, encouraging prod.

2. Many of these men are on probation for having assaulted or threatened their spouses. It is a matter of protocol that I contact these victims as 'collateral contacts'. The victims usually confirm that "something has changed". They frequently say something such as "At least now he is trying".

Almost to a man, the last thing these men do during our final probation appointment is thank me for referring them to Dr. MacQuarrie. They frequently add, "It changed my life". One weekend![3]

So what are the reasons for Dr. MacQuarrie's success with 'Difficult To Serve' clients? Again, I will not attempt an assessment of theory or methodology, but only describe anecdotal observations.

For me, honesty and authenticity are a major key. Dr. MacQuarrie presents himself as a full and transparent human being, flaws and all, and this is an essential component of his successful therapeutic intervention[4]. The 'I-am-the-unflawed-expert-trained-to-assess-and-fix-you-approach' is a disaster.

A related component immediately apparent in Dr. MacQuarrie's work is the atmosphere of trust and encouragement he sets up[5]. In my experience, Dr. MacQuarrie's demonstrated success in creating trust and encouragement follows his practice of asking clients to honor their past behavior as a survival strategy learned out of necessity. No shame here. No blame. Just look and be aware. So when change is invited, it is a change of strategy, not a change of worthiness --- the worthiness has always been there. The strategies were chosen, usually at a very tender and vulnerable age, from the repertoire available to that individual at that point in his life. The client is urged to

---

3. A few of these men, but a minority, have continued to attend weekly group-therapy with Dr. MacQuarrie. I am sure more would do so, but many of these men do not have their own transportation and Dr. MacQuarrie's therapy centre is located about forty-five minutes to an hour's drive from where my clients live, and it is not served by public transportation.
4. In fact, one of the most successful means of convincing my clients to participate in Dr. MacQuarrie's group-therapy is to disclose to them that I attended myself. I unabashedly stole this approach from Dr. MacQuarrie.
5. Of course, few therapists will admit they fail to do this in the same way few people will admit to not having a sense of humour.

honor the young child that found a workable survival mechanism, but now is invited to review it from the perspective of an adult. But how?

Here is where real therapeutic skill comes in. How does the client identify strategies learned long ago under duress at a vulnerable time of his life. My experience of Dr. MacQuarrie's work is that he recognizes the emotional and somatic constitution of these strategies and takes an emotional and somatic approach to identify them. "What's that physical gesture about?" he might ask a client. "Do it again. Notice the feeling it aroused. Where are you feeling it in your body? When's the first time you felt like that? Do you want to do some work on that?"

Note: no verbal identifiers; no shame-bearing labels; no omniscient conclusions; no abstract vaguely understood classifications; but rather, felt-feelings in the physical body, directly perceived by the client, undeniably real, something concrete to work with.

Then comes the invitation: "Can we examine it further. Is there some physical action that might act as a metaphor for what's going on emotionally. Would it help to act it out physically[6]. Try this if you like. Is that it? Is that what's been happening all these years?"

So now the client has the opportunity to 'get it.' Something's going on for him. There's that 'old familiar discomfort'! What's it about? How can the client find its origin, befriend it, examine it in safety, honor it for its role in his survival, be willing to question if he needs it now as an adult in different

---

6. This is a strategy contrary to much of the dogmatic ideology in the 'Anger Management' field. The received wisdom is that to encourage men to act their feelings out physically will lead to acting out violent behaviour in less appropriate contexts. I have not heard these claims verified by controlled empirical studies.

circumstances.

The next step is to offer a number of constructive strategies that might be effective when that 'old familiar discomfort' arises. I find that the probation clients remember these strategies and can describe situations in which they have applied them successfully. Various clients who attended the same weekend will often return having been struck by the possibilities of personally selected strategies that seem workable in their particular situation.

What strikes me most, however, is the way post-MacQuarrie probation clients communicate that 'something is different': they often say they "feel more relaxed, can "let things go", feel more capable of making choices about whether or not their emotions escalate, especially over trivial matters. And I find that this is often borne out in their behavior.

It appears that by approaching emotional troubles using emotional and somatic means is an effective approach that results in a kind of holistic, intangible outcome that de-escalates emotional intensity and frees up the cognitive processing skills to do their job more successfully. I have not found the opposite strategy --- that of using cognitive intervention to de-escalate emotional intensity --- works nearly as well with probation clients, and frankly, it doesn't work very well for me either.

JS"

****

In closing, let me say thank you to clients who have been my "more hardened characters." I have learned much from your integrity in holding on to your anger and rage until such time as you have found tools that are effective for you.

Printed in the United States
149001LV00001BA/2/P